W9-ASC-640

FREEDOM'S
CHILD

Also by Carrie Allen McCray

Piece of Time

Photo captions from left to right:

MARY'S MOTHER, MALINDA RICE,
FREED SLAVE.

MARY RICE HAYES ALLEN
AT AGE SIXTEEN.

MARY'S FATHER, BRIGADIER GENERAL
JOHN ROBERT JONES, CSA, RET.

FREEDOM'S CHILD

The LIFE

of a CONFEDERATE GENERAL'S

BLACK DAUGHTER

—

CARRIE ALLEN McCRAY

Algonquin Books of Chapel Hill 1998

Published by
ALGONQUIN BOOKS OF CHAPEL HILL
Post Office Box 2225
Chapel Hill, North Carolina 27515-2225

a division of
WORKMAN PUBLISHING
708 Broadway
New York, New York 10003

© 1998 by Carrie Allen McCray. All rights reserved.
Printed in the United States of America.
Published simultaneously in Canada
    by Thomas Allen & Son Limited.
Design by Anne Winslow.

For permission to use excerpts from copyrighted works, grateful acknowledgment is made to the copyright holders, publishers, or representatives named on page 270, which constitutes an extension of the copyright page.

LIBRARY OF CONGRESS CATALOGING-IN-PUBLICATION DATA
McCray, Carrie Allen, 1913–
    Freedom's child : the life of a Confederate general's Black daughter /
    by Carrie Allen McCray.
        p.   cm.
    Includes bibliographical references.
    ISBN 1-56512-186-4 (hardcover)
    1. Allen, Mary Rice Hayes, 1875–1935.   2. Jones, John Robert, 1828–1901.
3. Afro-Americans—Biography.   4. Afro-American women civil rights
workers—Biography.   5. Racially mixed people—United States—
Biography.   I. Title.
E185.97.A36M38   1998
973'.0496073'0092
[B]—DC21   97-32659
                                                                      CIP

10 9 8 7 6 5 4 3 2 1
First Edition

To the memory of my mother, who, in her red hat,
went out to fight for justice and equality for her people;
and to all of our forebears, who helped to make her
the person she became

For my people standing staring trying to fashion a better way from
confusion, from hypocrisy and misunderstanding, trying to fashion
a world that will hold all the people, all the faces, all the adams
and eves and their countless generations.

—from "For My People," by Margaret Walker

Contents

Author's Note

All of the characters in this book are real; however, two or three
pseudonyms are used to protect the privacy of those families.

Acknowledgments

—

Many have helped me on this journey. Thanks, first, to a higher source, who has allowed me to be here at this age with mind intact (at least most of the time). My deep appreciation also goes to my mother, for being the person she was, and to my father, for being what a real father should be. Thanks go to all my forebears, who, through their struggles, brought me to this place. As the old Yoruba proverb says, "If we stand tall, it's because we stand on the backs of those who came before us."

I want to thank my brother Hunter Reed, my sisters Rosemary and Dolly, and my niece Elberta. They reminded me of many of the family stories. And a special thanks to Rosemary, who often traveled with me to assist in the research and encouraged me all along the way.

I could not have written this story without two special people. The first is Anne Spencer, the poet and my mother's dearest friend. Before she died in 1975, I interviewed her several times and listened to exciting stories about Mama and her father, stories we never heard from Mama. The other significant person was Dale Harter, a student at

James Madison University when Rosemary and I first went there to find information about General Jones. Thanks go to Chris Bolgiano, of the Special Collections Library at the University; she referred us to Dale, who was writing a book about General Jones. Dale gave me a windfall of information about General Jones, in which was confirmation that he was Mama's father. Dale also asked a friend of his, Dale McAllister, for information on Mama's Rice family, who lived in Singer's Glen, the McAllisters' hometown. Dale McAllister and his father have done extensive studies on the families of Singer's Glen and I thank him for invaluable information.

Dale Harter also suggested I go to Duke University's Perkins Library, where General Jones' scrapbook is stored. I learned a lot about General Jones, the person, through that scrapbook. Without Dale Harter, I could never have written the complete story, and I can never sufficiently thank him.

I thank Tom Johnson of the South Caroliniana Library for sending me to James Madison University in the first place, and for referring me to Ann Carmichael, who was also very helpful, as was Laura Costello of the South Caroliniana Library regarding Ota Benga ("Otto").

In my research on Mama's first husband, Professor Gregory Hayes, president of Virginia Seminary, I must especially thank Dr. Ralph Reavies, professor at Virginia Union University. I also thank Virginia Seminary and College and Oberlin College for information on Professor Hayes. I must thank my friends Louise and Mac McCoy. Louise and I spent six hours at the Library of Congress while her patient husband waited for us outside. I am indebted to the late Reverend Norman Fletcher of the Unitarian Church in Montclair, New Jersey, for his letter to me with his memories of Mama.

I'd also like to thank John A. Williams, who edited and published my first real literary venture, *Adjos Means Goodbye*, in his anthology *Beyond the Angry Black* (Cooper Square Press, 1966). It has been reprinted in a book for schoolchildren and has also been used in a theatrical production at Luna Stage of Montclair, New Jersey, produced to raise consciousness of prejudice and how it hurts us all. Prejudice is what Mama fought almost all of her life. Thank you, John Williams.

Acknowledgment also goes to Scott Reagan, who spearheaded the founding of the South Carolina Writers' Workshop, and to the members of the Columbia Chapter of that organization. Their varied talents helped me significantly in the writing of this book. As always, thanks to Suzanne Wenzell Shearer, who not only types for me, but inspires me with her enthusiasm. Thanks to Chauncey Spencer for photographs of his mother and mine. Thanks, too, to my friend Lois Shearer and my late friend Muriel Davis, who were so helpful early in the writing. Thanks to Sondra Zeidenstein for referring Gloria Steinem to me and to Gloria Steinem for referring me to the Charlotte Sheedy Agency and to that agency for its interest in my work. And thanks to old friends in Montclair, New Jersey, especially Mrs. Hortense Ridley Tate, Norma Holcombe McCain, Florence Hampton, and Anne Slaughter, for their helpful stories, and to my friends at B&B Quickprint, Larry and Kimberly Barrickman, and Deborah Young, whose interest and encouragement keep me writing. I'd also like to thank Bret Lott of the College of Charleston for his encouragement.

And finally, I thank my editor, Shannon Ravenel, for getting me on the right road and helping me all the way. It has been a wonderful journey together.

FREEDOM'S
CHILD

Part One

DIGGING UP TRUTH

1875–1895

I have a friend
And my heart from hence
Is closed to friendship

—Anne Spencer, "I Have A Friend"

Chapter 1

STORIES FROM THE POET

When we were very young, we lived in a big yellow house across the road from the campus of Virginia Seminary in Lynchburg, Virginia. In Mama's bedroom there was a huge four-poster antique bed, the "birthing bed" where all except one of her ten children were born. In that same room, on the mantelpiece over the fireplace, was a picture of a white man in uniform. I don't ever remember asking who he was. I don't ever remember being told. In later years my brother Hunter told me it was a picture of Mama's father, a Confederate general named Jones. Somehow I could never think of him as anything except my mother's father, as if he had no connection to us children, nor to all the future generations of children yet unborn.

Mama never talked about her father. The hush-hush of the times covered the truth like a shroud. Years ago nobody talked about things like that except perhaps someone like Mary Chesnut, who says in her Civil War diary, "God forgive us. Ours is a monstrous system. . . . Like the patriarchs of old, our men live all in one house with their wives and their concubines, and the mulattoes one sees in every family, exactly resemble the white children."

The "monstrous system" continued long after the last shots of the Civil War were fired. Young black girls, though free now, were going to work as maids and housekeepers and had no protection against the men in those homes. Mama's mother, Malinda Rice, was one of those girls. In 1873, at age sixteen, she went to work in the home of General Jones. On March 2, 1875, Mama, the daughter of Malinda Rice and General Jones, was born in Harrisonburg, Virginia. They named her Mary Magdalene Rice. For many decades this was all we knew. A curtain was drawn to hide the truth about Mama and her father.

I always wanted to know more about Mama's father, more about her mother, more about all the people around her when she was growing up. I wanted to know what it was like for her, born into such a situation. And I wanted to know what combination of people, places, circumstances, and events set Mama on her course, dedicated to fighting for freedom, equality, and justice for all people.

In the late sixties, I traveled to our former home in Lynchburg to talk with Mama's dearest friend, the poet Anne Spencer. J. Lee Greene says in *Time's Unfading Garden* "Mary Rice was one of three women whom Annie considered almost as close as a sister." We called her Aun' Tannie. (She always laughed and said that before we moved north, we'd called her "*Ant* Annie.") I figured that Mama and Aun' Tannie, as young women, must have shared stories of their lives, stories that they'd kept to themselves. I was right.

Aun' Tannie's home at 1313 Pierce Street in Lynchburg is now a national historic landmark. When she saw me coming up the walk in 1969, she greeted me as she always had every summer when Mama took us "back home."

"Here comes Jonathan's Winter Apple," she said in her slow, soothing, poetic voice. I loved the name she'd given me. A chubby, rosy-

cheeked child with what blacks back then called bad hair, I was sometimes called the ugly duckling, but not by Aun' Tannie.

She looked just the way I remembered her. At eighty-seven, she
was still beautiful. She still wore long, thick braids, only slightly gray.
She still had her leathery Indian complexion and still wore those silk
Japanese pajamas she loved. Years ago, when this was daring garb, she
would say she wore them to give gossipy women something to talk
about. Her mind and memory were still as clear as crystal.

We went inside the house I loved. I followed her into the sunroom,
overlooking her garden. All kinds of flowers were in full bloom. After
she'd brought me some cookies and a glass of ice tea, we sat and talked,
first about the family, to catch her up on everybody's news.

Then I told her that I had come to talk about Mama, that I wanted
to write Mama's story. She got up, walked over to the window, looked
out at her garden. She stood there, her back to me, softly reciting her
poem "Lines to a Nasturtium":

Flame Flower, Day Torch, Mauna Loa
I saw a daring bee, today, pause and soar,
into your flaming heart.

"Mary loved nasturtiums as intensely as she hated pretension and
prejudice," she said, then sighed. "It was never a time for Mary to die."
She rubbed her fingers along the windowsill, her buried grief resurfac-
ing. She kept her back to me, trying to conceal the tears I saw when she
turned at last. She came and sat once again beside me.

"Mary didn't have a chance to finish her work. We still don't have
full freedom," she said, as if she truly thought it would take Mama to
bring that about.

Well, in a sense, Mama's children thought that too. "Full freedom"
was an expression we heard all during our growing-up years. "We will
not stop until we have full freedom," Mama would say, pulling her red
felt cloche hat down on her head, on her way out the door to the

"fight." Although we children weren't certain what this full freedom was, we knew if Mama was putting on that red hat, she was going someplace to tell somebody, "We want full freedom, and we want it now."

Aun' Tannie took my empty glass and put it on the table, then shook her head. "Young people today think they're the original protestors. They didn't know Mary," she laughed.

I laughed, too, and commented about all those other protestors reaching way back in time. "Tell me some things you remember about Mama," I asked.

"Sometimes there's pain in digging up truth," Aun' Tannie warned. "Like an old tree stump, hard to get up, and when you do, it can look so ugly lying there. Then you just have to remember it was that old stump that made the tree beautiful."

"Almost everything you say has a poem in it," I told her.

"That's from a long time living it." Then she added, "Your mama's life and my life could be chapters in a novel, though. We lived a novel. I remember Mary telling me once about an old woman in Harrison-burg who was supposed to have a second sight. That's what they called people who could see the future."

I reminded her that we had had one living with us once, in New Jersey, named Mizannie. Mizannie had told my sister Dolly she was going to marry a man who would have lots of chickens. The man she married years later had a chicken hatchery—thousands of new chickens every month. Mizannie could predict some things that came true.

"Not that old lady," Aun' Tannie said. "The one I mean told people Mary was born out of trouble and trouble would follow her all her life. She didn't know Mary. Mary knew how to handle trouble, hers and everybody else's."

In Aun' Tannie's opinion, Mama had a charmed life, as well as a father who adored her and who made certain she would get a good education. There were three men in Mama's life that Aun' Tannie thought influenced her. Her father (who Mama's family called "General") gave her a sense of self-worth. Her Uncle John, the ex-slave who raised her, passed some of his self-esteem on to Mama. And Mama's first husband, Professor Hayes, was a militant fighter for equality in education for Negroes. Aun' Tannie felt his philosophy must have influenced Mary too. She got her gentle, ladylike behavior from her mother and from her Uncle John's wife, Aunt Dolly. Mama was very fortunate.

Aun' Tannie explained that her own life was somewhat different from Mama's. Although she was proud of her father, Joel Cephus, because he would not work for white folks like they had to do in slavery, he was not around while she was growing up. It was her mother, Sarah, who saw to it that Aun' Tannie got a good education. And Sarah was proud that Joel saved his money to open his own business, but distressed that it was a saloon that served only white laborers. He would take the four-year-old Aun' Tannie to the saloon and sit her up on the bar to perform for "grubby old men." No place for a child. "Grubby old men" or not, I sensed the excitement attached to that memory as she told it. Aun' Tannie's mother was from an aristocratic family background, so different from her father's that they couldn't make it in the long run. The family broke up when Aun' Tannie was five years old.

In her view Mama, though born of the strange situation so prevalent during those times, had a more stable life. Malinda Rice was a woman of beauty and dignity and Aun' Tannie believed that Malinda and the General must have had a warm, loving relationship. "Even though they could never marry, their relationship endured until your grandmother's death."

I found myself squirming as she spoke the words. I was not quite ready for them. Aun' Tannie went on to discuss the culture of the times —strange times. Some white wives accepted their husbands' having mistresses, but they must have smoldered underneath. "Some kept it tight in their bosoms, and others took their hurting out on our girls.

They should have been taking it out on their rascal husbands," she said.

General's wife, however, must have been a kind, gentle woman. She was sickly and had no children. Even after Mama's and her brother's births, Malinda continued working and living in the Jones home and taking care of Mrs. Jones. During that time the children lived with their Uncle John and Aunt Dolly. Once General's wife asked Malinda to bring Mary to see her, which she did. Before they left, General's wife gave Mary a porcelain-headed doll that had belonged to Mrs. Jones when she was a child.

A porcelain-headed doll? Mama had kept a porcelain-headed doll in a box in her wardrobe. It was a doll she would not let us play with. This revelation stirred some undefinable feeling of circles being closed. Then Aun' Tannie told me that when Mary thanked Mrs. Jones and hugged her, Mrs. Jones reached over and kissed her on the forehead. Mrs. Jones asked Malinda to bring Mary back, and Mary visited her often before Mrs. Jones died.

"Evil and pain were back there, but so was a kind of humanity— in smaller doses, but it was there," Aun' Tannie commented. "It's hard to understand some things from past times, when you're not living it."

That story finished, she moved on to another one. Mary's father taught her how to read before she entered school and was proud of her quickness in learning. He also taught her to love poetry. When she was fifteen or sixteen, he sent her to Hartshorn Memorial College in Richmond, where she first met Professor Hayes. He was there to speak, and Mary had to present him with the gift from the students.

Aun' Tannie backtracked. She said that Mary's father had taken her many places with him. He even took her into an ice-cream parlor where Negroes were not supposed to go. One time when they were there, Mary's father heard a white man whisper, "That's his little nigger bastard," so he went over and knocked the man off the ice-cream-parlor stool. Aun' Tannie clearly enjoyed telling this story. But then in a more serious tone she described Mary's situation as "a mixed blessing." She was sometimes called such names by Negroes as well as by whites, and Mary was troubled by the fact that her father never took her darker-skinned brother, Willie, whom Mary adored, with them. Aun' Tannie believed that was one of the reasons Mary staged her first protest when she was just twelve years old.

The challenge is to become part of the
struggle to make a positive difference.

— David Satcher

Chapter 2

THE LADY REBELS

*B*reakfast was at the table in Aun' Tannie's sunroom. It was one
of those mornings you want to fold and store for bleaker times. The
sun filtered through the window, warming me as I listened to more
stories about Mama.

"Your mother and I were born rebels," Aun' Tannie said. "That's
what Will, your daddy, called us. 'How are the lady rebels today?' he'd
ask. Some people are born to rebel, and Mary and I were two of them.
I guess that's why we were so close."

"I've often thought of that," I said. "Both of you were wonderful,
free-spirited women. I can hear Papa calling you rebels. He was very
conservative, wasn't he? Quite different from Mama."

"Yes, and we were freer than some old gossipy women around here
in Lynchburg thought we ought to be. You know, I never would ride in
the back of the trolley car—oh no!" she laughed. "I'd thumb a ride in
somebody's buggy, wagon, or car, if they had one. Some of my suppose-
to-be friends would say, 'Annie, that's unbecoming to a lady.' It might
have been unbecoming, but it was great for the spirit. They'd just shake

their heads when I told them it was more unbecoming to a lady to ride in the back of a trolley car."

"Yes, I agree," I said. "There was more dignity in that wagon with you."

"Not only that, but it gave me an opportunity to know and talk with many different people. I learned a lot about the earth and planting from farmers who picked me up in their wagons. High-society folks can be so boring talking about their furs and diamonds."

"You and Mama were very much alike on that too. It's amazing how many parallels. When we moved to Montclair, many of Mama's closest friends were those who worked in service." I told Aun' Tannie how once when Mama had a party and, as she always did, invited all of her friends, one of her "bourgie" friends, as young people call them now, hands heavy with diamonds, asked Mama if it was necessary to have "these people" there.

Before I could finish Aun' Tannie laughed. "I know who that was and I know what your mama told her. 'We are *these people*,' your mama said. Then she added, 'Bad enough for white folks to divide us, but when we do it, it's a sin—just didn't make its way into the Ten Commandments!'"

We both had a good laugh. "I can just hear Mama," I said, "and never raising her voice."

"No, but Mary's responses sometimes could be like a velvet-edged knife, quietly cutting to the core."

"Mama always told us if we screamed and hollered while trying to make a point, all people would remember was that we screamed and hollered. She certainly wanted them to hear every word *she* said."

"Some of the women around here thought we should let the men take care of our fight for equality, but Mary and I were right there in the middle of it," Aun' Tannie said. Then she told me about James Weldon Johnson coming to Lynchburg to organize the NAACP branch there. She'd arranged for the meeting to be held at the library. "Mary," she said, "was elected secretary or treasurer. I don't remember some details at this age, like exactly what date, but it was either 1917 or 1918.

"One reason Jim [James Weldon Johnson] was working so hard with the branches all over was that there were so many lynchings during that time. We needed to fight for an anti-lynching bill. One of the senators, I don't remember his name, introduced an anti-lynching bill."

"Was that the Dyer bill?" I asked.

"I guess so, doesn't even matter now. Mary and I were working hard on this end. We took petitions around, spoke out in meetings against lynchings, and talked with people about writing letters to President Wilson. Jim later went up to Washington to lobby for the anti-lynching bill. It passed in the House but not in the Senate. No anti-lynching bill was ever passed. Never was." Her voice reflected disbelief.

I smiled at the thought of these two women, in the early years of the century, setting out against the grain. While some women were drinking tea and crocheting, Mama and Aun' Tannie were out there on dusty roads, going from house to house, crying out against the hanging tree.

"Your mama started early in her life fighting for equality. When she came to the seminary she was just nineteen or twenty, a strikingly beautiful young woman, fair skin, hazel eyes, soft reddish hair, and a sprinkling of freckles. When she walked into a room, she captured the attention of everyone there. We became friends right away and shared our greatest joys and deepest pain."

"That's why I came to talk with you," I said. "I know you must have many stories we've never heard."

She leaned back in her chair and told me what had happened to Mama when she was just twelve years old, in the later 1880s when things had gotten pretty bad for Negroes. Segregation was becoming formalized as it had not been earlier.

"Not many young people at twelve went up against that old bugaboo segregation, but Mary did," Aun' Tannie said. "When Mary told me this tale, seven years after it happened, I could see it still troubled her."

I listened entranced as Aun' Tannie told me the story of what Mama had done at the ice-cream parlor, embellished, I am certain, by Aun' Tannie's natural flair for drama.

"Mary must have been upset about being treated better than her brother because of her fair skin. All those years her father would take her—but never her brother—to places Negroes couldn't go. I call this story 'The Awakening,'" Aun' Tannie said. I pushed the breakfast plate aside and leaned in to listen to every word as Aun' Tannie told me of Mama's first protest.

One day, Mary was walking down the street with her friend Sudie, and they passed the ice-cream parlor. As if some idea had struck her, she turned, grasped Sudie's hand, and walked back to the ice-cream parlor.

"Come on, we're going in here to get some ice cream," Mary said.

Sudie drew back. She knew this was not a place for her. "Mary, you're crazy. We can't go in there."

"I've been in here with my father many times."

"Yes, but you look—well, I mean, they never would know, your father being—."

Sudie did not finish either sentence. "White" was the word she swallowed. Some folks taunted Mary with "half-white nigger." Others, like Sudie, kept the word "white" like a lump in the throat. No need. Everybody in Harrisonburg, Virginia, knew Mary was General Jones' daughter.

"We're going in here, Sudie. You're my best friend and we're going in." Before Sudie could resist further, Mary pulled her into the ice-cream parlor. She told Sudie to sit at the table while she went to get the ice cream.

"Can't you just see Sudie now, poor thing?" Aun' Tannie said. "Probably afraid to lift her head, sitting there counting those little marble tiles they had on ice-cream-parlor floors in those days."

When Mary walked over to the counter, one of the customers, a big, strapping man with a thick crop of red hair, grabbed her arm and yelled to the owner to come out of the back room. "Somebody here is trying to be smart," he yelled. When the owner came out, the redhead pointed to Sudie. "Miss Smarty, here, brought *her* in."

"What! Mary, what are you doing bringing a Nigra in here?"

"She's my friend." Mary spoke softly.

"Get out of here, both of you—*now*." He grabbed the two twelve-year-olds by the arms, ushered them to the door, and pushed them out into the street. Sudie fell down, skinning her knee.

"I told you, I told you," Sudie cried, tears running down her smooth brown cheeks. Why'd you have to go and do a fool thing like that?"

Mary was not crying; she was mad. This was the weekend she was visiting her father. General Jones by that time often brought Mary to his home to spend time with him. Mary walked toward the house with a determined stride. "Come on," she said. "When we get home I'm gonna tell Papa what he did."

When they got to the house, Mary walked up the steps, each foot stomping the bricks. Sudie followed her, completely subdued. They went into the kitchen, where Sudie's grandmother, General's cook, was preparing dinner. When Mary related the ice-cream parlor incident, Sudie's grandmother turned on her, her dark brown eyes flashing.

"What's wrong with you, chile? Don't you ever do that again. Poor li'l Sudie. Don't you ever do that again. Something bad coulda happen to y'all. It's all right for you, 'cause you half white and look white so your papa takes you anywhere, but not so Sudie."

I know Mary felt the sting of those words. Some children yelled bad words at her, but Sudie's grandmother's scolding, even without the bad words, cut deeper. Mary did not want to reveal her hurt. She straightened her shoulders and started out of the room.

"Well, I'm gonna tell Papa about being pushed out of the ice-cream parlor," she said, confident that Papa could set everything right.

When her father came home, she did tell him. The response was not what she'd expected.

"Mary!" He was shocked. "You can't take Sudie in the ice-cream parlor."

"Why not, Papa?"

"You just can't, and don't ever go in there without me, especially after what you did. Do you hear me? And don't ever take Sudie in there. Do you hear?"

Mary persisted. "Why can I go in there and Sudie can't, Papa?"

"It's not up to you to ask questions. Just do as I say."

"But I don't like it, Papa."

"You're getting beside yourself. Go up to your room, Mary, and stay there until you're called to dinner." Annoyance in his voice now.

So Mary went out into the hall and climbed the spiral staircase, slowly, as if carrying a heavy sack. She walked down the hall to her room and sat for a long time looking out the window. Her eyes were fixed on the big oak tree at the other end of the garden; the empty swing moved slowly with the wind. Her father had put the swing there and she had enjoyed it all those years. Now the swing made her think of her brother, Willie. Papa never brought him here. Never pushed him in this swing. Whenever he came to get her, she pleaded, "Papa, please let Willie go." His answer was always the same. The feeling of joy of going with her father was overshadowed by the picture of her brother, Willie, standing there waving good-bye, tears rolling down smooth brown cheeks, as she, the fair child, rode away in the buggy with her father.

Mary knew for certain now. She had reached into dark corners and found something ugly there, something she had been a part of all her life. She could not define it, but she knew it was there. First, her brown-skinned brother, Willie, now her best friend, Sudie. "I don't like it. I don't like it at all," she said aloud. "And I'm going to do something about it," she vowed silently. She did not know what, but she knew she would do something.

When Aun' Tannie finished the story she commented, "I will always believe that was the spark that set Mary to spend her life fighting for equality and justice. She saw injustice even in her own family."

"That's some story," I said.

"Do you understand now why your daddy called your mama a rebel? She never changed."

WHEN I LEFT Aun' Tannie, I carried with me many stories about Mama, her father, her mother, her Uncle John and Aunt Dolly, who raised her, and her brother, Willie. I returned to Alabama, where I was teaching at Talladega College and, with my colleagues in the Sociology Department, organizing grassroots movements to mobilize the black community of Talladega to fight for equality and justice.

I tried then to write Mama's story, but finally realized that the Birmingham church bombings, the water hose, the dogs, and the assassination of Martin Luther King had filled me with rage. Debilitated by anger, I could not write an honest story. As I struggled with the narrative, I heaped my rage upon Mama's father. I put this story down, but I also visited Aun' Tannie twice more before she died in 1975, and I learned even more about Mama's early life — from her soul mate, the poet.

I did not pick the story up again until the late 1980s. And when I did, I decided to go on a search, a search for the father my mother never talked about.

Traveller take heed for journeys undertaken in the dark of the year
Go in the bright blaze of Autumn's equinox

—Margaret Walker, "October Journey"

Chapter 3

TRUTH SEEKERS

—

October 1990

We drove through the beauty of the Shenandoah Valley, my sister Rosemary and I, on our way to Harrisonburg, Virginia—the childhood home of our mother, Mary. Somewhere here we'd find the truth. I pulled the car over to the side of the road. We stood in silence, looking out at the quiet mountains—secrets of the past stored in their tight bosoms. Autumn sunlight through the pine trees created soft filigree patterns. Tranquility. But my childhood questions, locked many years ago in the fragile recesses of my mind, began to stir.

Who was here before me? As I stood there I felt ancestral ghosts surrounding us. This idyllic place, denying with its calmness what was. No sign of the big house or the cabins. No sound of galloping horses, or singing in the fields. My answers hidden in the shadows. Somewhere here we'd find the stories we never heard as children. There were no griots to take us back in time beyond our beginning, no Genesis list of *begot*s defining the strain of us. Only grown-up talk reaching young sensitive ears. Our mother's father was some Confederate general named Jones, a truth we'd rejected for a long time. That day we came looking for him.

We had started out at the South Caroliniana Library, where we were given the name of a librarian at the James Madison University library. There we were led to the Carrier Special Collections librarian. When we explained why we were there, the librarian took a Civil War book from the shelf and searched through the pages until she found General Jones' name.

"This must be your mother's father," she said. "General John R. Jones.

We still weren't certain that this was the man we were looking for. There was no information yet to connect him with Mama. The librarian, seeming excited about it, said she would have a student, doing research on General Jones, call us at our hotel that evening.

Rosemary and I spent the afternoon poring through books Chris Bolgiano gave us on Harrisonburg, Rockingham County, and the Civil War.

From John W. Wayland's *A History of Rockingham County, Virginia,* we learned something about the setting into which Mama was born. Rockingham County, in the western part of Virginia, was unlike the large slaveholding counties in other parts of Virginia. There were many religious groups: "the Mennonites, Dunkers [German Baptist], Methodists, some of the Lutherans and Reformed and United Brethren opposed the Institution of slavery," Wayland reported. "Their well-known attitude on this question subjected them to no little unpopularity and to some persecution."

These religious groups had apparently been working against slavery for a number of years. Wayland says in 1790 all of the Negroes in the county were reported as slaves. There were apparently no free Negroes there at that time. However, due to the work of the "Methodists and the other religious bodies in behalf of emancipation, by 1810, there were 200 free Negroes in Rockingham County."

We wondered if any of our ancestors were among this number. We'd always heard that Mama's mother was born a slave, but we have never known upon what plantation.

John Wayland's book told us that in 1875, the year Mama was born, Harrisonburg "had a colored policeman, Joseph T. Williams, who was also a barber. In 1889, James Cochran, colored, was a member of the grand jury." This information gave us a warmer feeling about Mama's old hometown.

Then we ran across a footnote in Wayland's *History of Rockingham County* that gave us our first information about General Jones: "John Robert Jones, son of David S. and Harriet Yost Jones, was born in Harrisonburg in 1828. As captain he served the South with distinction in Florida, March 1861; in April following, he enlisted a company of 104 men in Rockingham County, VA. and joined General Johnston at Winchester, his company a little later being made Co I, 33 VA Infantry, Stonewall Brigade. In August 1861, he was made Lieutenant Colonel of the 33rd Regiment, and in July 1862 was promoted to the rank of Brigadier General. He was captured at Gettysburg, and held prisoner at Johnson's Island and at Fort Warren until July 1865." There was also a reference to General Jones quoted from the *Richmond Times* of April 4, 1901. At his death, survivors were listed as Clay Jones of Alexandria, Virginia, David Jones of Abingdon, Virginia, Samuel Jones and Dewit Jones of Washington City, and Jacob Y. Jones of California. All of these brothers had served in the Confederate Army. Rosemary commented, "Whether we want to admit it or not, if this is General, these were Mama's uncles."

We still had no proof that this was Mama's father, but it seemed likely, and knowing the details of his involvement in the war on the side to defend slavery was unsettling.

"When you think about it," Rosemary said, "he was fighting to keep our grandmother in slavery."

"That's a tough one to swallow," I responded.

When it came too close, we were both silent for a moment. Then, as if wanting to move away from that, we looked over such mundane information as typical weather in Harrisonburg and population.

Before we closed Wayland's *Historic Harrisonburg* we read his summary of the conditions around Harrisonburg after the war; he spoke of the progress since the "wreck and matter caused by the unnatural and fratricidal war." In that citation we found General Jones mentioned again. He was given credit for helping restore the area after the war. The following excerpt from the *Rockingham Register* quoted in the book states: "General Jones of Agricultural implement fame, has done a great deal, by his indefatigable business qualifications, toward building up the fortunes of the husbandmen of our county. He has furnished the farmers and others with labor-saving machinery, upon such conditions as enable them to purchase, by which to sustain themselves and retrieve their losses."

As the afternoon dwindled, Rosemary picked up *My Recollections of Rocktown — Now Known as Harrisonburg,* by Maria G. Carr, written in 1892, when Mrs. Carr was eighty years old. In her book we found reference to the home of Harriett and David Jones, General Jones' parents. Later we visited the spot where that house had been.

Rosemary pointed out a passage, as we read Maria Carr's book, that showed she must have been one of those troubled by slavery: "It was a common thing to see Negro men driven through the town chained together going south to be sold—women and children following in wagons singing the most mournful songs."

That evening the student interested in J. R. Jones called the hotel, identified himself as Dale Harter, and asked, "What is your connection to General Jones?" I said I wasn't sure if we were talking about *the* General Jones, but that my mother's father was *a* General Jones from Harrisonburg.

"What was your mother's mother's name?" he asked.

When I said Malinda Rice, he gasped. "Malinda Rice!" he exclaimed. Then in a more subdued, apologetic tone he asked, "Do you mind if I tell you something?"

"No," I said. "I'm looking for truth, whatever it is."

"Well, I was in the courts the other day and found the divorce papers of General Jones' second wife." He hesitated. "You sure you won't mind?" he asked again.

"No," I said. "You're a researcher and I know you search for truth. That's what I'm looking for. I tried to write a story based on assumptions, but now I'm looking for truth."

"The papers said that General Jones' second wife divorced him 'on grounds of adultery with one Malinda Rice.'"

We were about to meet my mother's father.

DALE HARTER WAS as excited to meet us as we were to meet him. He was friendly, enthusiastic, and knowledgeable. We wasted no time, moving immediately into an exchange of stories, his about General Jones, ours about Mama, her mother, Malinda, and the other family members on that side that we knew about, Uncle John and Aunt Dolly.

Dale Harter had not known about our mother, though he knew that General Jones had a second black mistress after Malinda died, and there were two sons of that union, and that he had left his whole estate to them.

I told him that there were two children with Malinda Rice — our mother and her brother, Willie, who we call Uncle Billy. Malinda's brother, John, and his wife, Dolly, raised our mother and Uncle Billy.

Dale Harter was thrilled.

"I can't believe I'm sitting here talking with descendants of General Jones, and hearing stories from the other side," he said.

Since he was so interested I told him about talking with my mother's dearest friend, Anne Spencer, and about the many stories she told us that we had never heard. I related the ice-cream-parlor incident, how her father had taught her to read and sent her to college, and the story of the porcelain doll. I also told about Mama calling General Jones "Papa Sir." As Aun' Tannie told it, Mama's Aunt Dolly was preparing her for a visit to Malinda's family in Singer's Glen. General was to pick her up and take her there in his buggy. Aunt Dolly told her to be a good girl and not to forget her manners. Be sure to say "thank you" and be sure to say "Ma'am" and "Sir," she told Mama. When Mama's father came to the door, she opened it and said "Hello, Papa, Sir." Loving the laughter she caused, she continued to call him Papa Sir.

I also told him the little bit we knew about the relationship Mama had had with "Papa Sir." When she was a young child, he took her often to visit Malinda's family in Singer's Glen and he made up little verses as they rode through the hills of the Shenandoah Valley and saw the cows on the hillside. Aun' Tannie remembered only one, which went something like:

I have a cow named Bessie
who gives me lots of milk
and when she isn't messy
I dress her up in silk.

We learned then why Dale Harter was interested in General Jones. Though he was the only Confederate general from Harrisonburg, there was little about him in the history books. There was no monument, no pictures in public buildings. He wondered why he wasn't romanticized like other Confederate generals. General Jones seemed to have had all the "ingredients" other heroes had. He'd been born on March 12, 1828, into a family with a strong military tradition. General Jones was described as a man of medium height and build, with stark blue eyes. Both his parents, David and Harriet Jones, had immigrated from Ireland in 1801. He'd enrolled in Virginia Military Institute in 1845, was seventh in his graduating class of twenty-four. His status, at graduation, was that of the highest rank of the Corps of Cadets, first captain. He believed in and adhered to the discipline of the Army.

What was keeping him out of the history books? We were beginning to understand.

Dwell with me, and
be unto me a father.

—Judges 17:10

Chapter 4

PAPA, SIR

—

The next day Dale Harter drove us to the white cemetery, Wood-bine. There we stood, looking at a tall, obelisk tombstone with the simple inscription

GENERAL J. R. JONES
DIED APRIL 1, 1901
AGE 74
AT REST

"This is the man your mother called 'Papa Sir.'" Dale smiled. "Here is your grandfather."

"Grandfather!" I exclaimed, not quite ready to accept that truth. I learned later that Rosemary had had difficulty with that too. In telling the story of our trip when we were back home, she said, "Carrie found out who her grandfather was." I laughed and reminded her that he was her grandfather too.

Now I wanted to speak to General, ask him questions. Aun' Tannie had spoken of love. Had he loved Malinda? I had not thought of love. I had perceived the "monstrous system" as the ravishing of *all* our women. Love, the purest of human qualities, may have been buried under society's rubble. Perhaps Aun' Tannie was right. We don't really know.

I wondered, too, if Mama's Papa Sir had ever told her any war stories. As close as they were, and as precocious as she was, did she ask questions? What were her feelings as she grew older, knowing her mother was born a slave and her father was on the Confederate side? Conflicting emotions must have tugged at her and must surely have had something to do with her course in life. As W. E. B. Du Bois says in *The Souls of Black Folk,* Mama, too, must have felt the "two souls, two thoughts, two unreconciled strivings."

Next, Dale took us to the black cemetery, Newtown. There we stood before a very small, plain tombstone marked

MALINDA RICE

BORN MARCH 19, 1856

DIED FEBRUARY 9, 1885

We had just seen General Jones' tombstone, and I spoke to Malinda: "He was almost fifty and you were just a young girl when. . . ." Anger kept me from completing that thought, an anger that was later softened by the one fact I'd known before I came. This General, whoever he was, was devoted to his daughter, Mary, and she to him. Softened, too, by what Dale told us that day during our lunch. He believed General Jones had been written out of history because of his recognition of his black family.

"Seems to me that's an honorable trait," I said. "If a man has children, he should take care of them, and I'm certain General Jones wasn't the only Confederate who had black children." But even I knew it was taboo to own up to that, that that was the unpardonable sin.

Freeman, in his *Lee's Lieutenants,* says that after the war 'if any [Confederate] veteran went over to the Republican party or consorted with Negroes, it never was forgiven him.'

Dale told us the evidence is there that history turned General Jones off because of his relationship to his black family. Prior to this relationship, General Jones was honored as a hero. He was invited to and involved in special Confederate celebrations and was a judge at some of the events. He was also respected and lauded for what he did in restoring the area after the war. He was elected trustee of the public schools and was commissioner of the court. It was after he acknowledged his black family that he was treated as a pariah. Dale showed us a letter that expressed the thinking of the time. Someone had written to Harrisonburg asking for information on General Jones. T. L. Williamson, a Confederate veteran, wrote the following letter in response:

> General Jones is dead, and peace be to his ashes, for they were not very clean. You would be well to drop his name from the list of Honorable men, if such is your roster when complete. . . .
>
> After graduation of J. R. Jones (from V.M.I.) he engaged in teaching in the South until the breaking out of the Civil War; when he returned to Harrisonburg and organized a company for the service in Virginia. He joined the 33rd Virginia Brigade —Stonewall Brg. promoted to the rank of Brigadier General in Stonewall Jackson's Division. In the Pennsylvania campaign he was relieved of his command for what cause I am not able to say. My information is he was captured and spent the remainder of the war in prison. . . .
>
> His subsequent life was a great disgrace to him and this community. I could write more but I think enough has been said. Draw a line through his name and be sure and have it *Black*.
>
> T. L. Williamson

"The line through Jones' name is remarkably thick," Dale told us, and went on to say that he wanted to erase the line from history. Not only did Jones not try to hide his biracial children, he had evidently cared for them financially and emotionally. And that, to his contemporaries, was the truly unpardonable sin.

Dale said some wanted to claim that the line through Jones's name had been drawn because of his lack of real military ability and because of a rumor about his leaving the field at Chancellorsville. The truth about Chancellorsville has never been uncovered, but some called him a coward even though the rumor had been started by a man who was not even on the field at the time.

Ernest B. Furgurson's 1992 book *Chancellorsville 1863: The Soul of the Brave* mentions General Jones several times, but does not mention any unmilitary behavior. Colston's second line is described: "Louisianians on the left, then John R. Jones' Virginians and E. T. H. Warren's mixed Virginia–North Carolina Brigade." Furgurson also includes General Jones in the descriptions of action: "Rodes called up E. T. H. Warren's Brigade from Colston's division in the second assault wave. Already that second rank was on the heels of Rodes' division, mixing with it as the attackers charged, flowed around thickets and knots of Yankees and rode on. Now Warren's and J. R. Jones' Brigade surged forward with the leading wave."

The book mentions one more J. R. Jones incident, which may be what made some call him a coward. Colston at one point was left with four brigades and only one general commanding them. Furgurson says, "One of Colston's Brigadiers, John R. Jones, had taken himself to the rear with an ulcerated leg, being relieved by Col. Thomas S. Garnett." Some seem to think Jones was not sufficiently injured to warrant his moving away from the battle. According to Dale, however, Freeman, in his monumental work *Lee's Lieutenants,* found it "most unpleasant" to associate Jones's name with cowardice, but was forced to do so rather than "bring several gallant men under suspicion." Dale believes General Jones "wasn't a hero or a coward, a saint or a sinner, but someone far more complex. I found an ordinary man."

Among other documents that Dale gave us was this letter about Jones's request to President Johnson for pardon:

Fort Warren
June 13, 1865

Hon. Henry Wilson
of Massachusetts

Dear Sir:

General Raymond Lee of Boston enclosed to me to-day your letter to him relating to your visit to the President in my behalf. Permit me to express to you my sincere thanks for this act of kindness and to assure you that I will quite fully remember it. I applied to the President on the 31st of May to be admitted to the amnesty oath, and I learn officially that the paper had been in the hands of the commissioner General of his at Washington some days before your call upon the President. That application contained all the facts upon which the President would want to know in reference to my past course and my feelings, and I greatly regret that he had not seen it. I am a "veteran" prisoner, having been captured on the *4th day of July 1863*, nearly two years ago. The date of my capture extends much further back than that of my group. I am therefore painfully anxious to be released, and my case, having some peculiar features, I think that it would have received the favorable consideration of the President. I know that no evil could result to the United States by my immediate release, and I am sure some benefit, for I am prepared to accept fully the result of the sword and to devote myself to peace and to the reorganization of society, with slavery wiped out and in submission to the authority of the United States. I mean to be as good and faithful a citizen of the United States as any one.

An order in yesterday's papers from the Attorney General states that an application to the President must be accompanied by the prescribed oath. I have no hesitation in taking the oath, but the authorities here are not authorized to administer it, so that I cannot comply with the condition.

Until other orders to the authorities here I am compelled to rest the matter upon the simple application to the President, which I have already made. Trusting to your good offices and the consideration of the President for my speedy release.

I am very respectfully

> your obedient servant
> Gen. J. R. Jones

When we returned home I had the weird curiosity to trace General Jones' *involvement* in Stonewall Jackson's 1862 Valley Campaign. I went to the South Caroliniana Library and searched books there, especially volume 2 of *The War of the Rebellion,* which gives detailed movements of the troops on both sides. There was one entry about how General Jones' troops drove the Union Army from the field; other than that it listed nothing of real military significance in relation to General Jones. There are a number of references to him in the Peninsular Campaign. The report said that on Monday, June 13, 1862, Jones' troops crossed the Chickahominy and set up camp. On Tuesday they moved toward Malvern Hill. There a piece of shell went into General Jones' knee and Lieutenant Cunningham took over.

Dale Harter's article "Ignored by History" maintains that General Jones was noted only as "distinguished" during the battle of Kernstown.

In fact, Dale reports that General Jones' most significant military mission during the Valley Campaign was not directed against Union forces. In late March, Stonewall Jackson assigned Jones the unenviable task of subduing a rebellion, known as the Rockingham Rebellion, in the Virginia militia. Jones shelled the woods where the militia were hiding and the rebels (his own side) surrendered to him. That seemed to me a strange twist, General Jones less involved in attacking Union troops than in quelling a rebellion of Confederate troops. It was, however, a twist I found easier to accept.

I wanted to find out more about General Jones and his thinking so Dale suggested I go to Duke University's Perkins Library and read General Jones' scrapbook. Rosemary and I traveled to Durham, went to the library, and pored over his scrapbook. This allowed me to get inside General Jones' head. It was strange to find so many ideas that paralleled Mama's. Coincidence? Perhaps. Values passed from father to daughter? More likely.

His concern for the homeless and the poor was often expressed, and a poem about the homeless was in the scrapbook. Mama, too, was concerned about the homeless and the poor and over the years of her life took in many people who were without a place to stay. If you came to her house with your story and your suitcase, you would be given the little spare room on the second floor, in the front. It was kept open for that purpose.

We found General Jones expressing compassion for Italians. I don't know what was happening at that time, but he states, "If there is one country on the globe which more deserves the sympathy of mankind than another, that country is Italy." When we lived in Montclair, New Jersey, in the 1920s, Mama championed the Italian immigrants' cause on several occasions, once in regard to what she considered the prejudiced immigration laws favoring the British and Irish. She learned about this when one of Papa's clients, an Italian, found he could not bring his mother over. And while we children went around the house singing *Sacco-Vanzetti, Sacco-Vanzetti* because it had a nice ring to it, Mama was writing to the judge handling the case to admonish him for his prejudiced remarks about Italians.

General Jones' humor was evident in many comments in his scrapbook. Mama's sense of humor was known to all. General Jones' love of poetry was clearly evident. He had copied many poems into his scrapbook. Aun' Tannie had already told me that Mama's father had instilled in her the love of poetry, just as Mama did with us. She bought us *A Child's Garden of Verses* and, later, books of poems by the Harlem Renaissance writers. Were all of these similarities just coincidental or did they represent the passage of values from one generation to another? Mama spent much time with "Papa Sir," and I'd like to think it was the latter.

If we stand tall,
it's because we stand on
the backs of those who
came before us.

—Yoruba proverb

Chapter 5

THE RICE FAMILY OF SINGER'S GLEN

James Baldwin says, in *The Fire Next Time,* that you have to know where you came from to know where you're going. Rosemary and I were slowly piecing together our Genesis. We had considerable information now about the white side of Mama's family. We needed to find out more about her black family.

We knew that Mama was raised by her Uncle John (Malinda's brother) and his wife, Aunt Dolly, who had no children and loved and cared for Mama and her brother, Willie, as they would their own. My brother Hunter and Aun' Tannie brought Uncle John to life for me. When Hunter was a little boy, Mama used to take him to Harrison-burg to visit her beloved uncle and aunt. Hunter remembered their white two-story house and the railroad tracks that ran diagonally in front of it. Hunter sat on the porch with Uncle John, waving at the passengers as the train whizzed by and calling out "God speed" to those in the Jim Crow car going north.

Uncle John worked at the livery stable and told Hunter many stories about horses, as he must have done with Mama. He also sang the ditty "All the Pretty Little Horses" to Hunter. I'm sure he sang that lullaby to Mama when she was a little girl.

> Hushaby, don't you cry
> Go to sleepy little baby
> And when you wake,
> You shall have cake
> And all the pretty little horses

When Uncle John shaved, he let Hunter come into the bathroom with him and watch. Then he'd lather Hunter's face with the big sudsy brush and take the lather off with the back of a knife.

According to Aun' Tannie, Mama adored Uncle John. Aun' Tannie was convinced that some of Mama's self-esteem came from Uncle John, a proud man who felt he was "as good or as bad as any man." He was personable and had a quick wit, and although he was illiterate, he learned about the world from the white customers who came into the livery stable.

His white customers liked talking with Uncle John. Aun' Tannie believed they liked Uncle John's "white lightning" as much as his wit. Once Aun' Tannie told me this, I looked at his picture a little closer. "You little rascal," I said, smiling. If he could have responded, he probably would have said proudly, "But it *was* the best moonshine around."

Aunt Dolly, Hunter has told me, was a warm, motherly woman, a wonderful cook who loved to feed people. Certainly she passed this on to Mama, who was not an especially good housekeeper but loved to cook and feed anyone who came by. "There is always enough to share," Mama would say. "When more come to eat than expected, and if there is only one pork chop left, cut it three ways and serve it with a smile."

Hunter also knew our grandmother Malinda's younger brother, Uncle Ben, and his wife, Jennie. They came to Lynchburg to visit their son, Gilbert, who lived with Mama while attending Virginia Seminary there. Hunter says Uncle Ben was a farmer who apparently worked hard and did very well.

Unlike Alex Haley, we have not been able to trace our family back to a specific place in Africa. Like most African Americans, our knowledge of our ancestors begins in this country. I have, of course, always wondered about my African forebears. Who was first captured and brought over here, and when? A few years ago, I stood, for the first time, in front of the old slave mart on Chalmers Street in Charleston, South Carolina. I spent a long, solemn moment wondering if any of us came through there. More slaves were brought through Charleston than through any other port in the country.

As I stood, looking at this old building, my Grandmother Malinda's face from the picture of her on my bedroom wall appeared before me; her soft face, gentle, her long sleek neck, lace collared, the small bowler hat atop her thick hair neatly pulled back into a bun. I spoke to my grandmother and later wrote a poem for her, part of which says:

... Woman of dignity bondage does not benefit you
sculpted beauty of what African strain
Ibo, Fante, Ewe
Did you come through here
or some earlier generation bearing the seed of you?

I know now my grandmother did not come through Charleston. She was born after the last entry of slaves. Thanks to Dale Harter, the young researcher, we are able to trace members of Mama's family back to the end of the 1700s. They'd lived in this part of Virginia before Mama's father's people immigrated from Ireland in 1801. Another Dale, Dale McAllister, who lives in Singer's Glen, shared his father's cemetery research on black and white families of Singer's Glen and then went on to further sources, compiling more information on the Rice family of Singer's Glen.

Abraham Rice, Mama's grandfather, was born in 1816, the son of

Anthony and Malinda Rice, who lived in this area before the end of the 1700s. The record says their son Abraham was born "in the brush." I don't know exactly what that means, but I do know that a number of slave children were born in the fields. I have read several slave narratives of mothers giving birth in the field and returning to work the rows of cotton only hours later.

Abraham Rice married Martha Veney and they had six children. In the 1870 census a *B* is beside Abraham's name, for black. His wife, Martha, has an *M* beside her name, for mulatto. Shirlee Taylor Haizlip, in *The Sweeter the Juice,* says, "The English word Mulatto is derived from the Latin Mulus, for Mule, traveling down through the Portuguese and Spanish; its original meaning was much the same: Mixed breed." Hunter remembered a picture of Mama's grandmother in Singer's Glen on the mantel in our parlor. He remembers that she was very fair.

The 1870 census also lists Abraham's brother, Robert, and his wife, Sarah. Robert, two years older than Abraham, was a "fine cabinet maker." Abraham was listed as a laborer. The two brothers owned property and lived side by side in a small settlement of blacks "near an old Black church." Abraham and Robert were illiterate, and all but two of Abraham's children were illiterate.

ROSEMARY AND I took ourselves to Singer's Glen on a beautiful day, blue skies, soft white shifting clouds. The area around Singer's Glen is dairy country and all along the approach cows were grazing on hillsides. I can imagine Mama as a child, in the buggy beside her father, riding down this same road on the way to Singer's Glen, and imagine him making up that little verse about the cow named Bessie. I can see Mary and Willie, in the wagon with their mother, Malinda, and Uncle John and Aunt Dolly, riding down this same road on the way to some family gathering.

Singer's Glen is an enchanting village with a post office, city hall, and a few buildings in the town center; small farms spread out around it. We took some pictures and walked around. It was exhilarating to know that we were walking on the ground our great-great-grandparents, Anthony and Malinda, walked on two hundred years before, that later Abraham, Martha Veney, and their children also walked on.

I could imagine Abraham and Martha Veney walking their six children, John, Malinda, Maggie, Benjamin, Nancy Bell, and Martha, down these roads on Sundays to the little church. I could even see Mama and Willie, when they visited as children, sitting in church between Grandpa Abraham and Grandma Martha Veney. I can hear them singing some of the same songs we sang in the little country church I attended when I lived in Alabama, songs that have come down from one generation to the other, singing slowly, soothingly:

I want to thank you, Father
For being a friend of mine
um-um-um-um-um
I want to thank you, Father
For being a friend of
Mi-i-i-ine

I can see the pastor of the little church in Singer's Glen, praying as black pastors always have, generation to generation, offering prayers like the ones James Weldon Johnson describes in *God's Trombones:*

O Lord, we come this morning
Knee-bowed and body-bent
Before Thy throne of grace . . .
We come this morning—
Like empty pitchers to a full
Fountain . . .
O Lord—open up a window of heaven
And lean out far over the battlements of glory
And listen this morning

We wanted to find Dale McAllister and thank him for introducing us to our forebears. We also wanted to see if he knew exactly where the extra land was that Abraham purchased. When we inquired at the post office, the clerk told us that Dale McAllister, a teacher, was at the school. We asked if there were any members of the black Rice family in Singer's Glen and were told that they had all moved away.

McAllister's research showed that Abraham Rice bought other land besides the land his house was on. Deed research indicated that "Thomas Brew of Singer's Glen sold Abraham Rice three acres of land in 1876." The land cost sixty-three dollars and was "to be paid with a twelve month bond." Abraham Rice died in 1879. This reminded me of another interesting thing about Uncle John Aun' Tannie had told me about. He had a very superstitious nature and claimed that when his left eye twitched it signaled bad news coming, though Aunt Dolly would say, "Go on, John, you just got the itch-eye." I wonder if that eye twitched twice in 1879? Missus Sarah, as Malinda called General Jones' wife, died in April of that year and Mama's Grandpa Abraham died in October of consumption, the census says.

The Rice family sold Abraham's land in 1895. Martha Rice, Maggie Rice, Benjamin Rice, Mary Rice Hayes, and Willie Rice deeded their three acres to a Mr. Mowbray. The land was described as "in the neighborhood of Singer's Glen." Benjamin and Maggie Rice, who could read and write, signed their names. Martha Rice signed with an *X,* and J. R. Jones signed for his children Mary Rice Hayes and Willie Rice (who no longer lived in Harrisonburg). "The land was sold for $1.00 in hand."

Abraham must have worked hard to pay off the bond of sixty-three dollars. And the land was sold for one dollar? I thought of all the other ex-slaves who bought land only to have the family lose it. Thousands and thousands of acres of land owned by blacks have been lost, many times because of crooked tax schemes perpetrated by both whites and middle-class blacks. One of Mama's causes later on in her life was raising money to help save land owned by blacks.

It is interesting that none of the girls in the Rice family married. Malinda never married; however, we have heard that when she was young, before she went to the Jones's home, she was in love with a young man in her church. As late as 1895, the date of the signing of the deed, Maggie and Martha's surnames are still listed as Rice. John and Benjamin, it seems, were the only ones in the family that married. John married Aunt Dolly, and Benjamin married Jennie Smith. I wondered if any of the other girls suffered the same experience as Malinda did. In many black families, after the war, when the oldest girl reached a certain age she went to work as a live-in maid. At thirteen, Malinda was listed in the census as living with a Benjamin Bowman family near Mount Clinton, not too far from Harrisonburg, and most likely, she was living there as their maid. I don't know why she left there, but three years later she went to work for General Jones and her life took a different turn.

Ambiguous of race they stand,
By one disowned, scorned of another
Not knowing where to stretch a hand
And cry "My sister" or "My brother."

—Countee Cullen, "Near White"

Chapter 6

BORN "OUT OF TROUBLE"

I sit here with a picture of General Jones' house in my hand and imagine my grandmother, Malinda, at sixteen, approaching it for the first time. She stands back looking at this L-shaped, two-story house with its gabled roof, paneled front door, and amber sidelights. It looks warm and inviting to her. She walks slowly up the brick steps, pauses for a moment, then lifts the brass knocker. Inside Missus Sarah, General's wife, is waiting for Malinda to arrive to be interviewed for a job as her personal maid.

I see Missus Sarah and Malinda sitting, with the kitchen table between them, and discussing the details of the job. How much alike they are. The Harrisonburg newspaper the *Rockingham Register* describes Missus Sarah as "gentle, meek and with generous, sympathetic impulses." My grandmother has been described as gentle, soft-spoken, with a quiet dignity. She must have been just the kind of person Missus Sarah, by then frail and sickly, needed, and so she was hired to take care of her as well as the house. It must have been Lucinda, the cook, who showed Malinda around the house. Uncle John called Lucinda "the captain of the kitchen," a tall, heavyset woman with smooth, dark brown skin and a commanding posture. Lucinda had been the cook in charge of the kitchen on one of the few plantations in the area. This position was one of authority and respect in the plantation household. I can imagine that she would have pointed out the various areas of the house to Malinda, with authority and possessiveness.

The inside of the house is very large and imposing. There is a wide hall with a circular staircase, the kind a young girl might fantasize descending to meet her beau. For Malinda, this would have been Caleb, the young man in her church she intended to marry. After showing Malinda the rest of the house Lucinda must have led her back to her domain — the kitchen. At the end of the hall a door opens up into that large room with its smell of hickory from the wood stove. From all appearances, this is a comforting setting, nothing to fear here.

Malinda, a slender, graceful, mocha-colored girl with fine features, would not have met General, a man almost fifty, until she served the family at the dining-room table. Did he watch her, with those stark blue eyes, as she moved quietly in the room? Was she aware that something might happen to her in this situation? Blatant sexual exploitation of black women during slavery and just after emancipation has been well documented. In fact, a long line of descendants still present visible evidence of this. As my father, a light-complexioned lawyer, would say, "We are exhibit A." Reading about it has always upset me. Why couldn't it be stopped?

I was surprised to find in my research that some Southern whites were also troubled by this exploitation and did try to put a stop to it. Elizabeth Fox-Genovese says in her book *Within the Plantation Household*, "By the late 1850's some jurists, theologians, and uncommonly conscientious masters were beginning to worry about total lack of legal protection for slave women, as women, and were beginning to argue that rape of slave women should be regarded as a crime. But," she adds, "convention and attitude militated against a serious hearing of their views. White male sexual power followed naturally upon white male social power, oppressing both white ladies and black slaves, however unequally."

Did Malinda wake up on the morning of March 2, 1875, with shattering pains and know this would be the day? Did she pack a small bag and go quietly out the side door so she would not awaken General and Missus Sarah? I think so. She would have had to get to the north section of town, where her brother John lived. Dolly, his wife, would deliver her baby.

I see her walking, heavy with child, through the gray early-morning streets, the blustering winds of March whipping at her long coat. I hear her praying as she walks, "Dear Lord, if it is in your wisdom, please let my child come here brown like me."

Dolly delivered Malinda's baby, who "loudly announced her arrival in this world at three-thirty that afternoon," or so said Uncle John. Her Aunt Dolly cleaned her up, put the tiny flannel gown on her, wrapped her in a blanket, and took her to her mother. If Malinda did pray for a brown child, it must have upset her to see the child lying there in her arms looking too much like General.

They named the baby Mary Magdalene Rice. It seems likely that General selected the name Mary, as there are several poems in his scrapbook related to his love of that name. One, on page 119, by L. T. Cist reads:

I have a passion for the name of Mary
Sang once the greatest bard of modern time
And so have I! 'Tis not imaginary
And merely said for the sake of spinning rhymes
But honest truth, for I of praise am chary
Save then with truth and honesty its chimes
But sooth to say, the name I think is pretty
Alike for country maiden or for city

There is another poem in the scrapbook that speaks of "gentle Mary." This second one really interests me because the handwriting looks more childlike and indeed it was "composed by Willie." I wonder if that was Mama's brother, Willie—and whether or not his father inspired him to write poetry as he inspired Mama's love of poetry. This poem reads in part:

> I love thee gentle Mary
> with love so fond and true
> As the young flowers love
> the dew
> > composed by Willie

I hope it was Mama's brother Willie's poem. If so, it might mean General spent more time with his son Willie than we have knowledge of.

After Mary's birth, I wonder if Malinda stayed in her brother's home longer than was necessary. If so, was it to be with her child or the thought of returning to the Jones home to face Missus Sarah that kept her there? Fox-Genovese says white women in situations like this often "displaced their anger at their husbands onto slave women." However, I don't believe Malinda had to endure anything like this. We know, after all, that Mrs. Jones gave Mama a treasured doll, which speaks of a more sensitive person.

In Mrs. Jones was some of that humanity Aun' Tannie spoke of. She was ill for so long that she probably felt no one could care for her the way Malinda did. Theirs was a strange, complex relationship. Underneath there must have been a "smoldering," each woman with her own personal pain. What brought them together, oppression by the male, also separated them. Malinda may have received more rebuffs from Lucinda, the cook, than from Missus Sarah. Aun' Tannie said Uncle John believed Lucinda resented Malinda's elevation to housekeeper. I can hear her commenting, "You coulda gotten mixed up with your own kind," or some similar barb. I can understand if there was no good feeling between these two women.

When Malinda finally returned to the Jones home, Mary remained with Uncle John and Aunt Dolly. They had no children and loved and cared for her as if she were their own. Mama always spoke warmly of her childhood with Uncle John, and my brother Hunter and Aun' Tannie told me enough to piece together what it must have been like. When Mary was a little girl she loved to curl up in Uncle John's lap, probably listening to a lullabye he sang to her as a baby, his voice low and comforting:

Paint and bay, sorrel and gray
And all the pretty little horses
So hush-a-bye, don' you cry
Go to sleepy little baby.

Apparently Uncle John did not care too much for General, and there was animosity between them from the beginning. So General would often come and take Mary to Singer's Glen, where Malinda's mother, Grandma Martha, was more accepting of him.

These visits with Grandma Martha must have been good and warm ones, Grandma Martha cooking one of her good, old Southern dinners, including her Sally Lunn, a kind of sweet bread that we had often in our home. Hunter says General visited Singer's Glen often. Perhaps he found an acceptance there with the warm, embracing Grandma Martha that he did not find with Uncle John or with his own people.

General Jones' recognition of Mama as his child caused some to turn against him. Some whites stopped calling him General Jones. The Rice family, however, always addressed him as "General," not with the Jones attached but in this more intimate manner. General and Mrs. Jones had no children, and perhaps this was one of the reasons he was devoted to his fair, hazel-eyed child with the lively personality. Whatever it was, General took care of his black family, which later included Mama's brother, Willie, three years younger.

Back then many white men had black children, but "honorable" men did not admit it. Today we deplore fathers who don't acknowledge and care for their children, but back then it was all right for a white man to have a black child and, to be "honorable," you denied it. As my father's mother, a former slave, used to say, "Sometimes I understands chickens and pigs better than us people."

I can imagine that this was a difficult situation for Malinda to be in, despite the security in it. Perhaps the black community was accepting of her first child, the result of something over which she had no control. But I can hear some of those righteous black church ladies talking about her "fall from grace" because of her continued relationship with General and for having the second child. We might wonder ourselves why Malinda stayed on in General's house. Was it for economic reasons? Did she care for General? Was it, as one former slave answered when asked that question, "just the way things was"?

While their mother was serving as housekeeper for the Jones family, Mary and Willie continued to live with Uncle John. In the early years of freedom, strong extended family ties were one source of survival for the black family and the black race. Grandmothers, aunts, and uncles took on the role of parents just the way Uncle John and Aunt Dolly did.

After the death of General's wife, however, the children lived for a few years with their mother. General sold his house and moved in with the Jonas Lowenbach family. Jonas, a queen's-ware merchant from Austria, and General, also a businessman, had become friends. It must have been at this time that General bought a small house for Malinda and his children. The 1880 census reports that Malinda Rice, twenty-four, was living in Harrisonburg "keeping house." Her daughter, Mary, age five, and son, Willie, age two, were reported living with her. It also said Malinda could not read nor write. The census designated Malinda and Willie with a *B* for black and Mary with an *M* for mulatto.

And so Mary was a child of two worlds, both nurturing. Aun' Tannie summed up Mama's attitude in flowery, poetic terms: "Your mother," the poet said, "was as certain of her importance in the scheme of things as soft spring rain, gift from her father, a Confederate general, gift from her Uncle John, ex-slave. Two men of divergent backgrounds granting Mary the gift of self."

Mama never believed she was inferior, and she spent her life trying to spread this belief in personal worth to her people. To instill a sense of pride in us as young children, she told us stories of our heroes. "You will learn about George Washington in school," she said. "You will learn about Booker T. Washington at home. You will learn about Stephen Douglas in school and you will learn about Frederick Douglass at home." A lifelong friend of ours, Anne Hampton Slaughter, told me recently that what she remembered most about Mama was that whenever young people visited our home Mama would tell wonderful stories from black history, stories they had never heard before, "making us proud." One of the other aspects about Mama that impressed Anne when she was young was that Mama always talked with them about the importance of getting their education. She would take time with each one, remembering their names, and talking with them "like we were real important."

It is clear how Uncle John and General, in their different ways, were responsible for instilling these interests and values in Mama — a sense of pride and the importance, as Uncle John would say, of getting her "book learning." Her father, a former teacher, was determined that Mary would get as much education as possible. We know that before she entered school he taught her to read and bought books for her. Although Uncle John could not read, he passed many stories on to Mary, encouraging her to get her book learning. Mary, born of that first generation out of slavery, was spurred on by one who had been in.

Listen to the striving
in the souls of Black Folk.

—W. E. B. Du Bois
The Souls of Black Folk

Chapter 7

Book Learning

—

One of the stories Uncle John told Mary was about an old slave named Jeremiah. It was one of Mama's favorites, and she never forgot it.

Once on a time (Uncle John always started his stories that way), there was an old slave man named Jeremiah Solomon. (I picture Mama snuggled close to Uncle John, little Willie right beside her.) Now, this old man's real name was Jeremiah Brent because he belonged to Masta Brent. But he was a very wise old man, so everyone called him Jeremiah Solomon; that is, everybody except Masta Brent and a mean old slave woman named Aunt Kreasy. Anyways, lot of slave people knew things from the Bible like the Twenty-third Psalm, "The Lord is my shepherd." Well, one night Masta Brent's son, Robert, stole down in the dark to Jeremiah's cabin and gave him a Bible, on the sly. Masta Robert loved Jeremiah. When he was a little boy he'd run down to Jeremiah's cabin and they'd sit there eating sweet potatoes Jeremiah baked in the fireplace. Anyways, when they finished eating their sweet potatoes, Jeremiah would set Masta Robert on his knee and tell him stories, all kinds of stories about animals and things. How the possum tricked old fox and the like.

Now when Masta Robert gave Jeremiah the Bible, he showed him where the Twenty-third Psalm was. Masta Robert watched Jeremiah finger them words—"The Lord is my shepherd." Then Jeremiah jumped up. "I'm reading," he shouted. "I'm reading. I'm reading." Jeremiah felt it was a blessing to know how to read and just kept on thanking Masta Robert, and then he looked up to Heaven and said, "Thank you, Lord." Then Masta Robert cautioned him. "Jeremiah," he said, "you have to hide that book under your floorboards. Papa will be angry if he finds out, and you and I will be in trouble. But if we keep our secret, I'll come by every now and again and teach you how to really read."

When Masta Robert left, Jeremiah took that Bible, kept fingering "The Lord is my shepherd" and smiling. Then he took the iron from the fireplace, pulled up a board of his cabin floor, and hid that Bible under it.

Jeremiah learned how to read real good. But one day he got in trouble because of mean old Aunt Kreasy. She was a skinny old woman, and meaner than a hundred mules. She took care of a lot of little slave children while their mamas was in the fields and some other ones who didn't have no mamas there. Masta Brent sold them away to somebody else, so he got Aunt Kreasy to take care of them. Aunt Kreasy would fix a little fat meat fried to a crisp, then take the grease, make a little gravy, and pour it over some cornmeal mush. Then she'd parcel a little out to those poor little children and say in her old creaky voice, "That's enough to hang on your bones. Give you anymore be too heavy to do your chores." Mean old lady, she was.

She the one told Masta Brent about Jeremiah having a Bible and reading. Masta Brent went down there fuming. Aw, was he mad. Made Jeremiah give him the Bible. He tried to get Jeremiah to tell him who gave him the Bible, but Jeremiah just kept saying, "A child of God, sir. A child of God." Finally, Masta Brent just stomped on away, Jeremiah's

Bible under his arm. But see, he didn't know his son had given Jeremiah some other books, so Jeremiah kept those. It was against the law for slaves to read. But Jeremiah, after he learned to read, he taught a lot of little slave children to read, on the sly. Yes he did. Yes he did.

The story over, Uncle John would say to Mary, "You go on with all that reading your papa teaching you and one day you'll be a teacher and teach little children like Jeremiah did, and y'all won't have to hide your books."

MARY WAS BLESSED, too, to be growing up in Harrisonburg, Virginia, where, in 1870, free public schools were established for black children at the same time they were for white children. John Wayland, in *Historic Harrisonburg,* describes the school she entered in 1881 as a 25-by-40-foot building that not only was used for education but was "the rendezvous of the colored citizens for quite a variety of purposes. Here were held the old time devotion meetings." Praise was sung within those walls by ex-slaves thankful for a place for their children to learn. The building, Wayland says, was also used for "sociables and political meetings." Did the ladies bring jelly cakes and perhaps fix the Virginia favorite of house servants called "syllabub?" A recipe for syllabub in *Housekeeping in Old Virginia* (published in 1879) reads as follows:

½ lb. sugar
3 pts. of lukewarm cream
one cupful of wine
Dissolve the sugar in the wine (or cider) then pour it on the cream from a height, and slowly, so as to cause the cream to froth.

Mama told us they used to have poetry readings and "song renditions" at most sociables when she was young. Perhaps here in her school they sang and read poetry at their "sociables." Wayland says that no building in Harrisonburg caused the "indulgence of more pleasant reminiscences by the colored people than 'the little old school house by the creek.'"

Mary attended that little old schoolhouse for only two years. By 1881, because of the enthusiasm for learning, there was a constant increase in the number of students and the building was inadequate. The "colored citizens" brought this to the attention of the school board members, Messrs. Avis, Conrad, and Compton. The board asked the colored citizens to select a suitable site for the new school. Effinger Street was their choice. The mayor and city council appropriated two thousand dollars for the school, a two-story, four-room brick building with a staircase in the center. Each room was heated by a stove. Wayland says that, although it was not well ventilated or constructed in "strict accordance with the most modern ideas of school architecture, it was a decided improvement on the past and the mecca of the aspiring young Negroes in this section." In 1883, Mary, one of those "aspiring young Negroes," moved with the other students to the new Effinger Street School.

The teachers at Effinger not only taught but inspired their students. The year after the war and for many years to come, there was, especially in the South, a strong focus on education for ex-slaves and their children. Many longtime freedmen started schools for those coming out of slavery. Lerone Bennett, Jr., in *Before the Mayflower* says that "by 1870 the freedmen of Virginia were supporting 215 schools and owned 111 school buildings. Between 1865 and 1870, according to an estimate by Du Bois, freedmen contributed $785,700 in cash to black schools."

In Harrisonburg, the first school for black students was a mission school established in 1868 in an upper room of the old Scanlon Hotel by two white ladies from Maine, Misses Martha Smith and Phoeby Libby. Wayland says that although the students had to "climb, jump and stoop to get into the room, boys and girls crowded to the place daily, so anxious were they to receive instruction at the feet of their benefactors."

The American Missionary Association (of the Congregational Church) and the Quakers had been at work organizing schools for freed slaves and their children for a long time. With the help of the Freedmen's Bureau and other organizations, schools were springing up throughout the North and South. As black churches developed, they, too, played a significant role in organizing schools. Mary's Uncle John wanted her to be a part of this great awakening. Black students were making progress in education and the white board of trustees of Harrisonburg wanted to let white citizens see how far they had come in educating the children of ex-slaves. In 1884, they invited white citizens to the "closing program of the colored school." But because by then segregation had become a way of life, and violence against blacks was rampant, the black churches in town were reluctant to lend their buildings for the program. There must have been much discussion in the black churches about the trustees' proposal. Deacons and trustees must have gathered in one after another of the black churches as they waited for the pastor to tell them why he had called them to this special meeting. Uncle John may have been there in the front pew at one church. Always the pastor's prayer came first. I grew up in a black Baptist church and can hear that prayer: Oh Lord, our Lord we come together this evening with a heavy burden on our hearts. We come on bended knee for your guidance in this matter. Lord, help us this evening to find the right answer. We don't always know the right answer, but You do. There is so much evil of the devil stirring around out there all over our land. Our homes are being burned, our boys are left dangling from the hanging tree. Lord, have mercy on us, have mercy on us, Lord. Guide us this evening and protect us from evil. And Lord, when our days are at an end, let us find love and peace in your gentle kingdom, where our weary souls will be at rest. Amen.

A course of *Amens* ripples through the group. Then the pastor tells them why he called this meeting.

"Some mighty fine white folk on the school board, Mr. Compton, Mr. Avis, and Mr. Conrad, want to have the closing program of our colored school in our church. They want to show everybody the progress our children are making in their book learning."

The group probably responds, *That's right fine* until he clarifies that they want to invite "the public," including the white citizens of Harrisonburg.

The response from the men probably varied from "That would be right fine, Pastor" to "I know but we never tried nothing like this before and even though we always lived peaceable here, the Ku Klux Klan is seeping into places even like our town." And another: "We might wake up and find our church burned down. No, Pastor, I think we need to thank them for their kindness but we better come on out and say what's what. Sometime good hearted people can't see inside the evil hearted. But we can. Oh! yes we can. I think we better say no Pastor."

The fear was based on a horrible reality. Although Harrisonburg was a fairly peaceful town during and after Reconstruction, in other parts of the state violence against blacks was rampant. The reaction of whites to the "freedom" blacks were securing was to do everything to stem this. Segregation was moving in on every hand. Just the year before, there was a cross burning in front of a church down in Danville, my father's home. This was because blacks and some whites had gathered there to work out something to calm fears after a race riot there, where four blacks were killed.

A more serious change in 1883 was the U.S. Supreme Court's decision to declare unconstitutional the Civil Rights bill of 1875. This bill had granted blacks equal treatment in public places. Now segregation was sanctioned by the government, creating an atmosphere conducive to violence by the Ku Klux Klan. That year there were fifty-three lynchings in our nation. With all of this as a backdrop, there was reason for fear in the black churches.

Even with this setback, the trustees of the school board were determined to have the program and to open it to whites. They wanted to demonstrate the work the teachers were doing with their students. A

black teacher from Washington, D.C., Miss L. B. Bragg, had been secured as principal and they were proud of her accomplishments. Not to
be outdone, the school board held the program at the Masonic Hall.
Colored and white people streamed into the building. The program
went well, and there was no trouble there.

On May 15, 1884, the *Rockingham Register* reported on the program with glowing comments regarding the teachers and the students.

Our Colored Public Schools
THE CLOSING EXCERCISES AT MASONIC HALL
ON MONDAY NIGHT.

During all the years of public free schools in Virginia, Harrisonburg has had its colored school and teachers, and from
year to year the sessions have begun and closed, without any
special interest being manifested by any of our citizens except
the colored children and their parents, and possibly an occasional visit from a School Trustee or County Superintendent.
At the beginning of the present session, Miss L. B. Bragg, a colored teacher from Washington, was secured as Principal of this
school, and, by her capacity, tact and industry, in the prosecution of her work, she has attracted the attention of our School
Trustees to a degree never reached by her predecessors, and so,
when the closing exercises were held last week, and efforts to
secure one of the colored churches for the exhibition failed,
Messrs. G. F. Compton, J. L. Avis and Geo. O. Conrad, the
Board of Trustees, determined that these colored teachers and
colored scholars should have an opportunity of showing what
progress they were making in the problem of education, and
so, on Monday it was announced that the exhibition would
occur that night at Masonic Hall. Invitations were extended to
many of our white citizens to be present, and we were glad to
see that a goodly number felt sufficient interest to attend, and

we know none now regret that they did so. For our part, it affords us pleasure to bear witness to the evidence of good training and marks of advancement shown in every feature of the entertainment. The programme was admirably selected, perfectly free from all objectional matter, and was rendered throughout with a degree of correctness, promptness and modesty that cannot be too highly commended. Of course many of the scholars were frightened, and naturally so, it being the first exhibition of the kind ever given before a mixed audience in a public place, but we do not think there was a single instance where a part was forgotten or a failure made.

The programme was announced by Miss Bragg, and every scholar did well. The fact was clearly demonstrated that for natural melody the voices of the colored people are superior to those of the white, and in some instances marks of cultivation were plainly discernible.

I had a good laugh over that generalized statement about the voices of blacks being superior. Of Mama's ten children, only one, my brother Bill, could sing. In the last book Langston Hughes wrote before he died in 1967, one of the humorous captions read: "Misery is when your white teacher tells the class that all Negroes can sing, and you can't even carry a note."

The next paragraph of the newspaper article read:

Intermediate Department—L. F. Simms, Teacher
My Country 'Tis of Thee—by School
Nannie Bell's Troubles—Josie Cooper
All About Two Dolls—*Mary Rice* and Josie Cooper [italics mine]

There was Mama! Mama, at nine years old, right there in the newspaper. I can just hear her reciting that poem with Josie. Stand up straight and throw your voice so it hits the back wall, she would say to us when we had to perform. And did we perform? All through our young years Mama had us performing in all kinds of programs, at the Y, at church, and when she had company always, always at home. Bill with his wonderful tenor voice usually sang some weepy Irish-mother song, Dolly tap-danced, Rosemary played "Meditation" on the piano, I recited one of Countee Cullen's poems, and Mama smiled proudly. Yes, Mama would have us performing, guests or no guests, a lot of the times just for her and Papa.

I was glad to see from the article that Mama had such a dedicated teacher as Miss Lucy Simms, a remarkable woman, like many of her time. Born a slave in 1855, she graduated from Hampton Institute, class of 1874, with Booker T. Washington. She devoted her whole life to teaching. Wayland in *Historic Harrisonburg* said she taught for fifty-six years and never missed a day until she fell ill in 1933. She died in July 1934. Appropriately, a "new school building for Negroes," erected in 1938, was named after her. An interesting note in this account was that the school "stands on a part of the Gray estate 'Hilltop,' where she was born a slave."

Mama had the best of all worlds in relation to her "book learning"—a father who was dedicated to her education and an uncle who inspired her to move on up that ladder. And then Miss Simms.

The article in the *Rockingham Register* intrigued me. So much was written and discussed back then about the inability of blacks to learn and their inferior intelligence, a notion that raises its ugly head periodically. This refutes that. Thank you, Messrs. Compton, Avis, and Conrad. Mary was the first one in her immediate family to secure any "book learning." I know her mother, her father, Uncle John, Aunt Dolly, and her brother, Willie, must have left the Masonic Hall feeling very proud.

I'm so glad
Trouble don't last always.

— Negro spiritual

Chapter 8

THE SCANDAL

—

*I*n 1883 a "scandal" involving Mary's mother was the talk of Harrisonburg. Dale Harter sent me the legal papers claiming that General's second wife had divorced him "on grounds of adultery with one Malinda Rice." Maria Carr in her book *My Recollections of Rocktown—Now Known as Harrisonburg* says the public spring was the "news depot for servants in town—a place where they met to exchange news." Certainly General's divorce would have been a choice morsel to bat around. "Chile, did you hear 'bout Malinda? She done caused that woman to leave her husband." "Well I knowed something was gonna happen. I heard my missus talking about that sometime ago." "Mine too. She a friend of Mrs. Jones and I heard her say that marriage wasn't going to last. It's a downright shame." "All y'all doing is talking 'bout Malinda. What about him? He the one got her into this mess."

Black maids have always gathered somewhere to pass on gossip about the families they worked for. That's why we knew more about the white folks' business than they did about ours. When we were growing up in Montclair, New Jersey, every Thursday, maids' day off, friends of Mama's who were "in service" would come to our house bringing stories about the "goings on" of rich white folks. One in particular, Miz Nettie, a woman of more than ample size, loved to rear back in her chair and laugh, "The maid that's going around white folks' table ain't just passing bread." Then she'd add, "And the grapevine from maid to maid is always bearing."

I imagine that General's scandal was not just whispered from maid to maid, but also discussed among the white men who frequented the livery stable where Uncle John worked: "Yep, guess the old man couldn't give up his chocolate drop." "That man, with his black children all over the place, is a disgrace to our community. That lovely lady never should have married a rascal like that in the first place."

I wonder how Uncle John felt listening to them talking about his sister. And how Aunt Dolly stood the church ladies whispering behind their fans as Malinda walked down the aisle: "It's a shame befo' God. Look at her. She better pray to the Lord to forgive her."

General Jones married his second wife, a lady from a socially prominent Maryland family, and moved into his new home in 1881. He not only continued to visit and care for his children, however, but also continued his relationship with Malinda. The law did not allow them to marry, and they probably would never have considered such a thing, but the relationship was strong and endured over the years.

This was not an unusual situation in the South during and after slavery. John W. Blassingame, in his book *The Slave Community,* says, "A number of white men sought more than just a fleeting relationship with black women." Mary Chesnut speaks of the "Patriarchs of old" and their "concubines," and in much of the literature of old England we find acceptance of mistresses. Perhaps the custom came across the waters, settling in the psyche of early privileged white society here. Even so, it certainly wasn't acceptable to everyone, especially the wives, who, like the black slave women, were powerless and passive. General's new wife, however, unlike the gentle Missus Sarah, found her own situation unacceptable, and decided to do something about it.

There was a poem in General's scrapbook that made me wonder if it had any connection to the failure of the second marriage.

They told me not to love him
They said that he would prove
unworthy of so rich a gem
as women's purest love

Maybe not, but at the very least it tells us something about General that he would keep a poem of this nature in his scrapbook.

General and his second wife were not married very long; after barely a year she started collecting information in preparation for a divorce. It was very rare for women back then to seek divorce, and it must have been a difficult decision for General's wife to make. I wonder, in preparing for the divorce, did she have someone follow General, or did she do it herself? The divorce papers report he was "seen going into Malinda's house on August 5, 1882, January 21st and 22nd 1883 and various other times."

The case was heard in Rockingham County Circuit Court on May 23, 1883, and General's wife was granted a divorce on the grounds of adultery. It upset me to see my grandmother, the woman Aun' Tannie spoke of as one of beauty and dignity, called a "lewd woman" in the papers. General was not, however, called a lewd man, nor was he referred to by any other derogatory term.

More than likely Malinda was rebuffed by whites as well as blacks in Harrisonburg. I know some must have spoken unkindly of Malinda. Since Mama was called "half-white nigger" by some blacks, what were they calling Malinda? It had to have been a terrible time for Malinda, to say nothing about how it was for Uncle John, who loved and protected his younger sister. And some of it had to spill over on the children. The breach, too, between Uncle John and General had to have been upsetting to Mama. She loved Uncle John and she loved Papa Sir, and children want those they love to love each other.

I wonder, too, how much Mama knew about what was happening. Sometimes when adults are upset about something, they talk, forgetting children are there. If Mary heard her Aunt and Uncle discussing the scandal, did she hear the word "divorce"? Did she hear them call her mother "lewd woman"? Careless adult conversation falling on young, sensitive ears. Mama, at eight, most likely did not know what those words meant, but tones and nuances let children know whether something is good or bad.

Mary and Willie may have been taunted by children in school: "Your mama a bad woman. 'Cause my mama said so." Children can be very cruel in passing on bad things they hear about others. I do know, however, from all Hunter and Aun' Tannie told me about the kind of man Uncle John was, that he had some answers that would comfort them. "Now, children," I imagine he said, "I know you don't understand all the things happening right now, but don't listen to what folks say. I want you to listen real good to Uncle John." (I picture Mama and Willie sitting there close to Uncle John, listening to his every word.) "Some things children find hard to understand, so do us old folks sometimes. But one thing for sure, your mama a good woman. She's gentle and kind to everyone she meets. You know how, after a long day's work she takes food down to old man Sawyer lying there so sickly. She don't have to do that. In her quiet way she just let a little light shine wherever she go. So who you gonna believe, your Uncle John or some of those old no-good flabber-mouth people out there?" How could you not believe Uncle John?

The Rice family suffered with Malinda through the "scandal." But as the old African Yoruba proverb says, "If rain does not fall, corn does not grow."

Lay me down beneaf de willers in de grass
whah de branch'll go a'singin' as it pass.
An' w'en I's a-layin low,
I kin hyeah it as it go
Singin' "sleep, my honey, tek yo' res' at las'"

— Paul Laurence Dunbar,
"Death Song"

Chapter 9

"In My Father's House"

—

*A*un' Tannie said she believed that Malinda's love and pride in her children helped her through many storms. She was proud that both Mary and Willie were doing well at the Effinger Street School. Every evening she watched Mary sitting with Willie, helping him with his schoolwork, the light from the oil lamp soft on their faces. She wanted the best for her children, and she knew, without a doubt, that General would see to it that Mary went as far in her education as she was inclined. She was not as certain, however, that he would give Willie the same opportunity, and that troubled her. She did know that her brother John would do all he could for Willie. A comforting thought. She envisioned a bright future for both of them, but did not live to see it.

Uncle John told Mama some years later that Malinda was suffering with a pain in her side and stomach and was losing weight. I wonder if General suggested it might be kidney stones, and if he recommended that she drink the water from Lithia Springs. Dale gave me an advertisement ("certificate" they called it back then) that claimed that General, who suffered from kidney stones, started drinking the spring water and was relieved of them. In the pamphlet containing his endorsement it said, "Lithia Springs is on the line of the Shenandoah Valley Railroad, Rockingham County, Virginia, near the base of the Blue Ridge Mountains." The water was said to be of "crystal clearness." On May 14, 1886, General Jones wrote this endorsement of Bear Lithia Springs water:

> "Between the summer of 1881 and the autumn of 1883, I had fifty attacks of nephritic colic, many of intense severity. I could get no relief except from morphia. At the suggestion of my doctor, Dr. J. H. Wolfe, I sent to Bear Lithia Springs for water, and drank it freely—. Since then I've had no attacks. I get five gallons at a time."
>
> J. R. Jones

If he had so much faith in this, he may have suggested it to Malinda. But even if he did, it did not help. For Malinda, the pain became more intense, and on February 9, 1885, she died.

Mary, who would be ten the next month, knew what death was now. She had seen the deaths of Missus Sarah and Grandpa Abraham, but this one was more real. Her mother lay in her parlor in the pine coffin, and family and friends gathered there for "sitting-up" night. I envision the next morning in the little church—Grandma Martha, even through the pain of losing her daughter, comforting the others, Willie and Mary leaning close against their Uncle John and Aunt Dolly. Malinda's death must have been devastating to Uncle John.

I can hear the pastor's sermon. Generation after generation, black pastors repeat John 14:1–2: "Let not your heart be troubled: ye believe in God, believe also in me. In my Father's house are many mansions: if it were not so, I would have told you. I go to prepare a place for you . . . that where I am ye may be also." I don't have to wonder if that was the passage. In black churches funeral services are designed to help you let out your grief, loudly, right there in the pews. No quiet tears. An unin-

hibited unleashing of emotion. I *know* the pastor set the scene for Malinda's "homegoing" dramatically: "Our sister Rice quietly left us for
her journey, journey to our Father's house. She is now up there within
the pearly gates, up there resting in the bosom of Jesus. She's smiling
down on us. Amen. Smiling down on you, her beloved children. Smiling down on you, her mother, and on you, her brothers and sisters.
Smiling down to let us know she is all right—all right, sisters and
brothers, safe in the arms of Jesus. Sister Rice was a kind, gentle, loving
person and God wanted her to join his angels."

Then the choir would have sung something like "Crossing over the
Waters," and the pallbearers would have lifted the pine coffin and
moved slowly down the aisle, followed by the family. I wonder if General was there in the rear of the church. One does not have a sustained
relationship over a period of twelve years without feeling loss. Would
he have acknowledged his loss in public?

If the graveyard was near the church, the pallbearers carrying the
coffin would have walked solemnly to the gravesite. If not, the coffin
would have been placed in a wagon and the family and friends would
have followed in wagons and buggies. Mary and Willie would have
watched the lowering of the coffin while the minister repeated words
they did not understand about "ashes" as their gentle mother was laid
to rest.

AFTER THEIR MOTHER's death, Mary and Willie moved back in with
Uncle John and Aunt Dolly, where they would remain for the rest of
their young years. Uncle John's house had always been as much home
to them as their mother's. They already had their own rooms there, had
spent the days there while their mother was at work, so this move was
not too unsettling. It was there they listened to the stories and wisdom
of Uncle John, wisdom that stayed with them throughout the years.
Wisdom that Mama passed down to us. One bit I remember well, as
Mama spoke it many times: "Be taller than your dog." I was grown up
before I understood that it meant set your standards high. Whenever

we would say something like, "Well, the other kids can do that," she would respond, "Be taller than your dog, be taller than your dog." Being taller than our dog may have kept us out of a lot of trouble, but it sure did limit what we thought would have been a high old time. Another bit of Uncle John's wisdom Mama passed down was, "We're all God's children. Always respect others." (Mama wrote that one in my junior high school autograph book.) Uncle John, as we already know, stressed education. "Press it down in your very bones," Mama would quote him. Then she'd add, "But don't let it stay there. Use it for our people." Mama was what was known as a "race person" back then. She believed that everything you undertook, you undertook not just for you and the family, but with the whole black race in mind.

Mama told us that living at Uncle John's was a school of life for her and Willie. Each had their daily chores. Willie fed the hogs, carried logs in for the fire, and did some of the heavier chores as he got older. Mama kept the backyard swept, set the table, and did the dishes. When Aunt Dolly was cooking, Mama loved to be in the kitchen with her. On Saturday nights Aunt Dolly let her knead the dough for the Sunday morning hot rolls. Mama loved to cook and carried this over into her adult life. On Saturday nights, Mama made the same rolls for us. She let us help her knead the dough. By the time we finished playing with it, it looked like a lump of gray clay; but on Sunday morning the best hot rolls in the whole world would come out of Mama's oven.

As Malinda had hoped, Uncle John spent much time with Willie. On occasion he would take the boy down to the stables with him. When Willie was older, he let him shoe and groom the horses. There was one horse Uncle John let Willie call his own, a beautiful chestnut filly, who danced whenever she saw Willie. Willie named her Dancing Girl.

Malinda was also right about Mama. When Mama was fifteen or sixteen, General started making plans to send her to college. I imagine he talked with someone like Miss Lucy Simms and found out about Hartshorn Memorial College, at that time one of the best schools for young black ladies. Hartshorn was founded in 1883 in Richmond, Virginia, by a white minister, Reverend J. C. Hartshorn of Providence, Rhode Island, "to honor the memory of his wife." A sum of twenty thousand dollars was donated to purchase land and erect a building. Professor Lyman B. Tefft, who was connected with the Roger Williams College, became the first president.

I'm certain that when General read, "The purpose of this institution is not to do the work of the common school, but receiving pupils, the most advanced and best," he thought, Yes, that would be for Mary. Hartshorn was one of the finest schools for teacher education at that time. It was dedicated to giving students "that instruction and discipline which shall develop the highest qualities of intelligence and womanhood." Yes, Mary would go to this school. When the time came, her father took her up to Richmond and enrolled her in Hartshorn Memorial College.

Parting they seemed to tread upon the air
Twin roses by the Zephyr blown apart
Only to meet again more close, and share
the inward fragrance of each other's heart

—John Keats, "Isabella"

Chapter 10

A Knight in Shining Armor

From all reports, Mary excelled during her years at Hartshorn. The catalogs list her as winning the second prize in an essay competition during both the 1891–92 school year and the 1892–93 school year. And Mary Magdalene Rice was listed among the students in class A. When I saw in the 1892–93 catalog that she won the first prize in dramatic recitation, my thoughts went back to the nine-year-old Mama reciting "All About Two Dolls" at the Effinger Street School. During Mama's final year in the normal course, she also won the President's Silver Medal for her graduating essay.

After graduation from the normal course, Mama was enrolled in "higher English and Latin courses"—first and second years. While at this college level, the students organized the Rachel Hartshorn Education and Missionary Society. I was not surprised to see Mama listed as the president that first year. Nor was I surprised to see that the purpose of the organization was to "awaken a deeper interest in education" and to raise funds for education and "be a helping hand of the institution." The importance of education was, as Uncle John used to say, "deep down in her bones." I can still hear her, repeating, as she always did to us, "Education is the road to full freedom. We must, as Negroes, get on it." As children, we didn't know exactly where that road was, but we did know one thing—we had better find out and get on it.

The Hartshorn catalogs also mentioned that Mary Rice received first *and* second medals "for excellence in instrumental music." The award was named after Rosa Kinkle Jones. That name caught my interest. Mama had often spoken of her. She was one of Mama's mentors, and as parents did then, Mama named Rosemary after her. When Mama was in school in Richmond, she spent much time in Rosa Kinkle Jones's home. She mentioned one overnight visit in a letter she wrote to Willie:

> Mrs. Rosa Kinkle Jones invited me over to her house to spend Saturday night and go to church with them the next morning. It was nice, all except the fact that I had to sleep in the same bed with their seven year old son, Eugene, who kept kicking me in the back.

Many years later, Eugene Kinkle Jones, the first executive secretary of the National Urban League, came to our house in New Jersey for dinner. While we were all sitting around the big table in the dining room, he made a comment that really startled me. "Mary," he said, "was the first woman I ever slept with." I was a teenager, and all kinds of thoughts ran through my head. I was upset, but there he was laughing. Papa laughed too, and Mama sat there smiling. I certainly couldn't understand Papa's response. It was not until later, much later, that I read Mama's letter to Willie. It was a relief to know that "slept" did not mean *slept*.

When Mary went home the summer before her last year in school, she learned that Willie had gone on the boat to Boston. He was working on the boat, and when he arrived in Boston, he decided to stay there. Mary was concerned. "But he is just fifteen," she said. She was protective of her little brother and was reluctant to let him go. Apparently Willie was quite capable of taking care of himself. He secured a first job in a livery stable, having learned the trade from Uncle John.

Willie, or Uncle Billy as we called him, later secured a job as houseman for a fraternity house on the Fenway. He lived and worked there for the rest of his life. When he would visit us, he'd bring many stories (some rather risqué) about the "goings-on" in that house, especially during the roaring twenties. One time they wanted him to answer the door in the nude, he said, but he declined. Mama took us to Boston to visit Uncle Billy, who was a tall, handsome man with an Indian complexion, a strong, muscular build, and a heavy head of straight black hair. What I remember most is his red, bulbous nose we always wanted to pinch. Uncle Billy liked to drink. We hardly ever saw him without a glass of something, but never saw him drunk. When asked, "How are you?" he'd always answer, "Everything is rosy-dosey." Everything *was* with Uncle Billy, including his nose. We adored him for letting us pinch it.

We also loved Uncle Billy because he thought wholesale. When he came to our house, if we told him there was no more ice cream, he'd go out and come back with four gallons. Once when we couldn't find the can opener, he went to the store and came back with a half a dozen can openers.

I remember well the day Uncle Billy brought his beautiful little girl to visit us. She was about four or five years old. It was winter and there she was, looking like a little Eskimo in a white fur coat and fur hat. Uncle Billy named her after his mother, Malinda. She had Uncle Billy's Indian complexion and his head of what colored folks back then called "good" hair. We could tell Uncle Billy worshiped her. Rosemary, Dolly, and I took her off to play with us. To us she was like a little doll.

Our trips to Boston to see Uncle Billy were even better than his visits to us. He always made codfish cakes (from fresh cod) and baked beans and brown bread for breakfast. After work, he would either take us for great walks around Boston or sit with us and tell one exciting story after the other. Mama didn't have a thing to worry about. Her brother, Willie, did fine up there in Boston and saw everything through rose-colored glasses.

It was Aun' Tannie who told me the story of Mama's "knight in shining armor." During Mary's last year at Hartshorn, Professor Gregory Willis Hayes, president of Virginia Seminary in Lynchburg, came to her college to speak at a student program. Mary was selected to present the gift from the students to him. Mama told Aun' Tannie that she was smitten when she looked into Professor Hayes' eyes. She wrote Uncle John that very night to tell him about the wonderful orator who came to the school and how, in some ways, he reminded her of Uncle John. For one thing, he was not afraid to say what he thought. And one of the things he'd said (that defined his philosophy throughout his life) was, "The Negro will never be free until he can control his own destiny and not look to the white man for everything."

Mary wrote to Professor Hayes to thank him for coming to Hartshorn. We found his response in an old box of Mama's.

Dear Miss Rice,

　　Thank you for your kind letter of 8 November. When you say I am the best orator you have ever heard, you overrate me and I daresay, at your young age, the number you have heard is limited. I did appreciate those words however, kind lady, and shall keep them close to my heart.

　　I pray your school is going well. I suppose you have been reading in the *Planet* that we are having some trouble here. The white Baptists want to control the Seminary and make it an industrial school and I am determined our Negro students will have the opportunity for both industrial arts and liberal arts. I will fight for this to my last breath. Some of my own people are not with me on this and think I want the impossible. They would rather I go along with the restricted education the white mission prescribes for us. Never! I know that a liberal education is very important for the enlightenment of our race, as well as for professional careers. We need good teachers, doctors and lawyers. I want my students to have the same education that I, a former slave, received at Oberlin College.

But my dear lady, I must not burden you with my problems, though they weigh heavily upon me.

With all good wishes to you in completing your work there at Hartshorn, a fine school.

> Respectfully yours,
> Gregory Willis Hayes

The romance started shortly after Professor Hayes visited Hartshorn, and the courtship lasted for only one year. The marriage record indicates Professor Gregory Willis Hayes and Mary Magdalene Rice were married in Richmond, Virginia, in the home of his parents on May 3, 1895. Professor Hayes was thirty-two years old, and Mary was twenty.

A picture taken after the wedding makes me wonder if only Professor Hayes' family was there to see them get married. There is no evidence that her father, Uncle John, or Aunt Dolly attended. Professor Hayes was a very commanding person, and this may have been the way he wanted it. Marriages are usually in the bride's home if it's a home marriage; and after all, Uncle John and Aunt Dolly were like Mary's mother and father. That piece of information is missing, so we can only speculate.

After the wedding, Professor Hayes took his young bride to Lynchburg, Virginia. During the coming years, they would keep the "pillar of fire" burning together, even through the storms that were gathering among Negro educators.

Part Two

THE LADY ON DURMID HILL

1895–1920

In young men like Professor Hayes rests the future of the race—modest, unassuming, brilliant, he stands tiptoe upon the threshold of success and justice bids him enter.

—G. F. Ritchings,
Evidence of Progress Among Colored People (1902)

Chapter 11

RIDING INTO THE STORM

I can just see Mary, the new bride, stepping off the old, dusty train in Lynchburg, Virginia. A black straw boater, trimmed in stiff white ribbon, sits saucily on her head. She looks stylish in her gray suit; its long flared skirt and short jacket with leg-o'-mutton sleeves is very fashionable this year. Underneath her jacket she wears a white blouse, a cameo pinned at the center of its high-standing collar.

Lynchburg is a town of seven hills. A buggy from Professor Hayes' college is there to take the newlyweds out to Durmid Hill, the rural outskirts of Lynchburg, where the train will stop only when flagged. The ride from town to Durmid is not far, but the poor old horse has several hills to climb before getting there. When the buggy finally stops in front of Mary's new home, her husband, Gregory Hayes, helps her down. Then the driver gives him a hand with the luggage and they walk up the long path to the big yellow house. Mary has known there are some problems at the seminary. Gregory had written her about it, even when she was still at Hartshorn, but little does she know how big a storm is raging over his presidency. This is May 1895, the end of his first term as president, and whether or not he will be re-elected will be determined at the Virginia (black) Baptist Convention in June. At this moment, however, Mary is excited about her new home and not worried about what is to come later.

"How lovely, Gregory," she says as they approach the square, two-story, Southern house with its long porch across the front. A wisteria vine covers one end of the porch, shading the swing from summer's heat. Mary follows Gregory and the driver into the house, where they put the luggage down in the large center hall. Mary stands still for a moment, looking around. There is a parlor on the left and Gregory's library on the right.

Gregory thanks the driver, then turns to Mary. "Come," he says, "I'll show you the rest of your home."

In the rear is a large kitchen with a wood-burning stove and good smells of something delicious baking in the oven. Mrs. Jackson, Professor Hayes' housekeeper, comes down the back stairs and joins them in the kitchen. Gregory introduces the two women. I remember Mama telling us years later, she knew from that very first meeting that she and Mrs. Jackson would be friends.

"Welcome, child," Mrs. Jackson says, her large, soft arms enveloping Mary, as they will later envelop all of Mary's children. "You gonna like it here." Then Mrs. Jackson goes to see how her pound cake is doing. "I baked you a little coming-home-after-the-wedding cake," she says with a smile.

"Oh! Thank you," Mary replies. It smells mighty good." And this is the beginning of a warm relationship that would last many years.

I imagine that Gregory then took Mary across the hall to the dining room, where she promised she'd serve him some meals deserving of its beauty. That would be no problem for Mary. Aunt Dolly had prepared her well for this day. Then, don't you suppose Gregory went out into the hall and picked up some of the luggage and that Mary followed him upstairs, where she first saw the big master bedroom with the huge four-poster mahogany bed, the same bed in which nine of

Mary's ten children were to be born? While Gregory went to get the other luggage, Mary must have walked through the other bedrooms. Marble-topped washstands with flowered washbowls and pitchers graced every room; chamber pots to match were under every bed in each of the large and airy rooms. This was a long way from the little white house Mary grew up in.

"What a beautiful home, Gregory." She certainly smiled.

"It's fit for my lady," he surely responded. "When you're ready, Mrs. Jackson will put our dinner on."

At dinner, she, Gregory, and Mrs. Jackson sat in the dining room. Professor Hayes took equality seriously and, unlike some Negroes, he never had separate eating situations for those working in the home. Everyone sat down together.

When they finished eating, Mary complimented Mrs. Jackson on the meal. She was anxious, however, to show her husband what a good cook she was and looked forward to cooking for him herself. She was so much in love, cooking for Gregory would be a joy. There is no doubt that she loved Gregory. On my last visit to Aun' Tannie before she died in 1975, she made that very clear to me. "Mary idolized and adored Professor Hayes," she said. Then, with an apologetic expression, she quickly added, "Oh! not that she didn't love your father too."

On that visit to Aun' Tannie, I listened to all the stories about Mama's first husband, a "courageous, dynamic man who fought hard for equality in education for Negroes, often at the risk of losing his position as president," as Aun' Tannie described him. "He was determined to see that we had available to us not only industrial courses, but the liberal arts courses he had at Oberlin College."

Aun' Tannie also spoke of the wonderful education she'd received at Virginia Seminary: literature, languages (Latin, Greek, German), sciences, philosophy, and psychology.

"He broadened my vision," Aun' Tannie said. "My writing, my poetry reflect the learning I received at the seminary under Professor Hayes' guidance." She also told me how he was always in trouble with the white American Baptist Home Mission Society because of his insistence on liberal education for "his people."

"Professor Hayes defied the American Baptist Home Mission Society," she said. "Professor Hayes was a disciple of Thoreau." At that, I mentioned that my students at the college where I taught then were drawn to Thoreau's essay "Civil Disobedience."

"The story I want to tell you is about that very essay," Aun' Tannie said. "Professor Hayes was drawn to it too, long before the current civil rights movement. Mary told me a funny story about that.

"One day soon after he married Mary, Professor Hayes dashed into the house, excited about something he wanted to share with her. Mary was, at the time, in the kitchen cooking one of her meals to impress her husband. Anyway, somewhere among his papers Gregory had found excerpts from Thoreau's essay 'Civil Disobedience.' You know, Thoreau thought if a law hurt the people, it should be broken." Aun' Tannie looked at me and smiled. "And when Professor Hayes saw a law or regulation related to limiting Negro students' learning, he was not afraid to break it. He went against everything the American Baptist Home Mission Society wanted him to do."

"He was a brave man," I said.

"Yes, but back to the story. While Gregory was quoting all those things Thoreau was saying, like if a law makes you carry out an injustice, break it, Mary's beef stew was burning. Mary was upset, but Professor Hayes just said, 'That's all right, Mary. We'll have bacon and eggs spiced with a bit of Thoreau.'

"You know, Carrie." Aun' Tannie spoke quietly. "Thoreau's peaceful revolution fit Professor Hayes like a glove. In the early part of this century Gandhi was influenced by this essay in developing his doctrine of passive resistance, a doctrine Martin Luther King adopted. Professor Hayes used it way back in the 1890s, long before Gandhi and King."

I WAS FASCINATED by Aun' Tannie's story and by the parallels between Thoreau and Professor Hayes in their methods of putting this doctrine into practice. Thoreau refused to pay taxes to a government that recognized slavery and the abuse of human beings. Professor Hayes refused to listen to the American Baptist Mission Society, which wanted him to limit the curriculum of black students to industrial courses. He also refused to report monthly to the society. He believed he should report to his board of trustees monthly and to the American Baptist Home Mission Society annually. This caused a conflict between Professor Hayes and the society, especially in the light of the compact that was signed at the 1891 Virginia (black) Baptist Convention, stating that Virginia Seminary would be a school affiliated with the society. The signing of this compact had infuriated some of the Negro ministers, who believed the seminary had "sold out." They argued that it was a school founded by Negroes and should remain autonomous. When Professor Hayes came in as president in September of that year, he defied the rulings of the compact, so his first term was a very stormy one. He believed in independence and self-reliance. Aun' Tannie was right. This was a dynamic, courageous man, who risked his position for his convictions.

His belief angered not only the American Baptist Home Mission Society but also the Home Mission Board of the Southern Baptist Board, which also contributed to the school. Dr. Ralph Reavies observes in *Virginia Seminary* that the "Southern Baptist Board, like the American, was very paternalistic."

Although they were both paternalistic, there were significant differences between the American Baptist Home Mission Society and the Home Mission Board of the Southern Baptist Convention. Their ideologies had grown out of different histories. At the 1840 Triennial Convention there was a split among the Baptists over slavery. The American Baptists, mainly from the North, were anti-slavery. As early as 1832 they had established the American Baptist Home Mission Society, which was, Ralph Reavies says, "concerned about the welfare of the Southern Negro." Early on they established schools and other services, and right after the Civil War they had Negroes on their board. On the other hand, the Southern Baptists were strongly pro-slavery, believed in the inferiority of the Negro, and, as later stated in their 1891 convention, felt the Negro should be "in a subordinate position to whites." Even though they believed in helping with education, their report stated further: "Whenever it [the Negro race] shall understandingly and cheerfully accept this condition, the race problem is settled forever." When I read this statement to my sister, we fell out laughing. I did a little jig, and said, "Yasah, boss, we cheerfully accept." I whooped, as Rosemary held her sides.

But time brings about a change, slow, slow, and a long time coming. It was heartening to go outside one morning (June 21, 1995), pick up the *State*, our South Carolina newspaper, and read the headline "Baptists Repent Racism." The Southern Baptist Convention had passed a resolution in Atlanta:

> We lament and repudiate historic acts of evil—and we hereby commit ourselves to eradicate racism in all forms from Southern Baptist life and ministry.

If the Southern Baptists had only spoken out against racism way back then, they might have helped avoid that dark and violent period in the history of our country. However, if the 1995 resolution is carried out, it will move us a long way from that dark period.

The American Baptists have moved beyond this too. They now have blacks in administrative positions. Dr. Walter L. Parrish II is, for example, an executive at their official headquarters. Not so, though, back in the 1890s, when they were opposing Professor Hayes' fight for equality and self-reliance. They tried in every way they possibly could to oust this uppity ex-slave who dared believe he was equal. Because of his beliefs and his actions, he was targeted by both the American Baptists, a Northern group, and the Southern Baptists.

Reavies says that in spite of this opposition, Professor Hayes went about his work securing the best teachers for the seminary—black teachers from Boston Law School, Yale University, Tuskegee Institute, and Lincoln University in Pennsylvania. He also raised the curriculum to a higher academic standard at all levels of the school: the preparatory, normal, and college. There were times, however, when they had to try to hide this development from the American Baptists.

In *Time's Unfading Garden*, the biography of Aun' Tannie, J. Lee Greene recounts a story she told him. It seems that whenever the American Baptist Home Mission Society visited, students had to hide their Latin, Greek, and literature books and pull out the sewing machines and industrial equipment instead. Once a Mr. McVickers of the American Home Baptist Mission Society arrived unannounced, and was outraged that Professor Hayes had introduced these courses of enlightenment. He threatened to withdraw the society's $1,000 contribution to Professor Hayes' salary. Professor Hayes held to his convictions, kept the courses, and forfeited part of his salary.

All this happened at a time when two distinct philosophies about the direction education and civil rights for Negroes were developing. In his famous 1895 Atlanta speech, Booker T. Washington said, "In all things that are social we can be as separate as the fingers, yet one as the hand in all things essential to mutual progress." To those who were fighting for total equality, Washington's statement split the cause of Negro education and civil rights down the middle. After that speech, there was the Booker T. Washington camp on one side and the W. E. B. Du Bois camp on the other. Professor Hayes was definitely in the Du Bois camp. My brother Hunter told me that Professor Hayes went to Tuskegee to see Booker T. Washington on two occasions. Whether those trips took place before or after the 1895 speech, I don't know. I do know they must have discussed the differences in their philosophies. Professor Hayes was not against industrial education, but he believed in choices rather than restrictions. For the Virginia Seminary, he elected to have strong liberal arts courses, for "enlightenment of Negroes," Aun' Tannie said. Higher mathematics, ethics, economics, foreign languages, Cicero, Horace, the *Iliad*, English literature, logic, and history, including Roman and Greek history, were taught at the higher level, all following a strong basic foundation.

For a while it looked like Professor Hayes might not make it another term. The American Baptist Home Mission Society was a strong force, and even some Negro ministers were leaning toward it. But Professor Hayes was a fighter. And he had, as one of his strongest supporters, John H. Mitchell, Jr., one of the trustees of the seminary. In the fight among the trustees at the convention of 1895, regarding keeping or ousting Professor Hayes, the *Planet* newspaper said John Mitchell "won the day." Reavies' book quotes the following from the *Planet*:

> Mitchell declared that Virginia Seminary was intended to be an institution established by colored people of the state, with a faculty made up of colored persons and the effort was to show what the Negro Baptist of the state could accomplish along this line. [Mitchell] opposed any change in this program. He learned that an attempt had been made to change Professor Hayes and he would oppose it. He would have traveled 3000 miles if it had been necessary in order that the grand work which [Professor Hayes] was doing should not be crippled.

During the 1895 Virginia Baptist Convention, a sufficient number of pro-Hayes trustees, such as Mitchell, were appointed to pave the way for Professor Hayes' election. He was re-elected by a narrow margin of five for, four against. This must have been a relief to Mama, who at that time had been married to Professor Hayes for only one month. The storm was subsiding, for the present.

In my search to find out more about this man, my mother's first husband, Gregory Willis Hayes, Ralph Reavies' book *Virginia Seminary: A Journey of Black Independence* has been an excellent source. Other books and articles shed some further light on this brave man. I found significant information at Oberlin College and traveled to Virginia Seminary for still more firsthand knowledge. My sister Rosemary and I also traveled to Richmond, Virginia, where Gregory's family settled after emancipation. With the help of our young researcher friend,

Dale Harter, who was then working at the Virginia State Archives, we learned more.

I was looking for the threads in Gregory's life that came together to weave the picture of the man Madison Allen, writing in the Virginia Baptist magazine *Expected*, called the "apostle of self-help." I wanted to know, too, how Gregory's beliefs influenced Mama. As the old Yoruba proverb says, "If you want to know the end, you have to start at the beginning."

You have seen how a man was made a slave,
you shall see how a slave was made a man.

—Frederick Douglass

Chapter 12

APOSTLE OF SELF-HELP

Born of slave parents on September 8, 1862, on a plantation in Amelia County, Virginia, Gregory Hayes was three years old when the last shots of the Civil War were fired. His father was a carpenter on the plantation, his mother, Lucy, a house slave. In the 1870 census, both his father and mother are listed as mulattoes, indicating they were of mixed heritage. I do not know whether either one was a child of the slave master, but I do know that mulattoes often had privileges other slaves did not have. Color as a criteria has always bothered me, as it did Mama. It's the same kind of injustice Mama protested when, at twelve years old, she took her brown-skinned friend Sudie into the ice-cream parlor. "Color prejudice is a divisive disease that festers," Mama used to say.

During slavery, the field slaves and house slaves were often treated differently, especially if those house slaves were children of the master. It could well have been the reason Gregory's family had been able to remain together on the plantation. Gregory's mother bore three children before the family was freed: Gregory's older brother, Willie, Gregory, and a younger brother, Charles. After emancipation, the family left the plantation and moved to Richmond. There, two more children, Minnie and John, were born. After a few early hard years, Gregory's father did well with his skills as a carpenter. He provided for his family, bought a home, and saw that his children were educated.

Reavies reports that when Gregory was old enough, he attended Navy Hill school, that he was a brilliant student, and that at age twelve was sent to New Jersey to Shooley Mountain Seminary. Later, he lived with an aunt in New York, served in the Navy, then worked on a steamboat between New York and Boston—probably the same line Mama's brother, Uncle Billy, worked on. When Gregory decided he wanted to go to college, he left his work on the boat and enrolled in Oberlin College. He spent seven years there, first in the preparatory school, then at the college, and finally at the graduate level. He graduated from Oberlin College in 1888, with a degree in mathematics.

Gregory excelled at Oberlin. The faculty at the college and the local press in Oberlin, Ohio, identified him as a student and an orator of superior performance. On one occasion, he was elected class orator. Reavies reports that the local newspaper covered his speech and quotes this from the account:

> For the first time in half a score of years a colored gentleman was chosen as one of the speakers. Mr. Hayes' delivery was second to none—some among the audience who had heard Frederick Douglass, compared Hayes' delivery to that great orator—[Hayes] delivered an admirable oration on the 'Bulwarks of our Republic.' "

What a wonderful place for any black person to be educated. Ever since I was a child, I have heard stories about Oberlin College and its courageous work on behalf of Negroes during and after slavery. In Nat Brandt's fascinating book *The Town That Started the Civil War*, he credits an African Methodist Episcopal minister as saying, in 1844, that

Oberlin College was the only place in the United States where a black man might get an inexpensive education and "at the same time, be respected as a man."

Oberlin College was located in a strong antislavery town and area. On the flyleaf of Brandt's book it says:

> Oberlin was in the Western Reserve, which was home to more than three hundred Anti-slave Societies, and was a major stop on the Underground Railroad. It had long offered refuge and opportunity to both escaped slaves, and many free blacks, who found a measure of equality there that was rare anywhere else in the United States.

The book tells the story of an incident in September 1858 when John Price, an escaped slave from Kentucky, was kidnapped. Students and professors from the college rallied around his cause and went to Wellington to free him from the abductors. They were arrested and indicted by the federal government for breaking the Fugitive Slave Act of 1850. All of them were jailed for three months, an action that in itself became a cause célèbre. This incident, Brandt writes, was said to have crystallized "positions on both sides of the issue [of slavery] throughout the nation." Thus, Brandt's title for the book.

By 1881, segregation had taken a stronghold in the nation and filtered even into once ideal settings like Oberlin. Brandt says that in 1882, a professor at Oberlin was incensed because a white student and a black student were rooming together. There had been an attempt to segregate living quarters at the school, but the alumni had protested this, still holding to the beautiful tradition that characterized Oberlin. Many professors still held to that tradition too, so Gregory fared well there. They recognized his special qualities. With his innate abilities, a strong, intact family committed to education, and big doses of self-esteem received at Oberlin, Gregory Hayes was destined to be a leader.

When he graduated from Oberlin, he received an appointment to teach pure mathematics and history at Virginia Normal and Collegiate Institute in Petersburg. There, he was also often in conflict with his superiors. Reavies quotes one newspaper as saying Hayes was "a man who was determined to fight unfairness toward Negroes, regardless of its source, and who was capable of showing deep resentment toward any form of racism, and who was confident of his own superior abilities and his right to use them."

At Virginia Normal and Collegiate Institute it was his attitude that kept the former slave boy in such constant trouble with the American Baptist Mission Society. They pressed the president of the college to fire him. Reavies reports four different stories of the reason he left Virginia Normal and Collegiate Institute. Frank P. Lewis, who wrote the history of black Baptist churches, said there was a cross fire not only between Hayes and the American Baptist Home Mission Society but also between Hayes and Governor McKinney of Virginia. When Professor Hayes made a speech that included the statement, "We must not just be hewers of wood and drawers of water anymore," the governor told the president of the college that Hayes was "a dangerous Negro" and ordered the president to get rid of him. Lewis says the president did just that. Other stories say he was not fired, but left of his own accord. Whatever the reason for his leaving, it was not incompetency, but much more likely his militant approach and belief in his people.

In the years just after the Civil War, any Negro who fought for equality and independence and had a strong consciousness of race was called a "race man." Gregory was definitely perceived as a "race man." Most Negroes placed a positive connotation on this. To them a "race man" was a man who fought for the rights of his people. White benefactors tended to interpret "race man" differently.

Even though Professor Hayes was considered a "race man," he was not one of those who wanted to leave the United States. He loved this country. Reavies quotes (from the *Roanoke Times*) a speech Professor Hayes made, in which he said:

> The Negro is now an American citizen and the place for American citizens is in America. We are the sons and daughters of old Virginia and we love her every hilltop. We love and honor her citizens with whom we have always lived and expect to continue to live.

The paper also reported that Hayes "impressed the fact that all citizens, both black and white, had an issue before them, and it was the duty of all to prepare to meet it." In this he believed citizens could work together toward a common goal of equality for all.

I have been particularly interested in how Professor Hayes became president of Virginia Seminary. While at Virginia Normal and Collegiate Institute, he was making quite a name for himself for standing up for rights and protesting unfairness. The story goes that a congressman, the speaker at commencement at Virginia Normal, said slavery had been a help to Negroes. Professor Hayes stormed off the platform in protest. Reavies says it was reported that some trustees from Virginia Seminary were in the audience and were impressed. They believed their school needed a man like Hayes. So in 1891, at the age of twenty-nine, Professor Gregory Hayes was elected president of Virginia Seminary.

Mary Rice Hayes was extremely proud of her husband and was a supportive wife and mother throughout the storm over education for Negroes. In 1896 she gave birth to her first child, a beautiful baby girl.

"She looks just like my baby sister," Gregory said. "We'll name her Minnie."

Minnie was her father's joy. He would come home and pick up his happy, laughing little girl, and the pressures of his work would slip away for the moment.

When Minnie was a baby, Mary took her to Harrisonburg to visit Uncle John and Aunt Dolly. General Jones must have seen his first grandchild at that time. The trip from Lynchburg to Harrisonburg was a pleasant one, and Mary made many visits. I assume she continued to see her father on these occasions.

I suspect, though, that there may have been some complications on these visits. After Mama's mother, Malinda, died, General Jones had another black mistress, Louisa Wells, with whom he had two sons. Dale Harter told me this and also that General Jones left all of his estate to his second black family. After all, Mama's father had provided her with a good education and a good life, and he must have known Mama had a comfortable life with her husband. It's likely that General Jones knew a good deal about Gregory Willis Hayes, and about his beliefs and activities. The struggle Professor Hayes had with the American Baptist Home Mission Society was well documented in the newspapers of the time. If General Jones did read about him, he must have known his daughter would be all right with so courageous a man.

The more I read about Professor Hayes, the more I understood some of the source of Mama's fire. I no longer had to wonder where Mama got the courage to stand up to governors, mayors, superintendents of schools, managers of stores, or whoever she felt she had to confront about injustice. She had great training from her first husband, Gregory Willis Hayes. Aun' Tannie was right. Three men in her life influenced the direction Mama would take. Her father and Uncle John granted her a strong sense of self-worth; Gregory gave her the courage to fight not only racism but sexism and any other unfairness wherever she saw it. All through our young lives, we watched Mama going out the front door in that red felt cloche hat, on her way to the fight for "full freedom." Now we understand. She was following in the footsteps of the "apostle of self-help."

> The ultimate measure of a man
> is not where he stands in moments of comfort,
> but where he stands at times of challenge and controversy.
>
> —Martin Luther King

Chapter 13

The Coup

*I*n 1898 there was again pressure from the American Baptist Home Mission Society for the trustees to fire Professor Hayes. Mary worried about Gregory but supported his continued fight to take the seminary out of the control of the American Baptist Home Mission Society.

Clearly, Mama loved Gregory totally, but it must have been a doubly stressful time as she was also experiencing an uneasy pregnancy. She wanted the child she was carrying and was praying she could present Gregory with the son he longed for. On the day she went into labor, a midwife was brought in to deliver the baby. Gregory was away, but Mrs. Jackson and a young student from the college, Annie Scales (who was later to become Anne Spencer, our Aun' Tannie), were with her. At one point it was thought Mary would not make it through the long, excruciatingly painful labor. Her face was hot with fever. Mrs. Jackson changed the sweat-soaked sheets. Finally, after many hours, the baby was born.

Mary was overjoyed when she heard the midwife say, "It's a boy."

Exhausted, she fell back on her pillow. The baby was having a hard time breathing; however, the midwife was working with him, and he came through all right. She cleaned the baby up, dressed him, and wrapped him in a blanket.

"Give him to me," Mary said. "I want to hold my son." She held the baby for a while, rocking him and humming. "He looks like Gregory," she said, smiling down on the little dark-skinned baby in her arms. "I can hardly wait for Gregory to get home and see his son." Mrs. Jackson and Annie agreed; he did look like Gregory. Mary finally asked Mrs. Jackson to put the baby in his cradle, which was right beside her. "We'll probably name him Gregory, but I'll wait and see what Gregory says. I know he'll want him to be named after him."

However, Gregory never saw his son. In the middle of the third night, with no symptoms and no warning, Mary's baby son died. Until Gregory came home, Mrs. Jackson and Annie Scales stayed close to comfort the devastated mother.

When Gregory returned home to the sad news, he, too, was upset, but assured Mary there would be other children and they would have a boy one day. Though it took Mary many weeks to regain her strength, once recovered, she stood by Gregory's side as he went through his own turmoil.

For the second time, there was a split among the trustees over the issue of retaining or firing Gregory. Gregory was aware there would be a showdown at the 1899 Virginia (black) Baptist Convention. In November 1898, to get his word out, he organized a congress at the college and invited many ministers from throughout Virginia to attend. He was going to fight to see that Virginia Seminary would "not descend to the level of a secondary school." He wanted to make it clear that the college "needed to be unleashed from the control of the American Baptist Mission Society." Many of those who attended were impressed with how well Hayes knew his foes. One of them, Reverend Phillip Morris, one of the founders of the seminary with a significant voice in deciding the future of the college, was particularly formidable. Gregory was alerted to Morris's position by an article in the *Planet* written by Elbert Ernest, who quoted Reverend Morris.

> The [American Baptist Home Mission Society] has firmly and irrevocably declared it will not cooperate with us, so long as Professor Gregory W. Hayes is President of Virginia Seminary. We have at last come to the point where we must choose one or the other. As for me, I am going with the white people. I am going where the money is.

It is exciting for me to see how politically astute Professor Hayes was and to imagine him rounding up his troops. Obviously, he was a very forceful man, with great oratorical skills. He traveled throughout Virginia speaking to large urban congregations as well as small country churches, delivering the message that "we must, as Negroes, take hold of the reins of our destiny." Elbert Ernest's article in the *Planet* described Professor Hayes's philosophy clearly. Hayes, Ernest said, wanted the kind of help that would allow the Negro race to "occupy the driver's seat." "He desires outside help," Ernest wrote, "but he wishes for it to be a ladder on which he may climb, rather than a pulley to lift him up in midair." Hayes, Ernest stated, believed that the Negro "desires to ascend and have help in the ascent, but he wishes to acquire the strength and agility that come from climbing, rather than the inertia and desuetude that come from being in a basket." These were flowery words but they spoke to the core of Professor Hayes's beliefs.

In his travels, Professor Hayes convinced many that his philosophy of self-reliance and self-determination was the right way to go. By the time the convention rolled around, it was evident that he and his followers had done their work effectively. The number of delegates in attendance was more than triple the usual two hundred. Reavies reports, "On the morning of May 9, 1899, Johnson [who was in charge of the convention], received a telegram advising him to prepare for 700 delegates, who were now waiting in Lynchburg to take the train to Lexington, Virginia." They had "come to Lynchburg by wagon, by buggy and on foot and occupied five cars of the train from Lynchburg to Lexington, the site of the convention." There, Reavies reports, the battle began.

The trustees must have thought that their dignity and their dark Sunday-go-to-meeting suits, set off by their white shirts and wing collars, would save the day. But in the heat of the battle, their dignity slipped away. Reavies reports it was a "knock-down, drag-out" meeting.

The Hayes supporters—Reverends Graham, B. F. Fox, Harvey Johnson, and John Mitchell—vehemently protested the recommendation of the anti-Hayes faction that he be ousted. The gavel comes down hard. "Gentlemen, gentlemen, one at a time." But in battle, gentle is not an appropriate word. The verbal battle was on. The scenario I envision might have been something like this: The chairman recognizes Reverend Graham.

"Mr. Chairman, McVickers of the Mission Society has implied that his plan is to demote this school to a preparatory and industrial school. We protest this with all our might. Professor Hayes has developed a college of high quality and we propose to keep it that way."

"And who will pay for this high-sounding idea?" one of the opponents yells out.

"We'll find a way, we'll find a way," one of the Hayes supporters yells.

However the meeting might really have gone, this session turned into a long and bitter fight with some name-calling, and it looked at one point as if Professor Hayes' opponents would win. But the Hayes supporters outmaneuvered the opponents, and during the election of new trustees several Hayes supporters were voted onto the board. Thus, the pro-Hayes group was, once again, victorious. Professor Hayes would retain his position as president by a vote of eight to six.

The next move was another blow to the anti-Hayes, pro–American Baptist group. Reverend Graham stood up and made a motion to "withdraw the school from the compact with the American Baptist

Mission Society." The motion was carried. There were shouts of joy among the pro-Hayes group, many *Amen*s ringing throughout the room. The school would once more be self-reliant.

Mary was relieved that the battle was over. Winning it had put a strain on Gregory and on Mary, pregnant with another child. One month after the convention, Mary gave birth to her third child, a girl. They named her Malinda, after Mary's mother. Mary went about caring for her two little girls and doing volunteer work at the college. She joined a women's group dedicated to raising money for students and to encouraging and tutoring them if necessary.

Most of all, Mary enjoyed her life as the wife of Gregory Hayes. She loved entertaining such distinguished guests as W. E. B. Du Bois, Booker T. Washington, and other outstanding Negroes in the educational, literary, and arts fields. Aun' Tannie told me Mama was an ardent disciple of W. E. B. Du Bois'. They were also friends, however, and on one occasion Mama admonished him for being arrogant and holding himself "above the people." Apparently, Mama told him in a friendly way he needed to "come down off the mountain and be with the people." Aun' Tannie laughed when she told me this. "He *was* arrogant," she said, and told me another story, about a visit he made to the struggling seminary when he refused to stay there overnight because he would have had to bathe in a tin tub. Aun' Tannie had the kind of plumbing he was accustomed to, so he stayed with her. Even so, Mama and Du Bois remained friends, working together for many years in the fight for equality. Aun' Tannie said Professor Hayes was more interested in putting money into good books and good teachers than into fine facilities, which was one reason she and Mama were annoyed that Du Bois felt he was too important to bathe in a tin tub.

Professor Hayes continued to work hard for the seminary. He traveled extensively to raise funds for the school, often visiting the New England states, especially Massachusetts, where some of the old abolitionists and their descendants were still interested in supporting the development of black schools without expecting to control them. After the "coup," things were less hectic for Professor Hayes and he could devote himself to enhancing the curriculum, expanding building facilities, and traveling to raise those always insufficient funds for the struggling school. Independence was costly, but the ideal of self-reliance was rewarding to a people not very far removed from slavery.

In October 1900, Mary presented Gregory with the son he wanted. He was a healthy, robust, chestnut-colored baby with a head of thick straight black hair.

"We'll name him Gregory Willis Hayes, Jr. He'll carry on my name," Gregory said.

If ever I cursed my white old man
I take my curses back.

—Langston Hughes, "Cross"

Chapter 14

TRANSFORMATION

❧

On April 1, 1901, Mama's father, General Jones, died in Harrisonburg, Virginia, from, according to the *Rockingham Register*, "the effects of the grip [sic]." I don't know whether Mama went to the funeral or even whether, at that time, she would have been allowed in the white church. Either way, his death had to have touched her deeply. Her father had sacrificed a great deal in order to care for his black families. Certainly he had provided Mama the foundation for a good life. From what Aun' Tannie says, Mama's memories of her childhood with "Papa Sir" were happy ones, memories that she could share only with her dearest friend and confidante, Anne Spencer. My guess is that she could not discuss "Papa Sir" with her husband, and that when General died, she may have had to suffer at home in silence, her sorrow released only when she could talk with Anne.

When my sister Rosemary and I visited the cemetery in Harrisonburg, the words on General Jones' tombstone seemed sparse and lacking in feeling. It gave only his date of death, his age, and the statement "at rest." I know he meant more to Mama than those few words would imply. He must also have meant more than that to his second black family, to whom he was a caring father and to whom he left his estate.

One of the many pleasures of my search for information about General Jones was the discovery of cousin Roberta Greenlaw. Roberta is the daughter of Percy Wells, one of General Jones' sons by his second black mistress, Louisa Wells. Dale Harter gave me her Chicago address and telephone number and suggested I contact her. Uncertain how she would accept me, I was, for a long time, reluctant to do so. Finally, in the summer of 1994, just before flying off to the Squaw Valley Community of Writers workshop in California, I wrote to her and sent pictures of me and my two sisters. I also sent my book of poems *Piece of Time*. Its afterword would tell her something about my family and my search for information on General Jones. I knew the risk of opening up sensitive areas in other people's lives, and I awaited—with trepidation—her response or lack of response.

One day while at Squaw I called my sister Rosemary, who was back in South Carolina. She was excited.

"You have a letter from Roberta Greenlaw."

"Open it, open it," I said.

When she opened the letter she took out a picture of Roberta.

"Oh!" Rosemary exclaimed. "She looks just like me."

Then she read me the letter:

July 25, 1994

My Dear Carrie,

When I pulled your brown envelope from the mailbox, I looked at the return address, studied it for awhile and said I don't know anyone in South Carolina. What a surprise! Here's a woman who has spent years researching the family tree and found me.

I have been aware of my father's father. Daddy always talked about it and wanted to take me to the gravesite, but Mother always kept those conversations short.

I'm an only child born July 4, 1922. I have only one son who also lives in Chicago. He works in the post office at night and teaches school in the day.

We've been living in a small world. I read in your book you were born in Lynchburg, Virginia, grew up in Montclair, New Jersey, and your father's home was Danville, Virginia, where you visited often. I taught school in Campbell County and lived in Lynchburg in the 1940's. I have friends and have visited them in Montclair and in Danville. We may have been in those places at the same time on occasion.

I've just retired after 38 years as a teacher here in Chicago, but stay busier than ever. Something has to be done, my friends say, "Call Roberta, she'll do it."

I'll keep in touch. Give my best to your sisters and your brother. Your book is really nice. I spent a Sunday reading and sharing with my friends. I'm going to order some so others can read it. I'm glad you found me.

Love,
Roberta

It's uncanny how much we have in common with our cousin Roberta Wells Greenlaw. We stay in touch by telephone and share our thoughts about our common heritage and about General Jones. I sent her a copy of Dale Harter's article about General Jones and she was pleased to know that he was also a caring father to our mother.

"I asked my mother about my grandfather," Roberta said during one of our many telephone conversations, "but she never wanted to talk about him. My father would tell me stories when my mother was not around."

"You were very fortunate," I said. "I had to learn about General Jones in books, through Dale Harter, and through Mama's dearest friend, Anne Spencer."

Roberta said if her father, Percy Wells, had lived until January 1994, he would have been one hundred years old. Her father was born the year Mama graduated from Hartshorn College, 1894. Mama must have known about General Jones' other black family. Roberta told me her father said General Jones would come to their house and have their mother dress the two boys up so he could carry them around town with him, just as he had Mama. From what Roberta's father said, General Jones seemed to have been proud of them. Roberta sent me a picture of her father. He was a very handsome man, light-complected, with a warm, smiling face and, in this picture, a head of heavy, straight, silvery hair. From what Roberta tells me, General Jones, in spite of ostracism by his own people, to his credit, continued to acknowledge and support his sons and Mama's half brothers, Percy and Harry Wells. Roberta seemed to have no difficulty calling General Jones "Grandfather."

Unlike cousin Roberta, I had to travel a long road to find out about the man Mama called "Papa Sir." It's interesting that two women, my mother and Roberta's mother, would not talk about General, but that her father did. I wish I could have learned all of it as a child, sitting at my mother's knees. What conflict she must have experienced, loving her father, yet feeling a shame that kept her from sharing her story with her own children. I have wondered too, if Mama was silenced by her first husband, Gregory Hayes, the strong "race man." I imagine he might have had some difficulty in accepting Mama's father. Since Professor Hayes was born into slavery, how did he feel about a man who fought to keep him and his family there? If Professor Hayes, like Uncle John, had some animosity toward General Jones, then there must have been conflict over this in Mama's first marriage. It is difficult not to talk about someone you love. Did she finally stop telling her stories about her father in order to keep the peace? Some things I may never know, but piece by piece I'm fitting our puzzle together.

I realize now that Mama was one of the few fortunate children born of the "monstrous system." I also realize that we cannot deny our heritage. Then, too, there's the strange reality that hit me in the middle of one night: if it had not been for General Jones, I would not be in this world, and I must say I do love being here. It took me a long time, many hours of searching, before I felt I really knew this man—a man for whom, in the beginning, I had nothing but anger. A man whom, for a long time, I kept at a distance by calling him "my mother's father." In the summer of 1993, while driving through the Shenandoah Valley once again, I stopped the car, got out, and just stood there for a while. A new feeling came over me, and I found myself talking to the man I can now call "Grandfather." When I got home, I wrote this poem:

CONVERSATION: PAST DUE
(On passing through Virginia—Summer 1993)

Are you really there, Grandfather, or
is this some transcendental joke, some
aberration
There is a strange sense of your presence
here in the shadows of the Shenandoah
This lovely valley, where you and my
grandmother
walked together in the season of a
different sun
You, an officer in the Army of the young
Southern Confederacy,
She, born of a million African moons

I see you there in the mist, a
puzzled smile on your face
The gray of your uniform angered
me for a moment
then dissipated by Aun' Tannie's words
"A good man, caught in a
time of evil. He loved your mother
and I believe he loved Malinda too."
Did you love her, Grandfather?
I had not thought of it as love

Perhaps there is a love that transcends,
that's unafraid, uncompromised
Perhaps there is a love that laughs in
the face of the shallow *Oh, mys*
of white-gloved ladies
Perhaps there is a love that says
"To hell" (pardon me, Grandfather)
"with false barriers,"
and stands there, unadorned,
in pure naked beauty,
like a field of wildflowers
unashamed of their unlike likenesses

The ease with which I call you
Grandfather bewilders me
First time allowing myself this truth
On rare occasions when I dared speak
of you at all
in muffled tones, I said, "My mother's
father"
Then you stepped out of the shadows, smiling
A whirl of conflicting emotions engulfed me
and I called you Grandfather

Anger is a bitter cup, from which I
no longer want to drink
Here in this place, this peaceful glen,
I want to reach out, reach out and see
if your hand is there waiting to take mine
You're offering me your hand, Grandfather?
You're offering me your hand?
Our steps are slow, measured, unsure
but closer and closer
We're almost there, Grandfather, almost

I want to see if we can walk
together
I want to talk more with you
and for that one day I will come
again
The distance seems shorter, the
truth is clearer, and I walk
freer

Sitting here now on my porch I think of my grandfather's life and how his life influenced my mother's, and ultimately how his life touched mine. His scrapbook speaks of his love of poetry and his compassion for the poor and homeless. These are the values that he passed on to his daughter and she to hers. I read of his death and think of his life, a life that is connected to mine.

"Good night, Grandfather, I have, at last, made my peace with you."

And who knoweth whether
thou art come to the kingdom
for such a time as this?

—Esther 4:14

Chapter 15

CARRYING THE TORCH

—

$\mathcal{M}$ary and Gregory had seven children. Though one was still-born and one died in infancy, there were five left to honor persons the parents respected. Back in those days, most children were not named after movie stars or soap opera stars, nor were they given African names. They were given names to honor others. Most of Mama's children in her marriage to Professor Hayes carried the names of ministers. Minnie's middle name was Tyler, after a certain Reverend Tyler. Wilelbert Galvin Hayes, born in 1903, was named after Elbert Ernest, the man who wrote so glowingly about Professor Hayes. Wilelbert was also named after a particular Reverend Galvin. Hunter Reed Moses Hayes, born 1906, and the last of Professor Hayes' children, was named after a Reverend Hunter, a Reverend Reed, and a Reverend Moses. Perhaps Mary and Gregory realized Hunter might be the last child and they wanted to make sure they honored everyone; so poor Hunter carries that long name. We always called him Hunna Reed. Malinda was named after Mama's mother, but her middle names were Ruvella and

Estella. I don't know who these two ladies were, but I'm glad they got honored before Mama had me.

Now that the college was no longer under the control of the American Baptist Mission Society, Professor Hayes continued his work under far less pressure. He proved wrong the Society's prediction that Virginia Seminary would fail without their support. There was wonderful response from black churches in support of the school. Professor Hayes's philosophy of self-reliance and his victory inspired an outpouring of financial support from those black churches. Reavies quotes the *Richmond Planet* from May 19, 1900:

> The financial success of our convention this year, saying nothing of the $1,000 raised and paid on the Virginia Seminary debt, saying nothing of the thousands of dollars raised by churches, associations, Sunday School conventions and our annual meeting which certainly would aggregate at least $15,000 was most wonderful.

Professor Hayes continued to travel, but now it was to raise funds for the school. In 1905 he even traveled to London, England, to attend an international conference, and while he was there, he appealed for funds for the seminary. On that trip he also bought the Bible that's still used for family documentation of births and deaths. All of Mama's children by Professor Hayes are listed in it. Later, when she married my father, and Rosemary, Dolly, and I were born, Mama registered our births there, too. Back in those days, the Bible was the usual place families kept their records. My brother Hunter, now the oldest in the family, keeps that Bible as a sacred trust, and I have used it several times in my research on the family.

Professor Hayes' diligence and the response of the black Baptist churches ensured the school's financial solvency (rather than the failure predicted by the American Baptist Home Mission Society). By 1906, however, what with expansion and increased hiring, funds got tight.

Money had to be borrowed from Adolphus Humbles, a prosperous black businessman in Lynchburg, to pay off a debt to the American Baptist Home Mission Society. Once that loan was repaid, the seminary did not suffer any drastic financial setbacks until the Depression.

Meanwhile, Professor Hayes continued his fight for equality and justice, not just at the college but throughout the nation. In 1906, he was involved in the protest black Baptist ministers were making to get the African Pygmy Ota Benga out of his cage at the Bronx Zoo. Professor Hayes offered to bring Ota to the seminary to begin his education.

In the history of man's inhumanity to man, the story of Ota Benga is one among many. A young African Pygmy from the Congo, Ota Benga was brought with other Pygmies to America by a white missionary, to be exhibited in the 1904 Saint Louis World's Fair. Though the missionary, Samuel Phillips Verner, returned the Pygmies to Africa after the fair, he brought Ota back to the United States in 1906 and left him at the American Museum of Natural History in New York City. The director of the Bronx Zoo, William Hornaday, seized the opportunity to exploit Ota at a time when there was great interest in Darwinism. He took Ota to the Bronx Zoo, placed him in a cage with apes, and exhibited him as the "missing link." A group of outraged black ministers demanded Ota's release. Though the ministers protested for some time, they got no help from New York's city government. Finally, when they threatened to sue, Ota was released and sent first to the Howard Orphanage in Brooklyn and then to Lynchburg, Virginia, to begin his education in the lower-level classes at the seminary. Ota lived part-time in Professor Hayes's home and part-time with Mrs. Josephine Anderson, the owner of a general store across from the Hayes home. Because of her generosity, everyone called Mrs. Anderson "Mammy Joe," and Mama named me Carrie Anderson Allen in her honor. Ota was given little jobs to do around Mammy Joe's store. His first trip to Lynchburg, however, was short, for Professor Hayes, his guardian, lived only a few months after he'd brought Ota to Lynchburg.

Gregory Hayes died just before Christmas, on December 22, 1906. He died of Bright's disease at Johns Hopkins Hospital in Baltimore, Maryland, leaving Mary and five young children. At this devastating time for his widow and his seminary, people came from across the nation to pay tribute to the "apostle of self-help." At some point, Ota was sent back to Brooklyn.

Professor Gregory Hayes is still honored on the seminary campus every November with a Hayes Day celebration. There is a statue of him on the campus, and one of the buildings was named Hayes Hall after him. The college has survived many hardships but still exists today, and, as someone there told me recently, "still carries on the philosophy of Professor Hayes, one of the heroes in the historical development of education for Negroes." A recent school catalog states, "The G. W. Hayes School of Arts and Sciences [a division of Virginia Seminary and College] was so named in 1988 in honor and memory of Professor Gregory W. Hayes, the college's second President." The mission of the G. W. Hayes School of Arts and Sciences is to "enable the student to achieve the highest possible degree of self-realization—to produce graduates who are well prepared to assume leadership responsibilities, who will meet life with knowledge, courage, understanding and faith." I think Gregory Willis Hayes would heartily approve.

When Professor Hayes died, some folks around felt Mama should take his place. Because she was so immersed in his philosophy, they believed that she could carry the torch. Aun' Tannie told me she and some others suggested to the board of trustees that Mary Rice Hayes could step into Professor Hayes' shoes. I have the impression Aun' Tannie was the leader of this campaign. She and Mama were teaching at the seminary at the time. Also, she was as much for women's rights as was Mama. My brother Hunter told me, too, that Mama did indeed serve as president of the seminary. I was dubious of this information, so I wrote to the seminary and received the following letter:

April 11, 1986

Dear Mrs. McCray:

I am in receipt of your letter dated April 7, 1986 in regard to the role of your mother, Mary Rice Hayes Allen, at Virginia Seminary and College.

Your mother succeeded Professor Gregory Willis Hayes as President. She served in this capacity from 1906–1908 (as Interim President). . . .

With every good wish

Sincerely Yours,
Thomas E. Parker
President

When Rosemary and I visited the seminary in 1990, we saw Mama's picture in the hall of the administration building, the only woman in the line of former presidents.

Aun' Tannie allowed as how there were several trustees who balked at considering Mama. "But," she said, "your Mother's charm and conviction won them over." Apparently, Mama requested a meeting with the trustees, walked into the meeting, sat down, and smiled at the group of austere gentlemen there.

"Gentlemen," she said, "thank you for allowing me this time. I came to volunteer my services as acting president of the seminary until you find someone."

Mary saw the shocked expression on the faces of the ministers sitting around the table, but continued: "I know this is unusual, but I do so because I know how my husband felt about the education of Negroes, his philosophy and his determination that Negro students would receive the best possible education. I would carry on his work and his philosophy if you allow me."

The chairman of the board cleared his throat, allowing him time for the proper words. "Mrs. Hayes," he said, "we appreciate your offer.

However, we've never thought of having a woman as president. I think we need to discuss all the ramifications of this."

"The only ramifications I see have to do with the fact that I am a woman. Does this mean you believe a woman cannot do the job? There are schools, as you know, where women are doing admirably in this position. I would only act in this transitional period."

There was much discussion, much buzzing among the trustees, but Mama just smiled and gave the trustees more food for thought: "Women, as you well know, gentlemen, have been in the forefront of education for Negroes before and after slavery. Many white abolitionist women from the North set up schools for ex-slaves. Many Negro women founded small schools for freed slaves."

"That's very true, Mrs. Hayes, but we have to consider the situation here," one might have said.

"Well, we cannot discount the heroic work of Mary McLeod Bethune down there in Daytona, who in just two years has established a flourishing school. We cannot discount that, now can we, gentlemen? I know the philosophy of my husband and of this school and would do my utmost to carry on the work my husband started."

I'm *sure* Mama got in that speech about women. Women's rights was also a continued battle of hers, and she was a charmer.

In any event, the trustees voted to have her serve as interim president. Thus Mama served as president of the Virginia Seminary from 1906 until 1908, when Reverend James Diggs was appointed president. While some black Baptist ministers are still preaching the subordination of women, it is amazing to me that as early as 1906, my mother was president of a black Baptist seminary. But the facts are there for all to see.

I can see clearly now.

—Johnny Nash

Chapter 16

REVELATION

—

We will never know the true story of how Mama met my father, William Patterson Allen. For years, Grandma, Papa's mother, and Aunt Maggie, Papa's sister, argued two different versions of the meeting.

"No, Mag, they met at the convention at High Street Baptist Church." Grandma's strong, but drawling voice was for me one of finality. I would never have questioned or disputed her. That's why it always surprised me when Aunt Maggie, who in all other areas of her life gave in to her stern, domineering mother, held onto *her* version.

"No, no, Mama," came the rebuttal from Aunt Maggie, a little lady who always walked on tiptoes and pitched her voice at high C. "No, it was at the Baptist Sunday school picnic, when Mary came to Danville to visit the Williamses. I remember because it was in July 1910, when Mr. Joseph Harmon was a corpse."

That's the way Aunt Maggie reckoned time. She attended funerals, those of people she knew and, just as often, of those she did not know; a stack of black-bordered mourning handkerchiefs lay clean, scented, and waiting in her top dresser drawer. I trusted her dates and preferred her stories. Hers were always more romantic, as was Aunt Maggie herself. A wiry, cheerful, chattery old maid, she would sit on the porch on Holbrook Street, wait for courting couples to pass, then call them in. "Come on, come on in, sit in the swing. I have a fresh pitcher of cool lemonade," she'd say, gathering up an audience for her stories, which always opened with either "Before Mama lost her leg" or "After Mama lost her leg," as if her life were divided into two long seasons—as indeed it was.

Aunt Maggie was supposed to marry a missionary who was going to Africa. She would go with him as his wife. After Grandma lost her leg, however, Aunt Maggie stayed home, dedicating her life to her mother and experiencing romance through others' lives. Which is why I believe Aunt Maggie's story about how Mama and Papa met. And anyway, I went to those Baptist Sunday school picnics when I was little. They were perfect for falling in love.

Whenever I hear the song "Come to the Church in the Wildwood," I remember our picnics. We'd go down a long dirt road, farms on each side, then through a wooded area, and into a clearing with the greenest grass and a rippling stream. A little white clapboard church sat pristine in the center of the greenness. Trucks, wagons, buggies, and a few Fords and Packards (owned by the doctors and undertakers) carried the happy picnickers to the idyllic spot. In all these vehicles there were big baskets filled with good food—fried chicken, Virginia ham, corn pudding, potato salad, homemade rolls, and pound cake. There were big wooden freezers of homemade peach ice cream and tin washtubs with huge watermelons cooling on ice. There were gallons of lemonade to wash all this down.

We younger children played the rhyming games, while the older ones played croquet or walked with their sweethearts under the watchful eyes of their mothers. The men in their straw hats went off every now and then with a jug of special lemonade, the laughter louder each time they returned and righteous indignation if anyone dared make the suggestion that they had homemade wine in that jug. The picnic is where I *want* to believe Mama met Papa.

Mama and Papa both enjoyed that perennial argument, and so they never clarified it. Papa used to tell stories not to us but to visiting guests about his courtship of the widow Hayes. Children hear many things not meant for their ears. "Courting Mary not only meant I had to travel on the train every weekend to see her, but it was hazardous," he'd say, and then he'd laugh and tell the story about Hunter, Mama's youngest, who was four years old at the time.

"I'm sitting in the parlor with Mary, and this little fella comes to the door, points at my bald head, and snickers, 'Mita Allen got a bean head,' then throws a marble that hits its target." Papa loved to tell this story.

Mama, a thirty-five-year-old widow with five children, still lived on Durmid Hill in Lynchburg. With all of these children she had no choice but to continue teaching at the seminary. Papa, a twenty-nine-year-old lawyer, not too many years out of the University of Michigan Law School, was practicing law in Danville. Theirs was a long-distance romance. They courted for a year, then there was talk of marriage.

A few years ago my cousin Mackye told me that Grandma "like to have blown a gasket."

"I don't know why Will is gonna marry that old woman with all those children," she confided in Aunt Ida, Mackye's mother.

Aunt Ida, a soft-spoken, straight-laced, Grant Wood sort of woman, answered her mother-in-law, "Perhaps, Ma, it's because she's beautiful, intelligent, and seems to love the whole human race."

Grandma was protective of her son, the youngest of her five children. Papa's parents, Robert and Lucretia Allen, former slaves, had moved to Danville, Virginia, from North Carolina. All of their children except Papa were born in North Carolina. Papa was born in Danville. When Papa was born, his oldest brother, James, was eleven;

his sister, Margaret, ten; his brother Robert, nine; and his brother Henry, eight. So Papa really was Grandma's baby boy. By the time Papa was nine years old, the other boys were up and out of the home.

Grandma was proud of Will, the son who achieved so much. His brother James, who had been working at a plush hotel in Newport, Rhode Island, for some years, found a job there for Papa as a waiter after he'd graduated from high school. In those days, Newport, Rhode Island, was the place where many of the wealthiest families of the country went for vacations. It was, for Papa, a good place to work. He worked hard, put himself through Lincoln University in Pennsylvania, and then through the University of Michigan Law School. He returned to the Newport hotel every summer and worked to save money for the next school year. Papa was one of the first turn-of-the-century blacks to finish the University of Michigan Law School. Grandma had every reason to be proud of him. He was an excellent student and became a brilliant lawyer. Still, that was no excuse for Grandma treating Mama as she did. Grandma tried to get Will to change his mind about marrying "that widow." She fought it right down to the day of the wedding, September 20, 1911.

Will and Mary married in Lynchburg, Virginia. The wedding itself was a compromise, as were so many things in their marriage. Will agreed to the location of the wedding, but insisted on having his minister, Reverend W. T. Hall, from Danville, perform the ceremony. Only now, after many interviews with Aun' Tannie, Mackye, and others do I sense some of the early problems in the marriage. As children, we never heard arguments; all we saw was a loving couple. Parents kept their arguments away from their children in those days. How in the world did they manage that? How can you whisper when you're angry? I'll never understand how they did it, but Mama and Papa certainly succeeded in keeping their arguments away from us. As far as we knew we were one big happy family enjoying lots of activity and laughter.

Mama and Papa were quite different from each other. Mama was a free spirit, Papa conservative and reserved. Because of their work, when they were first married, Papa lived in Danville, Mama in Lynchburg. The house in Lynchburg, where Papa spent weekends, was already bulging with people. Not only were Mama and her five children living there, but also an assortment of other people: Mrs. Jackson, Gilbert Rice (Mama's cousin who was attending the Seminary), and Ota Benga, the African Pygmy, who had wanted to return to Lynchburg because he "had friends there," and whom Mama had taken back in. Then in rapid succession Will and Mary had three girls: Rosemary, born in 1912; me, Carrie, born in 1913; and Dolly, born in 1915.

Nine of Mama's children were born in the big yellow house in Lynchburg. Dolly, however, was born the year Papa insisted Mama move to Danville. That move, for Mama, lasted only two "miserable" years, as she described them to Aun' Tannie. After those two years, Mama, who had kept her house in Lynchburg, refused to tolerate Grandma's indignities any longer. She packed us up and moved us back to Lynchburg.

Grandma was certainly a very harsh person. Perhaps her childhood years in slavery had made her this way, or the fact that in freedom she had lost a leg to Jim Crow. After a train wreck, the hospital would not admit any of the injured Negroes, and so she didn't receive medical attention for some time. Finally, a white doctor took her into his office by the back door and examined her in his supply room, but it was too late. Gangrene had set in. She remembered the cold words of the doctor. "That leg's got to come off, Auntie." Perhaps this misfortune made her as she was or perhaps she was always a harsh woman, without cause. Whatever the reason, she took her vengeance out on Mama, whom she never accepted.

Another compromise in this long-distance marriage affected Rosemary. Since Papa could not have the whole family there, Papa took Rosemary, when she was five, to live with him in Danville. The Williamses, who lived up the street from Papa, took care of her during the day. Rosemary says this was a very unhappy time for her. The

Williamses, a rather snobbish family, had decided that none of the children around were good enough for Rosemary to play with, so she spent
lonely days in the house with adults. She remembers how sometimes
she looked out the window at the other children having fun playing the
rhyming games and longed to be with them. Then too, Papa was so
busy, she did not see him often. He saw her mostly when he brought
her home to Lynchburg on some weekends. She would always cry
when it was time for her to go back to Danville; and she sometimes had
to travel not with Papa, who had business elsewhere, but with someone
or other who happened to be going to Danville. After almost two years,
Mama insisted that Rosemary be brought back home to Lynchburg.
There was a real tug-of-war in the early years of that marriage.

I didn't know any of this when I was a child. All I knew was I was
happy there in our home in Virginia. As we always do, I hold onto very
pleasant, selective memories, especially those of our Virginia days. I
loved our big old house that sat on top of Durmid Hill. I loved its big
back porch with the latticework and the long table where we ate in
good weather. It made meals seem like picnics. I loved the seminary,
where in summer we'd run yelling through the empty hallowed halls. I
loved the primary school there and my teacher, who taught me to write
my full name, Carrie Anderson Allen. I loved going across the road
after school, to Mammy Joe's store, knowing that she saved one of those
saucer-size sugar cookies for me, her namesake. I loved being invited
to dinner at Professor Drewry's home. His wife knew I loved homemade peach ice cream and always gave me an extra helping. I loved
going over to visit our white neighbor, Mrs. Limbaugh, who in summer always sat with us under her grape arbor and made us cold glasses
of lemonade. I loved running down the hill to the old weathered shack
of our favorite playmates. Even in winter, with paper stuffed in the
cracks and the sound of wind coming through, their home holds the
warmest memory for me. Our friends' mama would fix big bowls of
turnip greens and cornbread and we'd sit around their stove eating,
telling stories, and laughing. Then their Mama would start singing,

"Oh! Li'l Liza, Li'l Liza Jane," and we'd sing and clap our hands with
her. That shack was one of my favorite places.

I loved our pet cow, sad-eyed Mary-cow, and our pet pig, Jefferson
Case. Papa had brought Case home from Danville one weekend, payment for a case he had settled for a Jefferson family. Papa justified
bringing home chickens and pigs with one of his eternal quotations
from Proverbs: "If thou hast nothing to pay, why should he take away
thy bed from under thee — Proverbs 22:27" or, even worse, in a more
ominous tone, "He that oppresseth the poor to increase his riches . . .
shall surely come to want — Proverbs 22:16." Papa, for whose use the
Proverbs were written, had one for every situation. Papa's view of life
meant we never had much money, but we lived comfortably enough.

Somewhere in the jungle are living some little men
and women. They are our past and maybe our future.

—from Michael Sanchez and
Eric Mouquet's C.D. *Deep Forest,*
about the gentle, peace-loving Pygmies

Chapter 17

OTTO

—

*H*is name was Ota Benga, but we called him Otto, the name that
was given him at the Howard Orphanage in Brooklyn, where he lived
before he came to Lynchburg. Otto, a Pygmy from the Congo, was in
our home when I was born, and he lived there until his death. I was so
young I remember very little, and certainly didn't know then his awful,
dehumanizing story. In 1904 the Saint Louis World's Fair planners had
gathered "species" of many races of color to exhibit, and a lower act
than that I pray we never encounter. One of the Pygmies, Latuna,
protested the treatment of the Pygmies at the fair. He said, "When
white men come to our country, we give them presents, sometimes a
sheep, goat, or bird, and divide our elephant meat with them. But the
Americans treat us as they do our monkeys."

As I've mentioned, when the fair was over, the missionary Samuel
Phillips Verner returned the Pygmies to Africa, but he later brought
Ota Benga back to America, where he ended up at the Bronx Zoo, in a
cage with apes, exhibited as "The Missing Link." The *New York Times*
and other newspapers reported that people flocked to the zoo to see

"the Pygmy in the cage." On September 19, 1906, the *New York Journal* said:

"The Black Pygmy in the monkey cage [is] an exhibition in bad taste, offensive to honest men, and unworthy of New York City's government."

Black ministers, outraged, protested, but the mayor, as the *New York American* reported on September 16, 1906, "snubbed the Colored ministers." The ministers continued their protest and threatened to sue. Ota was then released and sent to the colored Howard Orphanage in Brooklyn, which was when Mama's first husband, Professor Hayes, offered the seminary as a place where Ota could come. The *New York Times* on September 19, 1906, reported that "The colored clergymen . . . will try to get possession of Benga, so that they may send him to Lynchburg, Virginia, to be educated."

So in September 1906 Ota was brought down to Lynchburg by one of Professor Hayes' students, William Taylor. Professor Hayes was his guardian.

When Professor Hayes, Ota's guardian, died in December 1906, Ota returned to the Howard Orphanage in Brooklyn. In 1910, however, he indicated he wanted to come back to Lynchburg to be with friends. Mama took him in. I remember the gentle, smiling man whose room was down the hall from mine, and I remember the gestures he made when he told us stories. He moved his arms like a bird's and imitated other animals of his Congo forest home. I don't remember too much else about Otto, as we called him, but my brothers remembered him well. When Otto died, Hunter was ten, Wilelbert was fourteen, and Gregory was sixteen. Through the years they told us many affectionate stories about Otto.

Apparently, Otto spent a lot of time with my brothers. He taught them how to make spears and arrows. He showed them how to shave the tips of hickory wood to a point so sharp no arrowhead was needed. He taught them how to cut a vine for the bow, just as he had learned to do in his forest. He found he could substitute vines from our woods for what he'd used from his forest. My brother said Otto did not speak much English. Mama was teaching him, so he knew some words and how to use them. "Good, good," he'd say, clapping his hands, when the boys made spears just as he'd instructed them to do. "Now we fish."

Otto taught my brothers to spear fish and to hunt wild turkeys with arrows instead of guns, so there would be no noise. He showed them how to approach the male turkey. "Keel him first," he told the boys. He didn't have to explain why — the boys saw the female turkeys flock around their fallen male. No wonder Hunter kept saying, "He was my teacher." When I read Colin Turnbull's *The Forest People*, I found much in there that reiterated what Hunter described learning from Otto.

Though Otto was only 4 feet, 9 inches tall, he was lithe and could run through the woods very fast, jumping over fallen logs with an agility that put him way ahead of the awkward teenagers. I guess he had to be swift in his forest home, sometimes to get away from animals and sometimes to capture them. The stories he told the boys about his skill in hunting elephants were conveyed through gestures. He drew his hand down from his nose, curving it up again, defining the trunk of an elephant. "Big, big," he would say, then pantomime stalking the elephant. Hunter, Wilelbert, and Gregory, wide-eyed, watched him make the kill. After the elephant was dead, he sang a hunting song, celebrating the successful hunt. Sometimes Otto would sing songs to the forest, which was cherished by the Pygmies. The forest provided everything for them and was respected as a spiritual source.

Otto would also join us in our ring games, as we sang, clapped our hands, and tapped our feet. Then he would sing one of his songs and dance for us, teaching us the games he'd played at home. Hunter says he and the other boys thought there was something magical about Otto, who could collect honey from bees without a single sting. My brother Gregory tried it once but failed, not knowing the secrets of the forest, and Hunter remembers that Otto laughed and laughed, fell down on the ground laughing as Gregory, covered with bees, ran screaming for Mama.

Otto loved to eat. He loved Mama's cooking, especially when she baked yams, which she often cooked just for him. He liked to fix his own lunch, though. Hunter said that no matter what Otto was doing, if he heard the 12:00 whistle at the cotton mill, he knew it was time for lunch. Lunchtime was when Otto fixed himself a special meal. "Gotta go cooka eat," he'd say.

Otto especially liked the activity around hog-killing time. The communal spirit must have reminded him of home. It was a special time for us, too, and was still so for the country folk when I lived in Alabama in the 1960s. Hunter says that when we were young all the men and boys worked together preparing the hogs, while the women cooked a feast to celebrate. To prepare the hogs the men and boys would place red-hot sandstones in a barrel of water. When the water was hot, they'd slide the freshly killed hog down into the hot water to soften the bristles, then take it out and place it on a long table. Otto loved scraping the hog while it was on the table. Then, while Wilelbert and Gregory cut the tendons of the hog, Hunter says Otto took an old broomstick and sharpened the ends like he sharpened his arrows. Together the men and boys would run the broomstick through the tendons and hang the hog up to clean him out. When all of this was done, hams were hung up in the smokehouse, sausages made, pork chops, chitlins. "Everything used but the squeal," Hunter says, "even the hair Otto scraped off. That was set aside for ticking."

Otto wanted to go back to his home in Africa as the missionary had promised he could, but there was never enough money for that. It must have been terrible for him. Even though he had wanted to come back to Lynchburg, he may not have been happy. I wonder, too, if going into the woods with the boys made him homesick. I wonder if our calling him Otto, instead of Ota, bothered him. Did he ever think, "Nobody knows my name"? When he took the boys spearfishing, didn't those waters remind him of happier days on the banks of his Kasai River?

According to Verner, the missionary, Otto had had a wife and children who were killed in a tribal war. Hunter says that over the years, Otto changed from the smiling, patient teacher of the hunt to a brooding man. Toward the end, he was no longer interested in the hunt. Trips up the hill to pick blackberries, outings to the river to spear fish ended. He became a silent, solemn man and often sat for hours, motionless under a tree, all alone.

On March 20, 1916, late in the afternoon, the boys watched Otto as he gathered wood and built a fire in the field between our house and the seminary. When the fire rose to bright blaze, he began dancing around it. Hunter, Wilelbert, Greg, and their friend Will Chigle watched in awe as Otto danced around the fire, faster, faster, faster, whirling around and around faster, faster, faster, making strange sounds as he danced, chanting, moaning. Sweat on his brow, faster, faster, faster, around and around, chanting, moaning. The boys stood back, confused and afraid. The dance had some meaning they could not comprehend, something mysterious, almost foreboding. They were frightened, but they stayed and watched Otto twirl around, and around and around, chanting, moaning, moaning the same sounds the slaves made, laying bare their sorrow.

That was the last the boys saw of Otto. That night while they were sleeping, Otto went into the old gray weathered shed behind Mammy Joe's store, uncovered a gun he had hidden in the hay, and shot himself. When the boys learned of this the next day, they were devastated. The shed was our place for hide-and-seek and for eating Mammy Joe's cookies, a place we'd go and fall laughing onto the hay-covered floor, clucking chickens strutting around us. To think of Otto lying there, blood oozing from his wound, was terrible. Hunter was upset for days. He felt the loss of a teacher, a friend.

I was too young to know any of this, neither the fire dance nor the dying. But I do remember that after that the room at the end of the hall was empty of morning smiles, and the bow from our gentle Otto was missing.

If you have a purpose in which you believe,
there's no end to the amount of things you can accomplish.

—Marian Anderson

Chapter 18

CARNIVAL PARTIES

—

Mama called them lawn parties. Aun' Tannie called them carnival parties.

"Lawn parties create an image of dignity and gentility," Aun' Tannie said. "Mary was genteel, all right, but these parties had a cause and, at them, Mary was up on a soapbox. The box may have had a little lace around it, but it was a soapbox nevertheless."

"I don't remember any causes," I told Aun' Tannie, "but I sure do remember Mama the producer getting us to perform for her guests on many occasions, out in the yard."

"Yes, I have a picture I'll give you, taken at the end of one of those parties," Aun' Tannie answered.

"What was the cause?" I asked.

"Saving colored folks' land. Your Mama would get very upset when she'd get wind of the fact that land was going to be taken away from some poor colored man by a crooked tax scheme—not only by the white man, mind you, but also by some of our affluent Negroes."

I didn't know this was the reason we were out there singing and dancing, but it feels good to know that now. During the early years of this century, many Negroes in the South did not own land. They were sharecroppers who inevitably owed their landowners money at the end of every year. When a black farmer was finally able to break out of this virtual peonage system, through extra work or by dint of land left to them in a will, it was extremely important for those working inside and outside of the NAACP to protest the taking of that land. Mama, who helped organize the Lynchburg branch of the NAACP, worked within the organization toward this goal. She also worked toward it on her own—thus the carnival parties. Her cause was a popular one with all blacks and there was always good response to her "call to arms." (That's what Aun' Tannie called Mama's land-saving fund-raisers.)

Aun' Tannie made it all more real by telling me of a specific family Mama helped. This happened, she said, in May 1918. The reason she remembered the year was because it was also the year of the influenza epidemic and the end of World War I. There was, it seems, a Miss Corruthers, a white secretary, who worked in an office in town. Whenever Miss Corruthers would get wind of the fact that there was a lawyer working with some unscrupulous client to carry out a land-grab scheme, she'd pass the information on to Mama. Everyone in Lynchburg—white as well as black—knew Mama was a fighter for causes.

The moment Mama learned from Miss Corruthers that Mr. Benjamin Waters was about to lose his house and land because he owed back taxes, she moved into action on his behalf. Mr. Waters was a poor farmer with a wife and eight children. If he lost his land it would devastate his family. So Mama organized a carnival party. Here's how a typical one would go:

"Is the lemonade ready?" Mama asks my oldest sister, Minnie, who always takes care of the beverages.

"Gregory, you and Wilelbert set the tables and chairs out on the lawn."

"Hunter, do you have film for your camera?" Hunter takes pictures and later sells them for five cents apiece.

We go into the woods and pick wildflowers to decorate the tables. (The flowers are withering by the time guests arrive.) Mrs. Jackson makes tea cakes, jelly cakes, and beaten biscuits. Jars of all kinds of homemade jam to spread on the biscuits are set out on each table. An area is set aside by Mama in front of the long porch, for the stage upon which her children will perform. Gregory and Wilelbert roll the piano out onto the porch. Minnie, who attended the New England Conservatory of Music, plays soft music as the guests begin to arrive. Once everyone is seated and served cold lemonade and tea cakes, the performance begins.

"My daughter Minnie will now sing for you one of my favorite songs, 'When You Come to the End of a Perfect Day.'"

Minnie is beautiful in her flowing pink empire dress with her long black hair parted in the middle and pulled back in a braided bun. She sits gracefully at the piano to sing and play Mama's song. When she finishes, she bows to loud applause. Mama claps louder than anyone. Mama is proud of Minnie, her firstborn, who is not only sweet and lively but very talented.

Next on the program is my brother Wilelbert. Mama introduces him: "My son Wilelbert will now recite one of Paul Laurence Dunbar's poems for you." Mama smiles at her other talented child. Wilelbert, the born actor, comes on with a flourish, clears his throat, and recites:

Little brown baby wif spa'klin' eyes
Come to yo' pappy an' set on his knee . . .

When he finishes, there is loud applause for him, too. Then Wilelbert announces that he would like to sing Bert Williams's song "Nobody." Wilelbert loves to imitate Bert Williams, considered the greatest Negro vaudeville performer of all times. (Recently, in fact, on A&E's program *Biography*, the narrator, in discussing the great Ziegfeld, stated that Bert Williams was "the greatest comedian of the twentieth century.") Everyone says Wilelbert is a second Bert Williams, and indeed he looks like that now. With a soulful expression on his face he sings:

> I ain' never done nuthin' to nobody
> I ain' never done nuthin' to nobody
> No time . . .

He is a smash hit, using the same gestures Bert Williams used. He finishes amid thunderous applause and takes an exaggerated bow.

The talent ends there, and so should the program. But Mama, blind to our clumsiness, deaf to *our* tone deafness and apparently defective vocal chords, announces with pride that "Rosemary, Carrie, and Dolly will now sing for you." We have no choice. (Sometimes I was sure I saw pained expressions on her guests' faces, but that did not matter to Mama. Although she accomplished much toward civil and women's rights, I believe she felt her children, flaws and all, were her greatest achievement.) Mama takes us by the hand, gives each of us a pot and a spoon, and leads us onto the stage. While Minnie plays the piano, we beat the pots and sing George Cohan's war song, a song he started writing the day he read that America had declared war on Germany. We squeal out:

> Over there, over there
> Send the word, send the word
> Over there
> That the Yanks are coming
> The drums rum-tumming everywhere . . .

We almost forget the words but there is the producer in the wings, singing louder than we are. When we finish, she calls out, "Bow, bow."

Fortunately, Mama has her talented Minnie ready to perform again. This time she comes out of the house dressed in Papa's black suit and black hat, and with a charcoal mustache. She does a perfect imitation of the new comedic rave Charlie Chaplin. Minnie receives the biggest hand of all.

The finale is all of us children doing "Ballin' the Jack." While Minnie plays the piano, we all sing and dance. When we finish the dance and bow, the applause is long and loud. Wilelbert keeps running back onstage and bowing. "Showoff," Hunter whispers.

This is the end of our part of the program. We have warmed them up for the main act.

Mama walks to the center of the stage. "We are here today to save the land of our dear friend Mr. Benjamin Waters. Mr. Waters has eight children, but what does that matter to some unscrupulous men, waiting in the wings to grab his property? Well, we're going to see that it does not happen."

There is applause from the adults seated at the tables. Mama continues, "Bad enough for white folks to take our people's land—and believe me they have taken plenty of it—but it's worse when one of our own is doing it. . . ."

Aun' Tannie said that at that particular carnival party, Mama looked straight into the eyes of Mr. Federson, one of the wealthiest black men in Virginia, who had amassed much of his riches through those shady deals that Mama was now protesting. He also owned a number of old, run-down shacks, which he rented to the poor.

Mr. Federson was a short, fat, "meriny" (the colored-folk word back in those days describing light-skinned Negroes with reddish blond hair) man. He had a pot belly, over which a gold watch chain jiggled when he laughed. It was his jowliness that caused Wilelbert to name him "Old Floppy Jaws." Isn't it amazing that Mr. Federson came to Mama's lawn parties?

Mama stands tall on her soapbox now. "Our people, who had nothing, have labored hard, scrubbed floors, picked cotton, to try to get little pieces of land for their families. How can our own stoop to taking it away from them? Well, we're going to make certain today that Mr. Waters keeps his property. As we come around with baskets, if you'd like to contribute to this cause, in whatever way you can, I know Mr. Waters will appreciate it." Mama uses the old "make 'em guilty routine," and it works.

Aun' Tannie said Old Floppy put more money in the basket than anyone else. Hunter took pictures and collected the five cents for each, with a promise to deliver the pictures as soon as they were developed. There was also a long table, on the side, with little odds and ends for people to buy. The carnival party was a success, and Mr. Waters' property was saved. This, Aun' Tannie said, was just one of many savings.

It was later that same year that Mama experienced her own loss and sadness. The 1918 flu epidemic grew to such proportions that gatherings were prohibited by law. Minnie, whose husband, Lieutenant John Sims, had returned from the war in 1917, was pregnant when she contracted the flu. At first Mama thought it was not a serious case because Minnie seemed to be getting over it. However, when Minnie lost the baby, which would have been Mama's first grandchild, she was weakened. Not too long after that Minnie died. Mama was devastated. As long as Mama lived, her eyes filled with tears whenever she heard the words, "When you come to the end of a perfect day, and you sit alone with your thoughts."

He who receives a gift
does not measure.

—Kenyan proverb

Chapter 19

THE BIRTHDAY PRESENT

One day, not long ago, the young historian Dale Harter came to see me. "Grandma Carrie," he said, a twinkle in his eyes, "I have a birthday present for you, but I'm not going to give it to you until your birthday."

"Okay," I said.

But when he got to the door to leave, he smiled. "No, I can't keep it. I have to tell you now."

"It must be something really good."

"You know I worked at the Library of Congress this past summer, and since you told me your mother was active in founding the Lynchburg branch of the NAACP in the early part of the century, I looked up those branch files. I also looked up the files of the Montclair, New Jersey, branch. They were all there.

"Grandma Carrie, you won't believe it. Those files are full of letters to your mother from people like W. E. B. Du Bois, James Weldon Johnson, Walter White, Arthur and Joel Spingarn, William Pickens. And there are some of her letters back to them. You need to go up there and check this out."

Dale also gave me a directory to guide me to the right spots in the library and to Jeff Flannery and Joe Sullivan, two friends of his there who could help me.

What a birthday present!

That night I called a childhood friend of mine, Louise Smith McCoy, who lives in Columbia, Maryland. When I told her about my birthday present, she was excited too. "Come, stay here," she said. "We'll get you to the Library of Congress."

The next day Louise's husband, Mac, not only drove us to the library but waited for six hours while Louise and I read and made copies of many of the papers. Louise wrote down on the visitor's information card, "Research Assistant to the Author." She is much more than that to me, a dear and close friend, but she served well as my assistant as she was the one to keep things straight. At my age, as the song says, "It takes two." It took more than that. Joe Sullivan was very helpful, as was Jeff Flannery. Joe Sullivan brought us the files and showed us how the library worked.

I saw Mama's writing—on a two-page letter—as soon as I opened the first file. When I turned it over to check the signature I saw that it was Mama's. The date on the letter was February 21, 1913. "My mother was pregnant with me when she wrote this letter," I said to Louise. It was a strange feeling. I was a part of the moment she wrote to the national office of the NAACP applying for membership, her first step in organizing the Lynchburg branch. The letter read in part:

> We the undersigned apply for membership in the National Association for the Advancement of Colored People and submit to you our constitution for consideration.

The list of names that followed included Reverend Woods, president of Virginia Seminary at the time. Others from the Seminary included S. H. Dreer, Latin professor; J. F. Chafin, professor of English;

R. C. Scott, professor of history. Also listed were T. J. Fawsett, physician; Reverend L. O. Lewis, pastor; E. D. Bonderaut. Aun' Tannie and Uncle Ed Spencer were on the list, and there was Mama, listed as secretary-treasurer of the fledgling organization.

Once established, the Lynchburg branch started off bravely, then seemed to flounder. A letter from the NAACP's national office dated November 25, 1913, asked:

> What has happened to the Lynchburg branch? . . . Never has the mood for workers been so great. . . . We are working hard for the cause. Will you not come in and help us?

I don't know what the other Lynchburg members were doing, but just one month before that letter was received, Mama gave birth to me, her seventh living child. Rosemary was sixteen months old at the time, and now Mama really did have her hands full. There were some follow-up letters from her to the national office, then a gap. I don't know all of what caused it, but I do know that in 1914 Papa insisted that Mama move us to Danville, and on June 10, 1915, Mama gave birth to Dolly, her eighth living child. After Mama left, I guess the Lynchburg branch must have died of natural causes. There's evidence that when we returned to Lynchburg, Mama expressed interest in reviving the branch. She wrote to the national office in 1918. A memo from W. E. B. Du Bois to James Weldon Johnson dated March 6, 1918, reads:

> Mrs. Mary Rice Hayes Allen, RT 2 Box 7, Lynchburg, Virginia, writes to know how the dead Lynchburg branch may be resuscitated.
>
> W.E.B.D.

Mama received a letter from James Weldon Johnson dated March 16, 1918, which reads in part:

We are advised that you are desirous of assisting in reviving the Lynchburg branch of the NAACP, which has practically been out of existence for some time. This is encouraging news as we are particularly anxious at this time, when there is so much work to be done along these lines, and especially in the southern part of our country.

J.W.J.

James Weldon Johnson was at that time field secretary of the NAACP. And it was during this period that Aun' Tannie and Mama walked dusty roads getting people to sign petitions for an anti-lynching bill.

There was an organizational meeting in Lynchburg on April 16, 1918. Forty-nine members were present. It's an interesting list since, in 1913, the membership had included mainly teachers at the seminary, doctors, ministers, and mail carriers, not a broad representation of the local Negro community. The 1918 list was much longer and included the same kinds of members listed in 1913, but also janitors, domestic workers, laborers, students, dressmakers, housekeepers, and farmers.

Mama received a letter from Walter White, acknowledging the list she sent him in May 1918 and welcoming the Lynchburg branch back into the organization.

On July 5, 1918, Mama wrote a letter to Mr. John R. Shillady, secretary at the national office of the NAACP. She reported that there were ninety-six members in the Lynchburg branch, all of whom were in accord with the current work of the national organization. She also reported the Lynchburg branch work:

A white policeman had accosted a young Negro girl several times before she defended herself against him. When she and a young boy hit the policeman with a rock, they were both arrested, fined fifty dollars, and sentenced to sixty days in jail. The NAACP took up the case. Mr.

A. W. Haynes and two other prominent members of the board solicited funds for a lawyer for the young girl. The case was heard and won. The girl was released with a fine of ten dollars. The officer was "removed from the beat with an investigation of his character by the police commissioner." Mama added, "Without the branch there could not have been the same manifest interest in the case."

Shillady requested that James Weldon Johnson answer Mama's letter. His letter reads:

Mrs. Mary Rice Hayes Allen
Route 2 Box 7
Lynchburg, Virginia

My dear Mrs. Hayes-Allen,
    I beg to acknowledge receipt of your letter of the third, and I note with a great deal of satisfaction the progress which is being made by the Lynchburg branch.
    We are also glad to see that the organization has already begun its activities and won its first victory. . . .

Yours very truly,
James Weldon Johnson
Field Secretary

Mama received another letter from James Weldon Johnson, dated October 1, 1918, which mentioned plans for a big public meeting being sponsored by the Lynchburg branch. However, another letter, dated October 17, 1918, recommended cancellation of all Virginia public meetings due to the ban on public meetings because of the influenza epidemic.

Another letter from Johnson, addressed to Mama and dated November 22, 1918, stated that he would not be able to come to Virginia until after the first of the year. He ends his letter with:

Thanking you for the interest and enthusiasm which you have
shown, I am

> Yours very truly
> James Weldon Johnson
> Field Secretary

In December 1918, Mama received yet another letter from James
Weldon Johnson, in which he enclosed the charter giving the Lynchburg branch a full membership. Mama continued to be a very active
member of the Lynchburg branch for another year, but in December
1919 something was happening in Mama's life that required that she
resign as secretary of the branch. Papa was up in New Jersey establishing his law practice there, and planning to move us all there as soon as
he could get settled and find a house. Mama was traveling back and
forth from Virginia to New Jersey and felt she could not carry out the
secretarial position as efficiently as she wanted to. The branch was by
then, as she wrote, "moving with vigor" and successfully handling local
cases. The new secretary, whose name is not clear on the reports, wrote
to the national office on December 6, 1919:

> We regretted exceedingly the resignation of Mrs. M. R. Allen
> caused by her [plan for] permanent change of residence, for she
> was a secretary of rare efficiency and clever tact so essential to
> the promotion of the affairs and the conduct of the fights of the
> local branch on discriminatory conditions which surround us
> in this city.

The new secretary reported another victory of the branch in the
courts. Against state law, brothels *for* whites had been established *by*
whites in a respectable Negro residential section, close to a Negro
school. On one occasion, the report says, "a white ruffian, visiting one
of these houses, shot and wounded an eleven year old school girl. The
NAACP branch secured attorneys. The outcome of the trial was the

conviction of the white man to two years in the state prison. Another victory was won against the "red light" houses themselves in the Negro neighborhood. The outcome was the prosecution of the owners of those houses and the jailing and fining of several of them.

On May 13, 1920, a report went to the national office concerning another fight:

> The branch is cooperating with the colored teachers here in their protest against a discriminatory salary scale, according to which the minimum salary paid the white teachers exceeds the maximum salary paid the colored teachers for the same grade and class.

The report also included news that twenty more members had joined the branch, bringing the number up to 120 members.

Mama not only played an important role in resuscitating "the dead Lynchburg branch," as W. E. B. Du Bois had put it; she worked in its many legal fights almost right up until the day of our move to Montclair, New Jersey—August 13, 1920.

Far from your native hills although you roam

—Vivian L. Virtue,
"To Claude McKay"

Chapter 20

GOIN' NORTH

—

*L*eaving Virginia was hard for Mama and for me, her shy, quiet almost-seven-year-old who wanted to cling to what *was*. It was so long ago and I was so young that I had to turn to my brother Hunter Reed for the date of our move.

"Friday, August 13, 1920," he told me, with authority. He said the date was firmly imprinted in his mind as Aun' Tannie had warned Papa it was bad luck to leave a place on a Friday the thirteenth.

Hunter Reed has an incredible memory and knows more than just about anybody in the world. Or at least that's the way my sisters Rosemary and Dolly and I thought of him when we were young. While we were growing up, he was the big brother who took care of us, read us stories, explained how those voices got in that box (the radio), settled many of our arguments and hinted at the facts of life. "Be careful of boys," was the most he ever said, but he said it in the same tone he used for "Watch out for snakes" and "Don't play with wild dogs." So we knew that those words, uttered from his great wisdom and knowledge, should be taken seriously. Thus you can see why

I turned to Hunter Reed for many of the details of this story of our life with Mama.

I may not have remembered the *date* of our move, but I certainly remember the day: a wrenching experience for the treasurer of the Friendly Five Club and overseer of the Sunday school class collection (a weighty responsibility as cross-eyed Freddie Johnson always thought we were passing out pennies instead of collecting them, and tried to kick me when I'd take them back from his grubby little hands). Seven is the age when there's lots of whispering, secret names, secret codes, and other secrets too numerous to mention. Mama said she almost had to drag me away, and I still get a tugging feeling when I drive through Virginia.

But Papa had bought a house in Montclair, New Jersey, and our Virginia time was running out. Here we were, standing down at the gate, waiting for the boys to put the luggage in the cars. The moving men were taking our furniture out of the house. We would soon be going over to Aun' Tannie's to stay until the furniture arrived Up North, and Papa would come back for us. He'd been Up North for almost a year, setting up his law practice and looking for a house.

While we were standing down at the gate, Mama decided to go back in the house one last time. She walked slowly up the path and I followed her. Aun' Tannie told me Mama did not want to leave this house where she had come as a young bride with her first husband, this house where all of her ten children, except one, had been born, this house where many of the early black educators, not long out of slavery, had gathered to talk about the future of the race, the meaning of freedom, and the importance of education. So she returned one last time to the house where, she said, "memories touch softly every corner."

While Mama was in the house, I returned one last time to my tree, the big oak tree that sheltered us from the sun on hot summer days, where we played our ring games, where our swing was. I sat in the swing, holding onto the ropes and dragging my feet in the dirt. Why do we have to leave our home? I looked up through the branches at the clear blue sky expecting maybe to find the answer there. In the middle of my musing, Mama came out of the house and walked over to me. "Come on, baby," she said, "we have to go." Then she took my hand, held it tight, and together we walked back down the path to join the others. Children may not always understand what's happening, but the light and dark shadows of adult conversation tell them whether it's good or bad. I knew that whatever the reason for leaving was, leaving itself was not good.

Caught up in what some current history books call the Great Migration, our family, like thousands of other black families, was leaving the South on the way to the "Promised Land." This was an exodus of black Americans that began around 1915 and continued significantly through the 1930s. Since migrations have definite patterns, it was almost predestined that our family would end up in New Jersey. Most blacks from Louisiana, Mississippi, Arkansas, and Alabama went north, up to Illinois, Ohio, and Michigan. Those from Georgia, South Carolina, North Carolina, and Virginia went northeast, to Pennsylvania, New York, and New Jersey.

Later Mama and Papa would tell two different stories of why we moved. Papa, a master at softening reality, would laugh and tell his story about the popcorn man. When he was practicing law in Danville, Papa came home only on weekends. Every Saturday we'd run down Durmid Hill to the little station shed to meet the nice man who brought us a big bag of popcorn, peanut brittle, bananas, and coconut candy. In his story, we'd be singing, "Here comes the popcorn man." So he decided he'd better move the family north and settle us all together in one place, so we'd know the popcorn man was our Papa. He always got a big laugh when he told this story.

Mama, on the other hand, blamed President Wilson for our move. In fact, Papa said, she blamed poor Wilson for just about everything. If Wilson had done so-and-so, we wouldn't be in this fix. If Wilson had kept his promises, things would be different. I didn't know what promises he had made to Mama, but she sure was mad at him for not keeping them. Everyone around knew that. Aun' Tannie said when Mama was in Virginia, angered because Wilson had reneged on his pre-election promise of "absolute fair dealings for Negroes," she wrote him some fiery letters admonishing him for taking away rights blacks had worked hard to gain. Wilson, one of the Progressives, ran on a ticket of "new freedom," a word that appealed to blacks, but this was not the freedom he had in mind. Rather than decreasing segregation and discrimination, his administration increased them. Under him, even the federal offices and cafeterias were segregated. Mama, a woman of action, organized letter-writing meetings. For several months a constant flow of letters arrived at the White House from the president's native state.

Papa's popcorn story did not hold up. The truth was that things were not going well in the South. Wilson's reversals created an atmosphere conducive to violence against us. The Ku Klux Klan was on the rise again just as an agricultural depression hit the South. Cotton and wheat were selling for half their former prices. In the Great Migration, workers left first, around 1915. After they established an economic base, in 1919 and 1920, professionals made their way north by the hundreds, Papa among them. Papa said practicing law in a town like Danville, Virginia, had become next to impossible, especially when he represented a black client against a white defendant. With the economic conditions as they were, many of Papa's clients had no money to pay him anyway.

Whatever the reason, here we were getting ready to leave our home and go over to Aun' Tannie's to wait for Papa. Uncle Ed and a friend of his came to take us over and we packed into two cars.

As the car I was in drove off, I looked around and saw Case, our pet pig. He looked so sad.

"Mama, could we take Case?" I pleaded.

"No, Baby, we can't take any pigs up there to Montclair, New Jersey. Anyway, we told Miss Victoria she could have Case and Mary-cow. Tell Case you'll see him next summer when we come back to visit."

Dolly and I were on the backseat looking out the window, watching our home disappear as the car turned at the bend in the road. I had tears in my eyes and I thought Case did too. We stayed at Aun' Tannie's for three weeks; then Papa came for us the day before we were to leave for New Jersey. When the cars taking us to the train station pulled up in front of Aun' Tannie's house, Papa and the boys took our luggage out to them. Uncle Ed, Aun' Tannie, their daughters, Bethel and Alroy, and their son, Chauncey, came out to wish us well. In later years Bethel told me she remembered three "fluttery little girls all dressed up in navy blue pleated skirts, white middy blouses, and sailor hats with red streamers, ready for 'goin' North.'" Parting was a mixture of excitement, sadness, and warnings.

"Be careful and let us hear from you," said Uncle Ed, usually calm, stable, a tower of strength, but now with concern in his voice. Something in the way he spoke made the unknown more foreboding.

As the cars pulled off, Aun' Tannie called out one last warning: "Remember, North is an old Narcissus, Will. Everything's not as straight up there as they'd have you believe." What she said puzzled us, but Papa must have understood. He answered, "We'll be careful."

I didn't realize until later years that there was indeed reason to worry. There was so much violence against us following World War I, and so much bloodshed, that James Weldon Johnson of the NAACP labeled the summer of 1919 the "Red Summer," and it has gone down in history books as that. The violence continued into the 1920s. I know now why Papa often reached into his fantasy bag, pulling out an appropriate story to cover up things in our lives that he thought might hurt us. The popcorn story was a kind of protective coating.

The train ride on the Southern Railway to Washington was a happy one. There was a communal spirit in the Jim Crow car. Everyone shared their fried chicken, pound cake, and bananas—a picnic in motion. It was dusk when the train emptied in Washington. Black families from Virginia, North Carolina, South Carolina, and Georgia stood on the platform waiting for the Pennsylvania Railroad. Mama stood watching the crowds of her people—farmers, sharecroppers, doctors, lawyers, domestic workers. From her backyard in Virginia she had seen trains whiz by, "going to the Promised Land." Now she was one of the pilgrims. All walks of life were milling around but still together, just as they had been in the Jim Crow car. Protective clustering. Some people were sitting on suitcases tied with rope, some carried paper bags and boxes. Some had brand-new luggage, others croaker sacks. They were people on the move in search of a better life.

On the Pennsylvania Railroad, we could sit anywhere we wanted, and the festive air of the Southern Railway gave way to more cautious behavior. Parents hushed their children, spoke softer themselves. Hunter said he felt funny riding with the white folks. Nothing kept us out of the shoe boxes though, and the picnic continued.

The conductor finally called out, "Next stop New-ark," and many of the families, including ours, started gathering children, baggage, and shoe boxes. The platform was packed with waiting friends and relatives, waiting for those now entering the "Promised Land." "Great balls of ice water," said Mama's brother-in-law Uncle Johnny (Professor Hayes' brother), who was there to meet us. Everyone else says "great balls of fire," but not Uncle Johnny, who, we were to learn, was not like everyone else. He laughed as he ran toward us, hugged Mama, then picked up Dolly: "Look at these children. My, my, my!" We girls, who had never seen Uncle Johnny, loved him from that very first moment. He was fat and jolly, with a laugh that made it seem like Christmas all year round. Papa pointed us out by name, giving deference to the eldest and coming on down.

"You sure got a passel of 'em," Uncle Johnny laughed, and then we moved on down the platform to wait for the baggage. Since all of us could not get in Uncle Johnny's car, Papa hailed a taxi to accommodate the overflow. On the drive to Montclair, when we passed through Uncle Johnny's town, Bloomfield, he laughed, "Yes, this would have been your home, if your Papa hadn't fallen asleep on the trolley car." And that launched Papa on another story, which he also told many times during those years. He said he'd wanted to pick a small town close to Newark, where his practice was to be, and one not too far from New York City. Aunt Georgia and Uncle Johnny were living in Bloomfield, which seemed an ideal spot. However, on his house-hunting trip, Papa fell asleep and did not awaken until the trolley car pulled into the car barn in Montclair. He got off, walked around the area, and, to his delight, saw a house with a big FOR SALE sign on it, just around the corner from the trolley-car barn. Certain that divine guidance and not old Morpheus had led him to this spot, he stood for a moment of reverence, then said to himself, "This is where the Lord wants me to be. Yes, I'll settle right here."

Papa finished his story as we came into a beautiful little town. Even though it was dark, it looked very special to us, with its gaslights blinking like stars. "Glen Ridge," Uncle Johnny commented, "nothin' but the rich here." We drove on and soon we went over a bridge. Uncle Johnny, with a sweeping gesture, said, "And this is Montclair, home of Wall Street's wealthiest." Uncle Johnny was always dramatic. "More money in this town per square foot than any place in the country. Streets are paved with gold." Then he chuckled as we looked out the window. "Just an expression, just an expression," he said, noting the disappointment on our faces.

We drove up the main street, Bloomfield Avenue, and turned in at Valley Road. Halfway up the block, Papa pointed out the white house on the left that was to be our new home. The drivers went up to the corner, turned around, and stopped in front of number 72.

"This is it," Papa said proudly, while paying the cab driver. Then he searched his pockets for the key as we all stood on the porch of the house that was to become so much a part of us. Finally Papa opened the door and hustled us inside. We started running through all the rooms. Dolly and I ran up the stairs and had the first of our many slides down that wonderful, long, straight banister.

"How do you like your new home, Mary?" Papa asked.

"I love it, Will. It's a charming old house, and a special place, the beginning of a new freedom," Mama said.

"And the end of the popcorn man." Papa smiled.

Part Three

THE LADY IN THE RED HAT

1920–1935

—

Do not follow the path. Go where

there is no path to begin the trail.

—Ashanti proverb

What is America to me?
A name, a man, the flag I see
A certain word, Democracy
What is America to me?
The house I live in . . .

— Earl Robinson and Lewis Allan,
"The House I Live In"

Chapter 21

THE HOUSE ON VALLEY ROAD

*P*apa was justifiably proud of the house he'd found for us on Valley Road, a white, two-story Victorian with a wraparound porch. "It's almost one hundred years old," he said. It seemed like every time he said that, a bit of the ceiling cracked and fell on someone's head to prove his point. There were other signs of aging in the house. Our first week there, Gregory's foot, a sizable one, came through one of Mama's "charming old ceilings" and the bathtub slipped off one of its clawfeet, unsettling the pipes, and showering water into the kitchen. In spite of all this, we came to love the house, which is still affectionately called "Seventy-two" by those who remember. Mama made it a warm, welcoming place, a cultural center, and a hub of social protest.

Through the years people told us their own stories about Seventy-two. Paul Robeson told Dolly that when he was young and visiting one of the beautiful Goode girls, he'd pass the house and wonder about the family living there. He said that sometimes, riding by on the trolley car, he'd hear the plucking of a ukelele and singing; other times he heard laughter and happy voices. "A veritable musical comedy in an otherwise staid community," he said. Another friend, Freddy Peniston, laughed and called Seventy-two the Overbrook Annex. Overbrook was the county asylum. The fact that we were just twenty-eight miles from New York City accounted at least in part for the attraction of exciting and fascinating people to our doors—Harlem Renaissance poets; early NAACP leaders; visiting speakers at the church and at the YMCA and YWCA; a distinguished gentleman from England; Me'la, a little African girl brought over here by one of the many missionaries to Africa; and best of all, our beloved Thursday people, domestic workers who came to our home on their customary day off.

When we first moved in, Mama spent her mornings walking through the house, leaving her mark wherever she could: changing a chair here, moving a small table there. But most of our furniture was so big it stayed where the moving men placed it. "Antique," Mama called the furniture. And it was, bought for her by her first husband. Aun' Tannie says Mama would hear about an antique sale at one of the old Virginia homes and would tell Professor Hayes about a certain piece she liked. More often than not, a delivery was soon made. Antiques or not, with our childhood lack of appreciation for finer things, we called them the "mahogany monsters."

Papa was irreverent, too, especially about the mirror over the big marble-topped sideboard in the dining room. In the left-hand drawer we kept the silver, the middle drawer, Mama's "miscellany"; and the right-hand drawer, Papa's bills. A large framed mirror with two scowling lions (or gargoyles) at the top hung over the sideboard. "Mary," Papa would say, "I don't like those monsters up there scowling at me because I'm in arrears." We laughed because he laughed, not because we knew what "in arrears" meant. The dining room had a hump in the floor, so one end of the table was propped up by one volume of the *Encyclopaedia Britannica*. (If there are specific deficiencies in our knowledge, that may be the reason.)

There was a mammoth hat rack in the much too narrow front hall. The rack was at least five feet long, with iron figures of old Hermes, the swift messenger of the Greek gods, seated on each end of its shelf. Mama entrusted her red hat to Hermes, but our less trusting friends held their hats to their bosoms, "lest the winged-footed messenger fly off with them." At least that's what Aun' Tannie used to say when she'd visit. She called Hermes the "master thief." She would recite lines from stories in Greek mythology:

The babe was born at the break of day
And ere the night fell
he had stolen away
Apollo's herds.

What a remarkable woman was Aun' Tannie, with a poem for every occasion. Professor Hayes' philosophy of enlightenment for his people really worked for her.

There were no family portraits on our walls. Instead, another huge mirror, the wide floor-to-ceiling mahogany-framed one in the library, reflected the personality of the family. Papa, the dignified one, practiced his conservative speeches before it; Hunter Reed, our gentle but strong brother, indulged his three adoring younger sisters and joined us and our friends as we danced, sang, and gave plays in front of it; Wilelbert, the handsome one, admired himself there; Gregory, the quiet one, contemplated there; and it was there that Mary Rice Hayes Allen pulled that red cloche hat down on her head before going out to let someone know, "We want full freedom and we want it now."

In *Hats in Vogue Since 1910*, Christina Probert says milliners of the time called the cloche hat "the helmet." What better name could there be for the hat Mama put on before going out to the "fight for equality." That red hat became a symbol, and the townspeople knew Mama early on as the "lady in the red hat."

I think, however, that what Papa liked most about Seventy-two was its closeness to the trolley-car barn. An Italian man named Joe worked there, and for years he and Papa solved the problems of the world over that fence. In the musical way Italians lift their voices, Joe would yell, "Hey, Willyama, *buon giorno*, what you thinka . . ." and for the next half hour we knew Papa and Joe would be tied up, talking about politics, religion, sports, and—trolley cars. Papa did love those trolley cars. Whenever we'd plead with him to buy a car, his response was, "See those trolley cars over there? They'll take us anywhere we want to go for five cents."

There was another wonderful thing about those trolley cars. Papa had opened his law office on the corner of Market and Broad Streets, in Newark, in very small, less than adequate quarters; however, he took pride not so much in how it was, as where it was.

"They say Broad and Market is the second-busiest crossroad of the world, second only to Times Square," he said, chest out. Whether it really was mattered less to us than the fact that, unlike at our home in Virginia, he could take those trolley cars and come home every night from that crossroad. But first he'd always stop at the corner store and pick up his newspaper and a bag of coconut candy, Mary Janes or peanut brittle for us.

Mama's favorite place in our new home was the big kitchen with its coal stove and the two big granitelike washtubs that had flat lids we could sit on. Mama hated housework, but she loved to cook, and our house always smelled of something good baking in her oven. The kitchen was also the place where all kinds of stories were told by visitors sitting around the coal stove and developing strategies for the "fight." It was by sitting quietly up on top of those washtub lids and listening to adult conversation that we learned what was happening in the "fight" during the early 1920s and 1930s.

The other place that Mama liked was her flower garden. She worked in the garden every day—weeding, planting, clipping. Our neighbor Mrs. Bengler had a flower garden that bordered Mama's. Sometimes both of them would be out there at the same time, but Mrs. Bengler never spoke to Mama.

One day Rosemary, Dolly, and I were sitting on the slanted cellar door watching Mama in her garden. She was talking to Mrs. Bengler as they dug around their flowers. There was nothing from Mrs. Bengler but silence. I felt uneasy waiting for Mrs. Bengler's response. Finally, I went into the house, where Hunter asked me, "What's the matter, Carrie?"

"Mama keeps asking Mrs. Bengler about her old phlox and her old petunias and she don't say nothing."

"That's nothing to get upset about. You know Mama told us we had to speak to our neighbors."

Yes, she did, and when we protested that they didn't speak back, her only response was, "I'm not raising them. I'm raising you."

Once we heard Mama say to Papa, "I'm going to keep on talking. She'll come around one day."

Then Papa looked at Mama. "There's a little bit of mischief in you, Mary." He smiled. Mama just returned his smile.

When we played in the side yard, we got in trouble if we stepped over the invisible line that separated our property from Mrs. Bengler's. She'd yell out, "Get out of my yard you little ———." She never filled the blank but we knew. We'd run under the house into a low dirt-floored room that had become our enchanted playhouse. Here we made our mud pies, played dollhouse and kept all our childhood secrets. It was here Dolly almost set the house on fire holding a celluloid comb over a candle, trying to make my hair straight like hers and Rosemary's. It was here we ran when Dolly would yell, "Take the keys and lock her up, old mean lady-o."

We felt safe in our playhouse, where we spent many hours playing on the cool dirt floor, away from the heat of the sun and away from the ire of our next-door neighbor.

On our second Sunday in Montclair, after a breakfast of hot rolls, salt mackerel, creamed potatoes, morning prayers, and Bible verses, Papa took us around the corner to the Union Baptist Church. Mama lined us up outside as a teacher does her class. Then she and Papa led us regally down the isle with Dolly between them. I never knew whether they held her hands so tightly out of parental protection or whether they were protecting the congregation from the ever uninhibited Dolly. Rosemary and I followed, holding hands, looking, I am certain, obnoxiously sanctimonious. Wilelbert and Hunter Reed were next, and Gregory came in alone as the rear guard. The man in the pulpit was tall and fair-complected. He looked just like pictures I had seen of Jesus. His name was Reverend Love, and didn't we sing a song called "God Is Love."

The service was long, but after the singing of "God Be with You 'til We Meet Again," the minister and many members of the congregation welcomed us to their town and to their church. There were many long, hardy, wrist-breaking Baptist handshakes and hugs, and then we started toward home, feeling the first glow of belonging—at least in our separate world.

After dinner, Papa said, "Come, we're going for the best ride of our lives." He marched us around to the trolley-car barn, and seated us by twos all over the trolley car, even in the back. He was proud, smiling, as we rode through the small adjacent towns. Mama told us that for Papa those trolley cars represented the first evidence of the "new freedom" he had pulled up stakes for. We could sit anywhere we wanted on the trolley. Every Sunday for a long time Papa took us up to the car barn for that "best ride of our lives."

No wonder he loved being close to the car barn. No matter how old Seventy-two was or how many repairs it needed, he was always thankful to God for finding this house for him. Whenever he told his story of how we ended up at 72 Valley Road, Montclair, New Jersey, he'd say, "God in His wisdom led me to this place."

No one can uproot the tree
which God has planted.

—Yoruba proverb

Chapter 22

THE TREE

—

$\mathscr{E}$xcept for Uncle Johnny, who came by almost every day in the beginning, our first visitor to the house on Valley Road was Mr. David Abbott, a member of our church. Mr. Davie, as we called him, was a butler for one of the richest families in town. He was very intelligent and, as a Bostonian, very cultured. Some people mistook the culture and called him "different" and other things, which the boys would snicker about. Mr. Davie wore soft, fine-looking tan wool knickerbockers and sweaters he had knit himself. He looked impeccable.

"Yes, Mary's got to make her speeches," Papa said to Mr. Davie on his first visit, "so I thought I'd better move her north and find a safer platform for her." It was evident from Papa's smiles, when he talked about Mama, that he not only endured but adored her, and indeed he must have. Papa introduced all of us to Mr. Davie, and when the conversation became more serious, he dismissed us with a nod of his head. Mr. Davie, Mama, and Papa stayed cloistered for a long time. Their low voices, serious tones, and scattering of audible words alerted my brothers to the fact that something was not going right. Wilelbert went into the front hall, stood by the parlor door, and listened.

"I don't know if you know it yet, Mr. Allen," Mr. Davie said. "I cawn't understand it, but your moving in here has caused some unhappiness in your neighbor."

Papa said he knew about Mrs. Bengler, our next-door neighbor, and the fact that something was brewing, then added, "Silence itself sends a mighty message."

"Yes, she has her first time to speak," Mama added.

"The Thursday grapevine says she's sending out petitions to get you all out," Mr. Davie continued. The Thursday grapevine. At that time, for most black families in Montclair, the main source of income was working in service for the wealthy white families of the town. Thursdays, the customary day off, all kinds of tales circulated around town about the happenings in town and the "goings-on" of the rich white folks. It was a powerful communication system, our own private intelligence service. Mama had already talked with Mrs. Price — they'd met in the grocery store — who worked for the doctor across the street. Mrs. Price had overheard the doctor talking about Mrs. Bengler approaching him on the matter of our being there.

Mr. Davie said he did not want to upset Papa, but thought he should be alerted in case of trouble. Mama said, "I can't understand this house being a problem. Negroes live all around us, down across Bloomfield Avenue, and the Negro church we attend is just around the corner."

"Well," Mr. Davie said, "I guess they're trying to protect these blocks along Valley Road, and I understand your neighbor's petition warned that if they're not careful, we'll be up on Mountain Avenue before they know it."

"Not hardly," laughed Mama, already aware of the economic impossibility of this. "What a paradox," she commented. "Here in what's supposed to be a better place, most of our neighbors don't even speak to us. Back home in Virginia, we had white neighbors all around us, children played together, families grieved together when there was a death, attended the funerals together, and identified each other's returning kin—'That's Jethro's oldest son, my he's done well'—and so on. We shared our troubles and joys like neighbors should. True, we couldn't ride the trolley car together, and we can't forget worse things, but with a lot of people on both sides, the deeper human feelings were there."

Mama, Papa, and Mr. Davie talked for some time. When Mr. Davie got ready to leave Papa thanked him for letting him know about our neighbor's plan.

One evening when Papa stopped at the corner store, Mr. Goldberg asked him to stay for a minute. Mr. Goldberg was waiting for one of the customers to leave, so he could speak privately with Papa. "You see that man that just left? That's Mr. Norman. Yesterday he was in here talking about you moving in up the street. Not to me but to another man who had come in. Sometimes they come in here and get to talking like I'm not even here with ears. But I heard it all right. Yes, old man Norman was saying to this other man, 'I guess the only way to get them out is to burn a cross in front of their house.' He laughed, but I thought he might mean it, so I was worried. In fact, I had thought once of coming up there and telling you."

"I certainly appreciate that, Mr. Goldberg. I've thought they might do something like that. Lot of that going on these days. I'll watch out for it. I'll also alert the police department and the fire department that this is a possibility."

The white world around us was becoming of more and more concern to Papa. He was receiving threatening calls, and our intelligence service, which had expanded, was reporting the seriousness of the situation. One of our main reporters was a lady from the church who we came to know as Miz Nettie. Miz Nettie was a big, round ball of laughter. Her face was the color and smoothness of caramel candy; her walk was light and airy, a contradiction to the two hundred pounds of flesh she was carrying. Miz Nettie came to visit the week after we went to church the first time. She and Mama became immediate friends. She played and talked with us for a while, then told Mama she had come on a "mission" and asked to speak privately with her, which prompted Mama to say, "Okay, children, run outside and play."

We obeyed, but became extremely thirsty in the process and were in and out of the kitchen a dozen times. With this on-the-spot coverage, Hunter Reed was able to hear snatches of conversation, which he brought outside, in confusing detail.

"It is about somebody trying to get us to move," he said, confirming his earlier news story.

"Why do we have to move?" Rosemary asked.

"I didn't say we were gonna, I said they want us to."

"Who wants us to move?" Rosemary pursuing the finer details.

Hunter Reed shrugged his shoulders. "I dunno—that's all I know." The news having gotten a little dull, we went on playing and forgot about it. But Mama and her caller still had their heads together in serious conversation. They were so intense they did not notice that Wilelbert had come in and was sitting up on the washtubs, listening. Papa came in while they were still talking. Mama introduced Miz Nettie, told him why she had come. Papa's only answer was, "If God be with us, who can be against us."

"Seems sometimes we take two steps forward, then you're pushed three steps back," Mama was saying. "That's why we have to keep up the fight, Nettie." They had reached a first-name basis already, and after she'd gone, Mama said Nettie was like someone she'd known all her life.

"Got to fight for every little thing. Ain't right—looks sometime like this country's going backwards," Miz Nettie said.

"We are," Mama concluded. "When President Wilson let them segregate those government offices, he gave a green light to segregation all over the country."

"Don't think Mary didn't write to the president 'bout that one," Papa laughed. "Oh, yes, he heard from Mary."

"We'll never give up, Nettie—never," Mama said. "They make us fight harder and harder, but a hard fight gives us more strength. The NAACP's been fighting segregation in housing. Won that fight a few years ago." She turned to Papa for specifics.

"Buchanan versus Warley, 1912." Not only could Papa quote laws and dates but he could extract their essence. "Defeated segregation through city ordinances."

"Yes," Mama said, "all across the country cities passed ordinances to keep us out of certain areas, but we beat them on that one."

"Doesn't do much good to have a law if other ways are used to keep us out," Papa said. "They're now writing in their deeds that their houses are not to be sold to Jews, Italians, or, of course, you know who."

"God don't love ugly," Miz Nettie informed Mama and Papa, "and one day it's gonna all come down, and when it does it'll be like fallin' rocks—big ones."

Mama said our troubles with this house did not compare with those some of our people in other northern cities were having: crosses were being burned and homes set on fire; ours were just mild threats and silence. Nettie believed our troubles were minimal because of the doctor across the street. "Sometimes," she said, "I think that doctor over there is helping more than we realize and certainly more than he realizes. Betty Price said they tried to get him to sign the petition and he gave them a piece of his mind, said he'd be minding his business and guessed you all would be doing the same."

"We always have to remind ourselves that they're not all alike. Sometimes it's hard, but I try to keep a balance, Nettie. For example, our neighbor on the other side has been very kind. She came to visit and welcome us. Later, when all this mess started, she brought the children some cookies. Although we never talked about it, I felt that was her way of saying she was sorry. Angels and devils come in all colors." A comment Mama often made.

One night shortly after Miz Nettie's visit, we lay awake, sensing something was wrong. The telephone kept ringing, and Papa responded louder each time:

"I don't care about your threats, we are staying; and if you keep this up I'll call the police."

They did keep it up, and Papa kept his promise. By then we were out in the hall, sitting on the top step, looking through the railing. Papa opened the door to a tall, heavyset policeman with a strong Irish brogue. It was McGinty. He and Papa had talked several times at the newspaper store. Papa liked him. He was friendly and full of funny Irish sayings, which Papa would bring home.

When the phone rang again, McGinty picked it up and said in an authoritative voice, "This is McGinty from the police department and I'd advise you not to call here again." There were no more calls that night, but although Mama came up and sat in our room for a while, our sleep was very fitful.

The next week the phone rang constantly, but the calls were mainly from our intelligence agents. Miz Nettie was one of the major reporters. "The people in one of those two-family houses across the street had a terrible argument about y'all," she informed us. "Seems like one of them says she thinks y'all have a right to live anywhere you want, and she was real mad about the fuss; but the other one, ooo-whee! is she upset. You know, it's like a house divided," she chuckled, pleased with her analogy. Things went on like this for a few weeks, then the fight seemed to gradually weaken. Finally one day Miz Nettie came puffing in with a late report: "Guess what I heard while servin' dinner last night? Mrs. Brewster musta been talkin' with someone 'bout the whole mess, 'cause she was saying to Mr. Brewster she thinks the whole thing will die down soon. I'm just listening. Every maid walking around the table ain't just passing bread," she laughed. "The Brewsters, they's friends to the doctor across the street and they don' like what's happening either. Seem like the doctor not only put your neighbor in her place but the lady down the street from him too. You know, Mary," Nettie continued with some demonstration of authority, "that doctor is the most respected person on the block and sometimes it only takes one big one to squelch all the little ones."

Mama was grateful. "Nettie, you don't know what comfort you and the others have brought us. I have been worried for the children and especially for Will, with those threatening notes and telephone calls. I'm so proud of the way he stands up to them, though. For everything they yell at him, he yells right back—'I don't care about your threats. This is our home and we're staying here, like it or not.'"

Yes, it was evident that we were staying. We loved sitting out in those big, dark green, reed-bottom rockers; and even with the profusion of the "cinnamon" vine growing over the side porch, there was no doubt about the color of the faces that showed through to the passersby.

We cannot afford to settle for being just average.
We must learn as much as we can to be the best
that we can. The key word is *education*.

— Bill Cosby

Chapter 23

HICKORY STICK

⟡

*I*t was a cool September morning when Mama sent us off to school, dressed warmly in our new clothes and smelling like asafetida, a fetid gum resin from some Oriental plant, and a popular folk medicine of the time. Having lost a daughter two years before, in the 1918 influenza epidemic, Mama was taking no chances in this colder climate. So we marched down Valley Road, asafetida lockets around our necks. The bad smell was enough to ward off disease, any enemies we might encounter, and possibly a few friends. Of Mama's ten children there were only six of us when we moved to Montclair. (Half the number of that wonderful Gilbreth, *Cheaper by the Dozen*, family. All three of us girls had Gilbreth children in our classes. Rosemary particularly remembers Lillian Gilbreth, who went through high school with her.)

Our first morning of school, Mama walked Rosemary and me up the rolling green hill to yellow-brick Spaulding School, where Rosemary would enter the third grade and I, turning seven in October, would enter the second. Hunter Reed walked on to the junior high school next door, and Wilelbert had the longest walk, up to the high school. Gregory had finished school and already had a part-time job. Dolly was not old enough for school yet.

We had passed our school many times when Mama had taken us for wonderful long walks through the beautiful streets of Montclair. "Don't tarry," she would say, "lots of wonders to see in this world." We always had to walk fast. Mama with her "Don't tarry" and Papa with his "Step lively, step lively." I never knew why, unless it was to dispel the old stereotype that blacks, like Stepin Fetchit of the early movies, just shuffled along.

On our first Montclair walk, we went down South Mountain Avenue. It was like walking through a fairyland. Some of the houses looked like castles, others like old English manors, and all of them stirred our imaginations. Kings and queens and princes had to live there. Then we left South Mountain Avenue and took a winding path up through the woods. Breathless when we reached the top, we could hardly believe the view. It was an unusually clear day and, in the distance way out over the trees of Montclair, we could see that mysterious, forbidden, and (as Papa warned later) "wicked" city, New York. He said that was one place he'd keep his girls away from.

But back to the first day of school. Everybody talked fast with clipped sounds, and nobody said "Yes Ma'am" or "No Ma'am" except me. It was "Yes, Miss Mellinger," "No, Miss Mellinger." When I did say "Yes Ma'am," Miss Mellinger corrected me and blood rushed to my face. That night I practiced "Yes, Miss Mellinger," "No, Miss Mellinger," "Yes, Miss Mellinger," until I fell asleep.

At the table every night, Papa asked each one of us how school was. Rosemary told us how pretty her teacher was and about a friend she had already made. Hunter Reed had also made a friend, who came home with him later that week. I said very little and would not let Papa know how unhappy I was. In Virginia, I went to the primary school attached to the seminary. There, everyone knew us. It wasn't wrong to say "Yes Ma'am," and we could run across the road after school to

Mammy Joe's store, where one of those saucer-size sugar cookies and a hug would be waiting for us if we'd done well in school that day. I had to say something when Papa asked, so I responded with a noncommittal "It's all right." Wilelbert, grinning impishly, told Papa everything was great up there at the high school, and for him it was. He wasn't telling it all, though, and Rosemary almost let the cat out of the bag one morning. "Mama," she asked, "did you see Wilelbert when he left for school this morning?" Hunter Reed kicked her foot. We had agreed not to tell. Wilelbert had left early, dressed out in a monkey-back suit, a forerunner of the zoot suit, similar except for the high waist and the considerable flair at the bottom of the jacket. He also wore pearl-gray spats and a derby. Rosemary didn't know what to do now; she had opened a subject she knew Mama would pursue.

"Was there something you wanted to tell me?" Mama left the coal stove, where every morning she cooked our Quaker oats, and came over to the table.

"No, Ma'am. Just the way he was all dressed up, that's all," Rosemary answered, the words rolling out slowly. Rosemary's Southern drawl never left her. Somehow it seems to complement her soft, feminine looks and Southern charm and has stayed with her throughout the years. And it helped that morning, too. Mama decided that Wilelbert's "dressing up" was nothing new and let the subject drop. What she did not know, however, was exactly how he was dressed, and why. He was wearing that outfit up to the high school for his performances. Some boys fight their way into new territory; Wilelbert was singing and tapping his. He would go into his act every afternoon, after school. Armed with a repertoire of his favorite songs, "K-K-K-Katy," "Melancholy Baby," "My Buddy," and "I'm Forever Blowing Bubbles," he was a smash hit. Everyday he'd come home with new stories for us.

"They asked me today where I came from," he said, leaning over to brush off his spats. "Know what I told 'em? I said, 'Ah come from New Ham-shiah.'"

"New Hamshiah!" Hunter Reed screamed. And no wonder: in the

black exodus from the South, nobody was going to "New Ham-shiah."
Most Negroes from the East Coast were going straight up to New
York City, or so the stories went. They said that even those who got off
in Newark, New Jersey, did so thinking the conductor had said "Noo
York." Though Wilelbert's inquirers were somewhat dubious about his
place of origin, he had an ever increasing fan club, which included his
admiring sisters. For Wilelbert things were going really great up at the
high school; that is, they were until Mama got a call from her primary
intelligence agent.

"Mary," Miz Nettie's voice thundered over the wires, "you gotta do
something about that Wilelbert."

"What's he done now, Nettie?" Mama's question implied no real
surprise at anything Wilelbert would do.

"Well, you know Miz Brewster, the lady I work for, her daughter
came home laughing and talking 'bout a colored boy coming to school
in spats and a funny-looking suit, singing, dancing, and clowning.
Turns out it was Wilelbert."

"Wilelbert!" Mama yelled up the stairs, "Come down here immediately!"

"Aw, aw," he said, gathering up his courage. Mama was waiting for
him at the bottom of the back stairs. She grabbed his ear and dragged
him into the kitchen.

"I'm not sending you up to that school to be a clown," she admonished. "They think we're nothing but clowns anyway. What are you
trying to do, *prove* it? We need something in our heads, not in our feet,
in our *heads*, and you're going to get that in *your* head," she said, swat-
ting him upside the head that was supposed to get something put in it.
"We need something in our heads if we ever expect to get full freedom." Wilelbert listened attentively, not really understanding how
"full freedom" would come if he stopped tapping and singing, but he
knew he must agree with the way Mama felt about education.

Education to Mama was the "road to full freedom." As a child I
often wondered where this road was, but Mama knew and was deter-

mined we were going to get on it for our own sakes, for the family's sake, and for the race. Since we were living in a time of heightened race consciousness and striving to restore pride that had been wrenched away, it was not unusual for black parents to think of their children's behavior in the context of race. In fact, Mama had us doing a lot of things for the race.

"We've got to lift up the race, so we can be proud," she would say.

"Or dead," Wilelbert would snicker under his breath, miming Atlas behind Mama's back. Lifting up the race was a solemn responsibility, but it was the one instilled in us from early childhood. And as far as Mama was concerned, getting a good education was crucial to the task. As a member of the first generation of blacks born out of slavery, Mama told stories that were filled with the drama of freedmen founding schools after the war, and she wanted Wilelbert and all of us to capture the same passion for education as the ex-slaves had. Now she used the example of his father to try to shake some sense into Wilelbert's head. "Wilelbert," she pleaded, "you have a good mind. Use it, as your father would want you to do. Du Bois says, 'The thinkers to think and the workers to work.' Your father felt every man, whether he is a worker or a high priest, needs to be a thinker. No matter what you turn out to be, be a thinker. Nobody can take that away from you."

Wilelbert usually enjoyed these philosophical discussions with Mama more than any of us, but not now. What she wanted meant giving up all the attention and admiration he was receiving up there at the high school. The white kids might have thought he was funny, but the colored girls thought he was divine. Not only could he sing, but he was tall, thin, a smooth medium brown, with dark eyes that sparkled when he sang. Now he was in great conflict, adoring Mama, who was asking too much.

Mama should have known Wilelbert just couldn't help it. He was a born entertainer. Even at home, he would burst into song without warning. In the middle of the breakfast dishes or as he was going out the door he would turn, sing one of his "eras," and leave us spellbound. Someone told him he had, of all things, a beautiful Irish tenor voice, so he sang a lot of weepy mother songs. His performances were priceless. First, he'd bow very low and announce himself in the following manner:

"Little Willie will now sing for you that be-ee-youtiful 'era.'"

Once when he sang "Does Your Mother Come from Ireland?" we all laughed and said, "No, and she don't come from New Ham-shiah either."

When Wilelbert wasn't singing, he was reciting Paul Laurence Dunbar's poems. He knew them all and liked especially those in dialect: "When Malindy Sings," "Little Brown Baby," and our favorite, "Jilted." We would all be practically in tears when he finished the closing lines:

> Somep'n's wrong 'bout my lung
> An' I'm glad it's so.
> Doctah says that I'll die young,
> Well, I wants to go

At this point Wilelbert, standing near the sink, would dab a little water in his eyes and start coughing:

> Whut's de use o' livin' hyeah,
> W'en de gal you love so deah
> Goes back on you clean and clear—
> I sh'd like to know?

Then, with a melodramatic, very consumptive cough, he would make a feeble bow and slump to the floor, dead. Sneaking a look at our sad faces, the devilish Wilelbert would jump up, grinning: "Got to ya that time, didn't it?"

Singing, dancing, and acting were just in Wilelbert's blood. But when reports continued to come in about his behavior, Mama knew she had a lesson to teach and took him off for "a serious Mama talk," which Wilelbert described as the last warning before Armageddon. Mama thought her lesson had taken effect, but she was to learn later, from the horse himself, that this was not so.

Two weeks into school, I was much happier. I had a friend now, Jane, whose mother said could come home with me one day. I was skipping down the hill from the yellow-brick school with Jane. Some of the words of the song we'd sung in assembly danced through my head: "Some think the world is made for fun and frolic — and so do I, and so do I." I wanted to dance and twirl and sing.

Rosemary, Hunter Reed, and Dolly were home. I proudly introduced them to Jane. A few minutes later Wilelbert came bursting in the door.

"I bowled 'em over today," he boasted. He was so excited, I didn't even get a chance to tell him about Jane, and I resented his intrusion.

"See it was like this," he preened. "All these kids gathered round and said, 'Come on, Billy, sing us a song.' Now, you can't disappoint your audience, can you?" he continued, gesturing exactly like Bert Williams, the great black comedian. He had everyone at school calling him Bill now, and he even told us to. Bill Hayes would look better in lights, he said, certain that one day that name would flash from some marquee in Harlem. (Later, having read Plato, he announced that Harlem was his Utopia. When I was older, Harlem of the '30s and '40s seemed that way to me too.)

"What'd you sing?" Rosemary asked the very question he wanted, an introduction to his act. He crooned:

Come to me, my melancholy baby,
Cuddle up and don't feel blue
You're my very foolish fancy maybe . . .

When he finished we all applauded; Jane was smiling and I, the proud sister, smiled too. He was forgiven; he had turned Jane's day into one even more special.

"That's not all," Bill said. "They kept saying, 'Do another one,' so I did my song-and-dance act, like this." And he sang and soft-shoed:

K-K-K-Katy
Beautiful Katy
You're the only
G-G-G-Girl
That I adore

Right in the middle of his act, Mama appeared in the door. His back was to her and he was so wrapped up in what he was doing, he never saw our eyes rolling or heard us clearing our throats.

"And I did a special step for them this time, like this. . . ." He twirled around and there she was. Mama, a woman of action and not without a temper when pushed too far, picked up the broom and swung. It missed the nimble Bill, but the message must have hit its mark. Bill stopped clowning at the high school, although he found many other stages upon which to perform, winning waltz contests at the YMCA, appearing on talent shows at the local theater, and performing at home for Mama's guests, or just for Mama whenever she would say, "Come on, kids, let's have us a program."

Mama's pleas to Bill paid off. All of his life he read philosophy, history, poetry, politics, and science. He did have a brilliant mind, like his father. Most of the books in our library were from the personal collection of Professor Hayes. It was there Bill found his poetry, his history, and all those philosophical quotes he'd bewilder us with. It was there I was introduced to Shelley, Keats, and Phillis Wheatley. It was there Papa read Bacon and Shakespeare over and over. But through the years, it was Bill, more than any of us, who read those books. I believe that if his father had lived, Bill would have been able to go to college. But after Professor Hayes's death, the opportunity for college was not there for Bill. This did not stop him. Though he never went to college, I'm certain he was more liberally educated and more "enlightened" than any of the rest of us, a worker and a thinker, with something in his head and in his feet.

I have a story fit to tell
in head and heart and song

—William Rose Benét,
"The Strong Swimmer"

Chapter 24

THURSDAY STORIES

On October 2, 1920, an article appeared in the *Montclair Times* stating that a Mrs. Livermore was encouraging women to vote and prophesied that "although the women of New Jersey have been voters for less than a month, they are already well organized and ready to do their best to restore sanity to the government of this country."

Mama's lifelong interest in politics was perhaps only partly due to the influence of Professor Hayes, who had been so politically astute. The passing of the 19th Amendment had excited Mama. She could vote not only as a woman, but as a Negro woman. Mama called Mrs. Livermore that very day to say she wanted to do what she could to encourage the Negro women of Montclair to vote and she'd appreciate receiving any literature she might be able to send. Mrs. Livermore was very responsive and told Mama that she believed that if everyone pulled together, New Jersey women would carry the state for the Republicans. (Out of loyalty to Lincoln, Negroes were still voting Republican and continued to do so until Franklin Roosevelt ran for president.)

Encouraged by Mrs. Livermore's enthusiasm, Mama gathered a small core of women, mostly our Thursday people, to organize and start getting the word out. "You've won the right to vote, use it" was Mama's call to arms at organizing teas, during which the core group encouraged the women guests to vote. The zeal of the women of New Jersey, as Mrs. Livermore predicted, must have helped in electing Harding, and Mama's Thursday ladies were a proud part of the victory.

Mama was active in politics all her years in Montclair. Hunter remembers that when Hoover was running for president, he came to Montclair. In the parade, Mama's car was the one just behind Hoover's. Mama left the Republican party in the 1930s and joined the Democrats. She worked hard with the county Democratic chairman, McMahon, to help elect Franklin Delano Roosevelt in 1932. And, as always, her Thursday people worked right alongside her.

Thursdays were special days for us. The kitchen would be full of people we liked when we came home from school. And they often came bearing gifts—chocolate cakes, sweet-potato pies, old clothes, and stories about rich people. Mama loved our Thursday people as much as we did. She liked their plain ole down-home honesty, something she felt was lacking in the so-called society Negroes striving so hard to keep up with the Joneses. "Noses held so high they can't smell the flowers. I want to smell my flowers." And she did, as did our Thursday people.

Mr. Davie, in his knickerbockers, came as regularly as Thursday itself. Among his gifts were fresh coconut cakes, gloves and scarves he had knitted for us, old Victrola records his "Madam" had discarded, and stories about the lives of great singers and composers. Mr. Davie loved all the "finer things of life" and at times would insist that we sit down and listen to some of these finer things. He brought us the wonderful voices of Caruso and Galli-Curci, the piano of Paderewski, and a record I will always remember because our brother Bill added it to his repertoire: "Macushla, Macushla, I still hear you calling. . . ."

Mr. Davie tried very hard to instill the finer things in us, and he did, though he was horrified to know that we thought Jelly Roll Morton's "Black Bottom Stomp" and Louis Armstrong's "Struttin' with Some Bar-b-que" were finer than his finest things. Our cousin James, from Danville, came up summers to work as a brick mason, and always brought us special records. James and his brother Leroy were working, as Grandma always said, "to make something of themselves"—and they did. James later became an undertaker, Leroy a doctor. The summer James had brought us Cab Calloway's "Minnie the Moocher," Mr. Davie happened to hear the Victrola and Cab Calloway blasting "Hi-de-hi-de-ho," and to see us with our friends—Ora, Pearl, Alice, Martha, Bessie, and Lovie—in front of the library mirror dancing the "snake hips," "the bump," and the "mess around." He was beside himself.

Then there was the lady we nicknamed "Miz Ruffles." She, like Mr. Davie, also came almost every Thursday. Miz Ruffles worked for a very frou-frou lady who was always giving her lots of maribou-feathered hats and old furs that smelled of mothballs, most of which Miz Ruffles wore most of the time. Whatever was left over, she gave to us for dress-up play. When I think of Miz Ruffles now, I remember maribou, dramatic entrances, and a shrill, birdlike voice. Come to think of it, I'm not sure we ever really saw her face for all the feathers and furs. Mama said she wasn't quite as down-to-earth as most of our Thursday people, imitating her Madam as she did, and putting on too many airs. But she was a good soul, always doing kind things for others, so Mama forgave the airs. We loved when she came over on Thursdays. She always brought old copies of *National Geographic* magazine, through which we traveled the world many times. But her stories were always about herself. Each week she would tell us with much excitement about a new tall, handsome gentleman who just adored her and wanted to marry her because he just could not live without her. Somehow, despite all her "beaus," she lived to be eighty-two without ever having reached the altar.

But our all-time favorite Thursday visitor and storyteller was Miz Nettie. She loved the stories we told on ourselves as much as we loved the stories she brought us. Funny stories were a family specialty in that kitchen every day. Everyone in our house considered themselves funny—Papa had his dry humor, Mama and Dolly their quick wit, and Rosemary her studied jokes (she usually forgot the punch line). Hunter Reed (he remembered the punch lines) laughed outrageously loud at his own jokes. Gregory had his mumbling humor (which no one quite understood). Bill had his teasing humor (which sometimes had us in tears). And I had my puns and corn (which often elicited loud *Oh no!*s from everybody).

Other times the stories were serious. Mama often read us articles from the *Crisis* about race riots and lynchings and about the NAACP's early fight for freedom and justice. Sometimes bits of adult conversation could be unsettling when it fell on the ears of sensitive children sitting on those washtubs in the kitchen, but there was warmth from the old coal stove and the interlacing of humorous tales with Mama's positive view of the future ("Things will be different") to keep the balance. "There are many good people, and one day the evil will be crushed...." We felt safe, loved, and protected from those vague "evils" somewhere out there.

A LOT OF learning took place in Mama's kitchen on Thursdays, too. Miz Nettie said she learned a lot from Mama about things she'd never known, like the way the NAACP started, for instance. Once when Miz Nettie was there Mama and Papa were talking about the coming election and how it was a shame so many of our people in the South were not allowed to vote.

"We need to do something about that," Mama said. After a pause she added, "We need more of that old Niagara spirit." Miz Nettie raised her eyebrows and looked bewildered, as the only thing synonymous with Niagara to her was honeymoon, and she expressed this thought to Mama.

"This was no honeymoon, Nettie," Mama said, and began to tell Nettie the story we had heard many times. Mama was as good a story teller as Miz Nettie, and always acted out her characters. The Niagara story: "Du Bois and a group of Negroes had met secretly at a little place near Niagara Falls way back at the turn of the century—1905, I remember because I was carrying Hunter Reed at the time," Mama said. "They met to draw up a program to protest all the injustices, and met again later at Harpers Ferry and announced to the whole country"—at this point Mama stood up to re-enact Du Bois's speech as if she were on stage—"We want our manhood suffrage, and we want it now, henceforth and forever. . . ."

"Right, right," yelled Miz Nettie, caught up in the story. Papa was smiling, pleased.

"That's really how the NAACP got started. Several white sympathizers joined the fight and together they later organized the NAACP. Some names we should never forget," Mama commented, "are Du Bois, who opened people's eyes and ears after Niagara, and Mary White Ovington, a white social worker, who was so stirred up about the race riots in Illinois. Also William Walling, a journalist who wrote about that terrible riot and expressed concern about what was happening to Negroes. They thought of getting people together—Negroes and whites from all over the country to talk about what was happening to us and how we needed a united effort. They joined with the Du Bois group. That's the way the NAACP started. By the way," Mama added, "have you paid your dues?" Miz Nettie opened her pocketbook, laughing. "Lawd, with a speech like that, how could I get out of it?" she said as she handed Mama her money.

Whenever Miz Nettie came to our house, she'd have a head full of stories. We could sit and listen to her for hours. Sometimes she would lean back in the chair and chuckle so that an epidemic of laughter, for which we wanted no cure, would spread around the kitchen. Other times she would tell scary stories of such suspense and danger we'd be afraid to go into the next room. All of her stories started with "Lawd, let me tell you what happened. . . ." Then, if it was to be a funny one, she'd say, "I almost died—with laughter, that is," or a suspenseful one, "I was so scared I like to have lost my skin," a sizable loss when you considered the bulk of Miz Nettie, three times the size of her sister Lettie, who she would bring with her sometimes. Miz Lettie was a mere wisp of a thing, with keen features and hair pulled back tightly into a small neat bun, accentuating the austerity of her drawn face, which seldom knew a smile. Miz Nettie and Miz Lettie worked as up- and downstairs maids for a very wealthy family and knew all of their top-drawer secrets, which they always told in two different versions, Lettie refuting and correcting Nettie all the way through hers.

Rarely did Miz Nettie miss a Thursday visit, and when she did, Mama worried. One Thursday when Mama was entertaining the Missionary Society of our church, Miz Nettie failed to show up. Mama needed Miz Nettie to back her up in a little controversy that was going on among the church ladies. Mama was asking them to take some time out from prayers and Bible verses to write letters to Harding requesting his support of an antilynching bill, a major NAACP concern at the time. One of the ladies, Mrs. Broland, protested, saying they were to be about the Lord's work and learning His word. It was Papa, not Mama, who usually quoted the Bible, but Mama borrowed from him that day, and countered Mrs. Broland's objections with an appropriate verse:

"For we are labourers together with God," she said, adding "First Corinthians, chapter 3, verse 9" and then, as a clincher, "God's commandment says 'Thou shalt not kill.' What better way to labor with God than to try to stop these killings." Mama won her point.

I'd never liked Mrs. Broland anyway. She was the church lady who always referred to me as the "ugly duckling" because I had what she called "bad hair." When I was about thirteen I ran across a poem of Countee Cullen's that, even now, reminds me of Mrs. Broland. During one of Mama's productions when we were performing for her guests, I recited this poem looking Mrs. Broland dead in the eyes, emphasizing the title, "For a Mouthy Woman":

God and the devil still are wrangling
   which should have her, which repel
God wants no discord in his heaven
   Satan has enough in hell

Mama sharply admonished me later for this too apparent appraisal of one of her guests, but I saw the edge of a smile as she turned away, a smile that I also saw on the faces of some of the ladies during my recitation.

Having won her own battle with Mrs. Broland, Mama passed around paper and pens for the Missionary Society's letter writing. She had already written to Harding, the day after his inauguration. Her letter read:

March 5, 1921

Dear President Harding:

   Congratulations on becoming the twenty-ninth president of our country. I know there is much that will require your time during your years in office. The road may be hard and some-times dark, but if we take the right road, we often find a light at the end. I will pray for you to find that right road. Among your many tasks along that road will have to be a concerted ef-fort to stop the lynching of our people. We urge you to push for the passing of the anti-lynching bill, so that our country can see that light. I want you to know, too, you will be hearing from me often.

   With the very best wishes during your days at the helm.

Respectfully yours,
Mary Rice Hayes Allen

And indeed, Harding *was* to hear from her—often.

When the missionary ladies' letters were written and the meeting was drawing to a close, we still had not seen Miz Nettie. Mama, worried, had even called the house, but there was no answer. Finally, after dinner, we had decided Miz Nettie wasn't coming. Then the doorbell rang, and Rosemary went to answer it. We could tell by the loud, warm greeting that it was Miz Nettie, and trailing behind her we heard the soft whisper of her sister Lettie. Rosemary brought them into the kitchen.

"Nettie," Mama exclaimed, "where on earth have you been? The children have worried me to death all afternoon. Sit down."

"Chile," Nettie said as the chair creaked from the weight of her, "I have been through some trials and tribulations this day."

"We," Miz Lettie corrected.

"I mean we—me and Lettie."

"What happened?" Mama asked, concern in her voice.

"Me and Lettie been at the police station since one o'clock."

"Twelve-thirty," Lettie corrected.

"Okay, okay, twelve-thirty, one, don' make no difference."

"What were you all doing at the police station?" Papa asked.

"They claim they had to be sure we wasn't mixed up with what happened last night. Thought we were protecting somebody. Even said 'You people don' tell on each other.'"

"Nettie, what happened?" Mama asked.

"I tell you, Mary, I got a story for y'all today." And with that Miz Nettie reared back in her chair and told a story I have never forgotten. I shall call it "The Ring."

"Well, last night . . ." She started off so ominously, we knew it was one of her tales of suspense, and drew in closer. "You know, Mr. and Mrs. Brewster are down at the other house and the chauffeur and cook are with them. So me and Lettie, we in that big house by ourselves. Well, last night we come in from choir practice and go on up to our room on the top floor. As soon as we turned on the light, Lettie went over and put up the window, then in her little voice said, 'Oh, pshaw, Nettie, I dropped my ring out the window, I'll be right back.' I didn't remember no ring on her finger—in fact, she don' have no rings, but I didn't think nothin' of it at the time. So I'm walkin' 'round the room, takin' off my things and hummin' 'Old Rugged Cross.' Then I went over to the dresser, and when I looked in the mirror, what do you think was stickin' out from under the bottom of my bed?" She stopped, put her hands on her hips, where her knuckles nestled in the soft, round rolls. Everyone shook their heads, acknowledging their denseness, but Dolly, the imaginative one, ventured a guess.

"A snake?" she asked.

"Aw, naw," Miz Nettie said, and it was evident a li'l old cobra or rattlesnake was nothing compared to what Miz Nettie saw sticking out from under her bed.

"Naw," she repeated standing now to make this announcement. "A man's two feet," she said, emphasizing "two," as if one foot would not have been quite as bad. "When I saw those two feet, I understood about the ring. I tried to keep calm and just kept singing 'Old Rugged Cross,' but it was gettin' kinda shaky now. I kept clinging to it though, and doing a little praying on the side."

Mama couldn't help smiling. "It wasn't funny, Mary," Miz Nettie laughed. "Seemed like Lettie was gone a whole hour, and here I was scared to go and scared to stay, so I just kept on singing. Finally, I heard a man's voice downstairs and knew it was the police, but so did the owner of those two feet. He got out from under the bed so fast, pushed past me, started runnin' down the back stairs. What a racket, what a racket. He's droppin' silver all down the back stairs, and I'm screamin' to the top of my voice, 'Oh, Lawd, help, help.' The police had started up the front stairs, but when they heard him running down the back, they ran back to try to catch him, but just like a flash he was out that back door and gone. They ain' found him yet."

"You should have called us from the police station," Papa said.

"I was so upset, I couldn't think of nobody to call on 'cept the Lawd."

"Pretty good choice." Papa smiled.

"I did later ask 'em if I could call you and they said we didn't need no lawyer. Kept askin' us if we didn't know him, kept sayin' this a small town, then kept sayin' 'Y'all don' tell on each other.' They asked me had he ever been to visit me."

"No," Lettie corrected, "they asked me that question."

"Okay, okay. They asked you. Me, you, don' make no difference. Wanted to know why he was in our bedroom, and all such things as that."

"My goodness," Mama said. "You know the implication."

"Yeah," Nettie commented, "us in all that danger, tryin' to save Madam's things, and then they act like that."

"I'm going to write to them about this," Mama said.

"Another letter?" Papa laughed.

"Yes, fifty of them if we need to. You all haven't eaten, have you?"

"No, not even bread and water!" Nettie laughed. Mama fixed two plates. Miz Nettie wasted no time attacking her heavily loaded plate. Miz Lettie picked at hers gingerly.

"And another thing," Miz Nettie said, putting her fork down, looking over at her sister. "Here I am in all that danger, up there in that room with the culprit, and after we convinced them we wasn't mixed up in it, who do you think they called the hero—her!" she exclaimed pointing to Lettie, who for once did not disagree with her sister's story.

Life-long, poor Browning never knew Virginia,
Or he'd not grieved in Florence for April sallies
Back to English gardens

—Anne Spencer,
"Life-long, Poor Browning"

Chapter 25

GOIN' BACK HOME

After two full years Up North, we started going "back home" to Virginia every summer. Many Negroes who moved North in the exodus did the same thing, so the umbilical cord was never really severed.

Mama would start making preparations in the spring. "It's always good to see spring edging winter out of the way," she would say. Then she'd add, "Spring is a time to cleanse ourselves, our souls, and the world of winter ills." Her way of cleansing for us was a big dose of sulphur and molasses; for the world, a dose of her fighting spirit.

With the windows open to the spring air we could hear again the sounds from the trolley-car barn. The Italians that worked there called out something that sounded like "Wellio, vene aqua." We always thought they might be calling the water boy. Italians were the next-largest minority in Montclair, and just as most Negroes' occupations were in domestic service, Italians worked mainly as laborers in construction and places like the car barn. Spring meant Papa would be talking over the fence with Joe again. They talked over that fence a lot in those days and became good friends. Joe began referring some of his friends to Papa.

So Papa had a number of Italian clients, and perhaps there was a good reason for it. In a social atmosphere of what history books call "100 percent Americanism" (meaning Anglo-Saxon Protestant), neither we nor the Italians were acceptable. Papa, however, had made quite a name for himself, and not just by divorcing people and settling real estate matters but, of all things, in corporate law. He had a passion for corporate law, delved so deeply into it, in fact, that even some white lawyers consulted him. They thought a black man who had graduated from the University of Michigan Law School at the turn of the century, and with so much knowledge of corporate law, was an oddity. Thus Papa was believed to be a genius in his field in Montclair, New Jersey. I don't know whether he really was, but that's the way he was perceived, and the perception served him well.

One of Papa's Italian clients was Mr. Vitale, a neighbor of Uncle Johnny's in Bloomfield. Mr. Vitale would come to see Papa on business and they would go upstairs to the "spare room," which Papa also used as his home office. When they had finished with their business, Papa would bring Mr. Vitale down to the kitchen for a cup of coffee and some of whatever Mama had baked that day. "Ah, how are my beautiful bambinos," he would say in that wonderful Italian way. We responded to his warmth with smiles, and a chorus of "Fine, Mr. Vitale."

Mr. Vitale was a short, stocky man with a round face, large sparkling eyes, straight black hair, and a great, big, lean-back laugh. He was bouncy and happy and he and Papa laughed a lot together. One evening, however, Papa told Mr. Vitale that as soon as we were out of school, he was taking us back home to see his mother. When Papa told him about this, tears shone in Mr. Vitale's eyes; it was the first time I had seen a man cry.

"Papa die. I sava money to bring my Mama here, now they say no." I didn't know who "they" were, but I knew they were mean old goats to make Mr. Vitale cry. It was much later in life I learned the real reason.

In *The American Nation: A History of the United States*, John A. Garraty reports that after World War I there was a significant increase in the number of immigrants coming to the United States. The number rose from 110,000 in 1919 to 430,000 in 1920, and to 805,000 in 1921. Garraty says, "Instead of setting some general limit on new arrivals, Congress, reflecting a widespread prejudice against eastern and southern Europeans, passed an emergency act establishing a quota system." For a given country, the formula allowed in 3 percent of the number of residents from that country that were in the States in 1910. This rule significantly favored the British and other northern and western Europeans. Since there was a much smaller number of Italians here in 1910, the number of Italians allowed in would be very small compared to the number of British and other northern and western Europeans. This was the act that made Mr. Vitale cry. The "old goats" were United States congressmen.

Papa and Mr. Vitale sat at the table for a long time, talking about this and other situations, and from their sharing of many similar human injustices, their friendship flourished.

JUST AS PAPA had said, there was excitement in looking forward to the trip back home, no matter how much we had come to like Montclair. Looking out the window, we could see tulips and daffodils blooming in Mama's and Mrs. Bengler's garden. By then, they were not only talking but sharing. The previous fall Mama had walked over to Mrs. Bengler's with a basket of tulip and daffodil bulbs. The bulbs had been given to Mama by one of our Thursday people, a chauffeur for a wealthy family who said, "Nobody needs that much of anything," taking the bulbs right from the gardener's abundantly endowed wheelbarrow. When Dolly was older, she challenged our moralistic Papa about all the things our Thursday people brought from their employers' houses.

"Papa," she asked, while he was enjoying a piece of probably confiscated ham, "isn't it a sin to accept stolen goods?" Papa just smiled.

"That's surplus," he said, trying to vindicate himself. "Sometimes their madams give them things to take home."

"And sometimes they don't," Dolly added.

Anyway, it was always a good feeling thinking about going back home, seeing our friends, and basking in the neighborly warmth of Holbrook Street, where Grandma lived. Everyone knew us and everyone spoke to us. Paul Robeson was right: except for us, our home in Montclair was on a rather staid block, mostly older and settled white people. Even now as I try to visualize families on our block, except for the Sterns down the street and the friendly Meads next door, they are faceless. We did not want for playmates, but aside from the Mead girls and Sidney Stern, we had to go some distance to find them.

There was a little girl named Susan on our block who had a freckled face and ash-blond hair. We'd been in our house at least a year before her mother allowed her to play with us. When she did, Susan always wanted one of us to be the maid. We got fed up with this and decided the next time she came we would be the "Madams" and she would be the maid. Dolly would be Mrs. Van de Vanter; Rosemary, Mrs. Van Astor; and I, Mrs. Van Elmore. Even at that age we knew that Van something spelled wealth, and Rosemary as Mrs. Van Astor had to be the richest woman in the world. Fortified with our rich names, we were ready for Susan. When she came, we told her she was our maid. She went home. We couldn't wait to get "back home" to Virginia, where things would be different. On Grandma's street there were many colored children for us to play with. The time could not come too fast.

Part of Mama's preparation for our trip was getting Mrs. Blakey to make our pongee and organdy dresses for church and buying bloomers and middy blouses for our playtime. Once school was out, the excitement around the house rose to a new level. The trunk was brought down from the attic and packed for our extended stay. Papa would go for just a week. The train ride was always a happy one. From Newark to Washington, riding the Pennsylvania Railroad was not too memorable, but once we got on the Southern Railway, even though we rode in the Jim Crow car, the communal spirit gathered us in. The shoe boxes loaded with good Southern food were on the overhead racks, for sharing and having a good time "goin' back home."

When the train pulled into the station in Danville, Cousin Winslow, Papa's cousin, an undertaker, had two cars waiting to take us to Grandma's house. Grandma lived in a two-story house with a long porch downstairs and another long porch upstairs. The house seemed made for children, as there were steps up into some rooms and down into other rooms. We always had fun jumping up into some rooms and down into others. Chickens clucked around in the backyard and one of our jobs, which we liked, was collecting the eggs. As if to celebrate the return of the prodigals, there was always a round of dinners, parties, picnics, and more dinners.

In the evening when it was cool Mama and Papa would sit on the porch with Grandma and Aunt Maggie, while we played the rhyming, singing ring games under the streetlight. I did not realize then, nor would I have cared, that these games are a significant part of our heritage and culture. In *Shake It to the One That You Love the Best*, Cheryl Warren Mattox says, "Those play songs were not just childhood amusements, but a vital link in my musical heritage as an African American. They sprang from the imaginations of children who lived —and played—many generations before me." Some of them were sung way back on the plantations. We always enjoyed Little Sally Walker, a ring game that was played in circle formation and to the song:

Little Sally Walker
Sittin' in a saucer
Rise Sally rise
Wipe your weeping eyes
Put your hands on your hips
And let your backbone slip

Shake it to the east, Sally
Shake it to the west, Sally
Shake it to the one that
You love the best, Sally

When the Beaver girls across the street came over with their brothers, we'd play the clapping, rhyming games that the slave children played. They clicked bones together for rhythm, but our boys just slapped their legs to the tune:

Hambone, hambone, where you been
Round the world and back again
Hambone, hambone have you heard
Papa's gonna buy me a mockingbird
If that mockingbird don't sing
Papa's gonna buy me a diamond ring.

Sometimes we'd make up extra verses. Those were wonderful evenings under the streetlight and unthinkable in front of our home in Montclair, New Jersey.

Aunt Maggie's favorite pastime was watching us as we sang and played the game All That I Desire. Aunt Maggie never married and seemed to enjoy the romantic quality of this game and its words:

All that I desire
All that I desire
Me and my gal
Gonna take a little walk
That's all that I desire

One summer when we went back home everyone went to the Baptist Sunday school picnic except Aunt Maggie and me. I was about sixteen then. Aunt Maggie had to stay home with Grandma, who was ailing, and I did not feel well myself. I hated to miss that picnic because there would be all kinds of good food: fried chicken, potato salad, corn pudding, lots of homemade peach ice cream, and watermelons cooling in big tin tubs of ice. However, if I had gone I would not have known about Aunt Maggie's "gentleman beau" whom she was supposed to have married. Everyone gone, the house was silent, only an occasional call from Grandma: "Mag, Mag, come, my leg hurts." Aunt Maggie would go and take care of her, then return. "It's always the leg she lost in the train wreck she complains about."

That was a family story we all knew too well, about how Grandma and all the other Negroes in the wreck could not be taken to the white hospital and so received no medical care, which was why the leg later had to come off. When Grandma finally fell asleep, Aunt Maggie said, "Come, let's go in the parlor." No one went in Grandma's parlor except on Sunday, so I knew this was special.

We walked into the musty, red-velvet room. Aunt Maggie did not open the blinds, but went over to the table and turned on the lamp with the rose-colored globe. Then she opened a drawer and took out a wooden box tied with a blue ribbon. She opened it and handed me a stack of letters. They were from the man she would have married, if Grandma had not lost her leg. He had gone to Africa as a missionary. I read them all. All of them expressed his love for her and ended "and I remain respectfully yours." When I finished the last one Aunt Maggie put them back in the box and tied the box with a blue ribbon. When she turned to me her eyes welled with tears. Even at the young age of sixteen I felt her pain. I also understood why Aunt Maggie invited courting couples to sit in the swing. She would give them glasses of cool lemonade and ask questions about their romance. "When are you getting married?" she'd say, and, "Oh, I know you'll have beautiful children."

The end of our summer visits coincided with the Baptist Sunday school picnics held in August. Although we loved these picnics, they meant our Virginia time was almost at its end. When we were ready to leave, Aunt Maggie would pack our shoe box full of her specialities. Papa had something special he carried in a small leather bag and protected on the trip. We learned later from our brother Bill that it was "white lightning," moonshine whiskey.

Papa always called his liquor "medicinal whiskey." This was during Prohibition. On January 16, 1920, the Eighteenth Amendment became law, making liquor, beer, and wine illegal. After this the Volstead Act was written to enforce prohibition. I don't know why anyone thought this act would work. Some political demands can be ridiculous. I remember a friend of mine, Annie Laurie Tucker, telling me some years ago, when she was working for the Department of Welfare in New York City, that she and her friend Lula Wilkerson were assigned to investigate the condition of the Children's Center. The mayor, Fiorello La Guardia, said, "Do a thorough job. Count the roaches." Annie says that was impossible. She didn't know whether a counted roach had fled and returned or if it was a new roach.

So it was with the Volstead Act. It didn't work either. Speakeasies flourished, women stashed flasks of whiskey in their stockings, and illegal whiskey-related crime escalated. One aspect of the Volstead Act worked for Papa, though. The act stated that alcohol for medicinal purposes was legal. Papa always looked the picture of good health to us, but sometimes he took broken doses of this "medicinal whiskey." It was reported that doctors prescribed it and druggists dispensed it and the number of patients increased significantly. But Papa did not have to go to a doctor for his medicinal whiskey. He had stashed away some good, old-fashioned, Virginia corn liquor.

When it was time for us to leave, cousin Winslow would bring the two funeral cars to take us to the train station. We would line up like it really was a funeral procession. Farewell hugs and kisses always brought tears to Aunt Maggie's eyes, which made us cry too. Leaving Virginia was always sad.

For the racial situation has become
like an irrational sea in which Americans
flounder like convoyed ships in a gale.

—Ralph Ellison,
Shadow and Act

Chapter 26

THEATRICAL PERFORMANCES

━

*M*ama put herself in the movies. She became a surprise star man-
agement had not counted on. This happened when a movie theater
opened up in the heart of Montclair, New Jersey. It was to be "the epit-
ome of progress," according to the ad that appeared in the *Montclair
Times* on February 17, 1923. "One of the finest amusement houses in the
country," it read, "probably no building ever erected in Montclair has
caused such a change in the aspect of the site which it occupies." An
ironic statement, as this building, so highly extolled, was to be our town's
first segregated theater. It would not sit well with the lady in the red hat.

One day Mama told Papa what had happened to several of her
friends who had gone to this new theater. She was fighting mad. Her
friends were, as were all Negroes, ushered to one side. When Mama
calmed down long enough for Papa to speak, he said, as any lawyer
would, "That's hearsay, Mary. Before you jump into this fight, you'd
better go and find out for yourself."

Mama kissed him on his bald head. "That's exactly what I'll do,
Will," she said, "and I'll take all the children with me."

The next Saturday Mama got all of us to "sparkle up" by promising, "Children, we are going to the movies." Armed with her children, "available in six different colors," she marched into the Clairidge Theatre and sat us all "smack-dab in the middle."

We were hardly in our seats when a very polite usher appeared. Hunter recognized him. They played football together.

"Hi, Hank," Hunter said.

"Hi, Hunt," the usher answered softly, then stumbled over his next words: "Pardon me, but . . . but you all will have to move to the side of the theater."

Mama turned to Hank and said, "We are quite comfortable here, thank you."

Hank fidgeted and timidly tried again. "You should sit over there, please," he said, pointing to the side aisle. "You really can see very well from there."

"We can see very well from here, thank you, Hank," Mama said, holding her head a little higher. Whereupon Hank retreated.

This segregation was not done with signs of COLORED and WHITE but in the Northern manner, which was more subtle, more devious, and with a politeness that belied the evil there. Sometimes the technique was so cloaked that one had the extra burden of deciding if it really was what it was. That Saturday afternoon though, there was no doubt. An usher of greater importance came to our row. He had bigger epaulets and a firmer voice. He bent down and whispered firmly but gently:

"Madam, will you please move your group to the side?"

This time Mama quit fencing and asked the usher to give her one good reason why she should gather up all of her children, climb over everyone, and move to the side. When he demurred, she asked him directly if the reason was because we were Negroes. Annoyed, the usher said in a firmer voice, "I don't make the rules here."

"Well, young man," Mama said just as firmly, "then take me to the one who does."

Mama was a great one for seeing managers when she couldn't get what she wanted. She was used to going right on up through the ranks to the boss's boss. I should add that Mama's meeting place with managers was not always on the battlefield. If there was something good about a place, she was just as outspoken in praise. I have run across copies of letters Mama wrote to stores and restaurants as their policies changed and they began admitting Negroes. I remember one in particular. It seemed to embody everything she believed and fought for as well as the femininity that was as much a part of her as her fighting spirit. Commending a large restaurant for "embracing a free democratic spirit" and giving us the "same courteous service for which your restaurant has been known for many years," she ended with, "and may I add that your apple brown Betty is every bit as good as mine."

Mama's letters of commendation revealed what she could do off the battlefield, but this meeting with the manager of the theater was called for the purpose of declaring war.

"Watch the girls until I get back," she said to Hunter Reed, and followed the usher to the manager's office. I can imagine the scene: she sat down in the chair next to the manager's desk, and said, "I suppose you know why I'm here."

The manager would have answered, "The usher told me you were causing a scene, and wanted to change the regulations of our theater."

"Only one regulation, the one about having all of us colored folks sitting on one side of the theater, and changing it is exactly what I want to do. We're not going to have it."

Then there must have been an exchange about what we were going to have and what we were not going to have. As she reported it later, the meeting ended with the manager's statement that she'd have to take her money back and leave, and Mama's statement, "I'll do just that, but I'll tell you one thing again—we're not going to have this." This grim declaration meant something entirely different to us children. For us, it promised many delighted returns to the movies.

My sisters and I couldn't quite figure out what was going on, but my brothers could. The scene had really upset Hunter Reed. Back at the school football field the next week, Hank walked over to Hunter with the ball in his hand. Without looking up he said, "I'm sorry about the other day, Hunt."

"Aw, forget it," Hunter said, not looking at Hank either. In fact, their eyes never met.

"Those crummy old people," Hank said.

"Yeah, those crummy old people," Hunter Reed repeated as he took the ball and kicked it as far as he could over the goalpost.

There were a number of strategy meetings at Seventy-two with Mama's Thursday people and with the good Baptist church ladies. Some of them, who had believed that going to the movies was a sin, were going now for a Christian purpose and would therefore be absolved. Always among them was the lady in the red hat.

The Montclair branch of the NAACP also took up the fight. The national office wrote letters protesting the theater's practice. Dr. E. S. Ballou was president of the Montclair branch and Mama was secretary. Papa, along with our minister, Reverend J. C. Love, and Mrs. Alice Foster of the colored YWCA and Mr. C. H. Bullock of the colored YMCA were among those on the executive committee of the Montclair branch of the NAACP. At the time, the national office was made up of some of its founders and other prestigious persons, such as Moorfield Story, Archibald Grimké, Reverend John Haynes Holmes, Bishop John Hurst, Arthur Spingarn, Mary Talbert, and Oswald Garrison Villard. The secretary was James Weldon Johnson and the assistant secretary, Walter White. Dr. W. E. B. Du Bois was editor of the *Crisis*, the NAACP's magazine, Robert W. Bagnall was director of branches, and William Pickens and Addie Hutton were field secretaries. These were persons Mama communicated with.

Mama made sure we heard about "good white folks." Her expression "Angels and devils come in all colors" was repeated often. With fighters like those named above, you would think the Clairidge would have been defeated, but it took long years to end segregation in that theater, such was segregation's stronghold across the country at the time.

The Clairidge was defeated early on one issue, however. In 1924, it planned to show the movie *The Birth of a Nation*. With all due respect to D. W. Griffith's direction, *The Birth of a Nation* is highly bigoted, characterizing, as it does, Negroes as inhuman rapists. Based on Thomas Dixon's *The Clansman*, it is a story of the Old South, Civil War, Reconstruction, and the rise of the Ku Klux Klan. It is a story of good and evil—the Southern white family good, the black man evil. At a time when lynchings were commonplace (there were 1,457 documented lynchings of blacks between 1900 and 1923), black leaders believed this film would serve to inflame whites to more lynchings. In *NAACP: A History of the National Association for the Advancement of Colored People*, Charles Kellogg states that a white man, leaving a showing of the movie, shot and killed a young black boy, at random.

In some cities the movie was also used to influence legislation to pass segregated-housing ordinances. Kellogg says that real estate men of a town in the Saint Louis area handed out leaflets to people as they came out of the theater. The leaflets implied that if these segregation ordinances were not passed, whites would have to live next door to the black character in the movie.

The national office of the NAACP protested the showing of *The Birth of a Nation* in 1915, the year it was released. The Clairidge Theatre was planning to show it in 1924. There was, in response, strong protest by the NAACP branch as well as by Mr. Kirk Brown, a respected white citizen. Mama sent the following letter to Mr. Robert Bagnall, director of branches at the national office.

September 8, 1924

Dear Sir:

I am sending you a letter written by Mr. Kirk Brown, leading white citizen of Montclair, as a protest against the coming of "The Birth of a Nation." I am wondering if you could find the time to write him a line of appreciation on behalf of the national office. Mr. Brown backed his letter with an appeal to his friends and to the Commissioners. There are so few dependable white folks here. If you find you can write this letter the branch will appreciate it. . . .

> Yours truly,
> Mary Rice Hayes Allen
> 72 Valley Road

Walter White, assistant secretary of the national office, wrote back:

> September 18, 1924

My dear Mrs. Allen:

Thank you for calling our attention to the protest made by Mr. Kirk Brown against the showing of the "Birth of a Nation." I have today written Mr. Brown a letter thanking him in behalf of the national office, copy of which letter I enclose herewith.

> Sincerely yours,
> Walter White
> Assistant Secretary

Enclosure

ww:o

Excerpts of Mr. Brown's letter were printed in an article in the *Montclair Times*:

"The Birth of a Nation" is a picture that appeals to "passion, hatred and bigotry," Kirk Brown of No. 79 North Mountain Avenue, wrote in a letter sent yesterday to the Board of Town Commissioners. The letter expressed the hope that the Commission may see fit to use the power invested in them to prevent the presentation of the photo-play. Part of the letter stated:

"The picture is offensive not alone to Negroes but to whites as well . . . in short it is a lying, sinister appeal to the passions of the ignorant and an attempt to set up one section of people against another." He continues that he had talked with Mr. Hinck, proprietor of the theatre, and offered to pay for some of his loss in not showing it. He also said in earlier years the picture had been banned in another theatre in Montclair and in other surrounding communities, and that the then Mayor, Mr. Louis Dodd, had at that time stopped its showing.

Mr. Kirk Brown and the Montclair branch of the NAACP were victorious. *The Birth of a Nation* was not shown in 1924 in Montclair. But not too many years later, the local branch of the NAACP had to again protest its showing, this time at the Bellevue Theatre in Upper Montclair. An article I found in the Library of Congress files from one of the New Jersey papers, not identified, and without the year of its publication noted, reads:

MONTCLAIR N.J. BARS "BIRTH OF A NATION"

Montclair, N.J. August 21: The talking film, "The Birth of a Nation," was withdrawn here at the last minute from the Bellevue Theatre at the request of Mayor Charles G. Phillips after a delegation of approximately 100 Colored residents led by the NAACP had presented a written protest to the Mayor. The NAACP's petition charged the film fosters race hatred and mistrust. The theatre manager offered to hold a preview and allow the objectionable parts to be cut out, but the Mayor requested the entire film be withdrawn.

Since Charles Phillips was mayor from 1928 to 1932, the article had to have been printed within that period. Though they've since passed on, I feel like thanking Mayor Dodd for the 1924 fight and Mayor

Phillips for the later fight, and certainly Mr. Kirk Brown, to say nothing of all the local NAACP members, among whom was Mama, the lady in the red hat.

Even so, the Clairidge Theatre seemed to be determined to keep its seating segregated. According to an April 4, 1928, *Newark News* article in the Montclair branch files:

> ### "SEGREGATION" IN THEATRE PROTESTED
> Montclair colored people's group says police aide theatre in violating law.
>
> Commission to investigate.
>
> A large delegation from the Montclair chapter of the National Association for the Advancement of Colored People protested to the Montclair Commission last night the alleged practice of police officers of the town aiding in "segregation of Negroes" in the Clairidge Theatre. The spokesman for the group was Dr. E. S. Ballou, who said, "A system of segregation has been going on in the Clairidge Theatre ever since the theatre opened."
>
> There was a witness there G. H. Hill who said: "A police officer of this town, who is supposed to protect all citizens, came into the theatre and ordered me to move" [to the section set aside for Negroes]. "This officer was patrolman Walsh, who was requested by the management to come into the theatre from his post in the traffic booth to put me out."

It was reported to the local branch of the NAACP that many other Negroes, who also protested removal, were ushered out by police. I know we were ushered out, along with Mama, many, many times, although I don't recall the police ever doing it. And the Clairidge continued to hold to its policy of segregation well into the 1930s. I know this from a response I received from Dr. Norman Fletcher, minister of the Unitarian Church in Montclair, active on the Interracial Committee.

I wrote to Dr. Fletcher because I knew he had been involved in the final defeat of segregation in the Clairidge Theatre. He responded:

September 2, 1981

Dear Mrs. McCray,

It was a great pleasure to hear from you and to learn you are writing a book about your mother. . . . I remember your mother as a fighter for equality and that I wrote about her in a letter to *The Montclair Times* years ago. . . . I do remember an incident that occurred early in the 1930s. . . . Thanks to your mother's fight and others, the Clairidge Theatre was open to Negroes (Blacks today!). However, they had a way of ushering Blacks over to the side aisle. The Interracial Committee heard of this and sent Blacks to the box office to see what would happen. Ushers insisted on placing them on the side aisle. The then secretary of the Washington Branch Y.M.C.A. [James Williams] and I went to see the manager about this. At first he denied it, but after we produced specific evidence, [he gave this reason]:

His ushers, mostly high school students, "Tried to keep a balance in the theatre audience"! . . . "If there were too many people seated in the center, they would steer newcomers to the side aisle. So many to the right, so many to the left"!

I grew more than a trifle sarcastic and replied that it was indeed amazing that such young (male) ushers had such a developed appreciation particularly in the matter of balance in seating. *We won out. Blacks were permitted to sit wherever they chose.*

Reading of the manager's frail reason for segregating, I thought of how many times people try to justify inequality with ridiculous explanations. I thought of a time back in the 1940s when sugar was rationed because of the war. My sister Dolly, Kay Davis, who sang with Duke

Ellington, and I went into a luncheonette in Detroit. We asked for coffee. The waitress was flustered and said, "We don't have enough sugar for the public." All three of us said: "That's okay, we all drink our coffee black with no sugar." She had to serve us. I usually hate coffee like that, but at that moment somehow it tasted sweet.

Dr. Fletcher's letter to me ended with this:

Although there is a change there are still problems and liberties to be won and organizations like the NAACP have much to do. Such progress as has been made is due to fighters like your mother who fought a much heavier battle than is required now.

I tire so of hearing people say,
Let things take their course.
Tomorrow is another day.
I do not need my freedom when I'm dead.
I cannot live on tomorrow's bread.

—Langston Hughes, "Democracy"

Chapter 27

ALL IN THE NAME OF FREEDOM

—

"Full freedom" wasn't coming fast enough for Mama. She was fighting to get a Negro policeman on the force. She was fighting prejudices in the schools. She was fighting stores that wouldn't serve us. It seemed like each day a battle would break out on a different front. Aun' Tannie's daughter Alroy remembered, "With your mother, the most casually uttered words might at any time draw you into the fight." She told me that once when she was visiting, she simply ran her hand over her head and said, "I need a haircut."

"Put on your coat," Mama said, "you're going to get one."

Little did Alroy realize that her harmless words were to become new ammunition for doing battle with the beauty shop of one of the largest department stores in New Jersey.

"Get ready," Mama repeated, "you're going to Newark to get a haircut."

"Oh, it can wait," Alroy said, beginning to realize what was in Mama's mind.

"No, it can't," Mama answered. "It's been too long already. I want you to go back to Newark and try to get it cut today."

"But . . . but . . . they wouldn't cut my hair. I already went there. They wouldn't cut it."

"I know," Mama said, "but you have to go again and again and again."

"I know they won't—"

Mama would not let her finish. "Well, you try it today. There are only two things they can say: 'yes,' which would surprise you very much, and 'no,' which wouldn't surprise you at all. But most of all, we have to try."

Mama had a way of saying things that could—for the moment—make everything seem all right, so in that kind of moment Alroy said, "Okay, I will try again." The moment, however, was over by the time she got on the trolley car. She looked at herself in the window. Her hair didn't seem all that long, she thought. Maybe she really didn't need to get it cut. She tried to think of all the ways this mission could be avoided. "A little accident would help," she thought. But the old trolley clanged blissfully along and arrived safely at the end of its run, which was all too near the store she was to enter and ask for—"a haircut."

Alroy dragged herself into the store and stepped on an elevator that whizzed up to the salon's floor in thirty seconds flat. As she stepped off, she straightened herself up, tried to look self-assured, and walked into the beauty salon.

"I would like to get my hair cut," she said softly to the receptionist, who was writing something in her book.

"One moment, please." Without looking up, the receptionist finished writing. When she did look up, she was so startled she gasped.

"Oh, oh! We don't have any openings today."

"Oh, thank you, thank you," Alroy said, feeling relieved and knowing that she could go back to "the lady" and say that she had tried again. She left the salon, stepped back on the elevator, and thanked those wonderful, wonderful Otis people as the elevator swiftly descended to the first floor.

The trolley car ride home seemed twice as long as the trip down. We all gathered in the kitchen to find out what had happened.

"Nothing," Alroy said. "They just didn't have any openings today."

Mama said, "That's possible, and I'm very proud of you, but when you go back—"

"Go back!" Alroy exclaimed.

"Yes, you must go back." Mama knew that deep down inside, Alroy had a fighting spirit, even with all her fears. Mama wasn't worried. "When you go back, if they say they don't have an appointment, just tell them you'll take one any time this week—and if they don't have one this week, tell them you'll take one any time this month— and if they don't have one this month, tell them you'll take one any time this year."

THIS WAS MAMA'S strategy, going back again and again to places that refused her. Once when she and my brother Gregory went shopping in Newark, she stopped for a thoughtful moment, then turned to Greg and said, "Come, we're going in here for lunch."

"In Brubers?" Greg exclaimed.

"And why not?" Mama said as she pushed the revolving door and walked in. Greg, self-conscious and unsure, followed her, holding his head down as he wove his way between the tables. He felt the curious stares as he passed. When he and Mama were seated, a waitress came over and made the remark that, for us, was to change my brother's name. For a long time after that we called him Shandu. This had nothing to do with his magic tricks. It had to do with his hair. Greg was the darkest one of us; however, the dark mahogany of his face was set off by a head of *straight* black hair, making him look like the darker East Indians, and therein lies the story of Shandu.

"Oh, my," the waitress said as she stood there waiting to take the order. "He's East Indian, isn't he?"

"No," Mama said, "this is my son"—which only confused matters, with Mama sitting there looking more like the Irish than the Irish.

"He looks very much like an East Indian," the waitress said.

"No," Mama said, "we are American Negroes."

"Oh, oh, I'm so sorry," said the bewildered waitress.

Mama smiled at her and commented, "I didn't say we had beriberi or the plague. I just said we are Negroes."

"I know, I mean, well, I didn't mean I was sorry about that. I meant the boss won't let me serve you. Could I just tell him he's East—"

"No, you cannot," Mama said. "We're not Indians—East, West, nor American, and we want to eat here as Negroes."

There was some to-do and the waitress went to the boss, who came over and said they had a big luncheon today and couldn't serve extras. Mama told him she would be back until he did serve them. She did go back a number of times. Whether she herself broke down the discrimination there, we don't know, but Brubers did finally open its doors to Negroes.

BUT BACK TO Alroy. She knew there was no turning around, and she found herself taking the trolley to the big department store in Newark several times, several times climbing onto its swift elevator, and several times stepping into its beauty salon—and still no haircut, several times. Her hair was getting longer and longer, and Mama had said, "Try not to get it cut for a while. You can't go into a shop and ask for a haircut when you've just had one."

Our brother Bill, whose humor was always sharp and biting, didn't help the situation. One day, as he opened the door for the shaggy-haired Alroy, he burst into laughter. "Come in, Rapunzel—*entre dans la salle,* and, as the French would say, *Liberté! Égalité*—and let me cutté le bushé. *Mais oui, mademoiselle*, I'll cut it for twenty-five cents," he bribed.

Mama heard him and started toward them. "Come on, Al, honey. Don't listen to that Bill. That's what's wrong with some of us now, too ready to give up the cause."

"Yeah, Mama, but the cause is gonna be hanging down 'round her ankles in a few more months."

"Oh, go on, Bill." Mama waved him off as she and Al sat down in the kitchen to plan the next move — Alroy's meeting with the manager of the department store.

"The manager of the whole store?" Alroy asked.

"Yes," Mama said, "since we can't get any satisfaction from the people in the beauty salon, here's what we'll do."

"Oh, brother," Alroy muttered.

A few days later she found herself at the store manager's office door. He had already received a letter from Mama, so he knew why she was there.

Even so, he asked, "Now, what is it I can do for you," as he showed her into the office.

"I want to get my hair cut here. I've tried and tried and they keep turning me down."

"Aren't there places nearer your home where you can get a haircut?"

"Yes, but that's not the point — and I'm not speaking just for myself," she said courageously. "I'm speaking for my whole race."

The manager gulped. "You mean you want appointments for . . ." But the thought of this was too much for him to express aloud, so he just sat there and shook his head.

"Yes," Alroy continued. "Anyone who has enough hair to be cut should be able to get it cut anywhere they want to. It's an American principle upon which our government was founded." She had gotten started now and could hardly be stopped.

He sat listening, then said, "You're a very courageous young lady, I must admit. But this is a bigger problem than you think. Well, I can't promise you anything, but I'll give it some thought," he concluded and walked her to the door.

It was several weeks after that when Alroy came by to tell Mama she would go only one more time, and after that she'd have to hand the torch to someone else and go get herself a haircut someplace else. Mama agreed with her and told her how proud she was of her, that there were so many who would not have gone the first time.

Alroy did go one more time, and to her utter surprise, bewilderment, astonishment, and joy — they cut her hair.

"And how would you like it?" the stylist asked.

Alroy smiled as she thought of Bill and said softly, "The boyish bob, please."

"Okay," the stylist said, and he started clicking the scissors.

On the way home Alroy kept looking in the window, pleased as punch with her haircut.

"Um, um," she thought, "it really does something for me." She thought it was the best haircut she'd had in her whole life.

We were sitting on the porch and saw her coming up the street, holding her head high. Dolly ran into the house calling to Mama, "She got it, Mama, she got it."

Mama came out just in time to see the triumphant Alroy coming up the steps. Bill wiped off the biggest porch rocker for "Her Majesty." Mama went over and hugged and kissed her.

"What did they say? What did they do?" We were full of all kinds of questions.

"He just said, 'And how would you like it?'" She looked at Bill and smiled. "And I said, 'The boyish bob, please.'" I'm certain there was much more assurance in the re-enactment of the scene than the actual performance.

"Oh, boy," said Bill, "just like I said — *Liberté! Égalité — 'le jour de gloire est arrivé.'*" This, of course prompted all of us to follow him as he started marching around the house singing, "*Allons, citoyens, le jour de gloire est arrivé.*"

"What's going on over there," Mrs. Bengler called.

"She got her hair cut," we yelled, still marching.

Mrs. Bengler wasn't certain she heard right. "She what?"

"They cut her hair, they cut her hair." Mrs. Bengler's expression was evidence that the message had not quite gotten through.

"Well, she's the first one to get her hair cut there." Dolly tried to clarify.

Mama went on over to tell Mrs. Bengler the whole story. Mrs. Bengler was a little uncomfortable but did manage to say, "Goodness, I didn't know a haircut could cause so much commotion." After the *liberté* march we went into the house and, with big hunks of gingerbread and glasses of milk, toasted Alroy's coup d'état.

As we were clearing away the dishes, Alroy's beau, Rawley, rang the bell. Dolly ran to open the door, and we could hear her in an excited voice telling him about Alroy's haircut. When he walked into the room, he took one look at Alroy and said in distress, "What in the world did they do to you?"

"They cut my hair. Isn't that what we've been fighting for?"

"Yeah, but they didn't have to scalp you."

"I wanted it like this. It's the latest style. Don't you like it—aren't you proud of me?"

"Yeah," he said, "I'm real proud of you. But gee," he said, looking at her somewhat wistfully, "I was beginning to like it better long."

"That's all right, honey," Mama said, hugging her. "Now you can let it grow, anytime and anywhere."

Just fifty years—a winter's day—
As runs the history of a race;
Yet, as we look back o'er the way,
How distant seems our starting place!

—James Weldon Johnson,
"Fifty Years—1863–1913," on the anniversary
of the Emancipation Proclamation

Chapter 28

THE NIGHT MY BROTHER HUNTER REED
WAS EMANCIPATED

—

*O*ur house put on its own celebration the night my brother
Hunter Reed was emancipated. My father had invested fifty dollars in
the purchase of an old Essex car, his first and only car. What this meant
was that Hunter Reed would no longer have to accompany Mama in
the cold January snow when she went to deliver her annual "freedom"
speech.

Every January, Mama was invited to speak at a celebration of the
signing of the Emancipation Proclamation, and every January its site
seemed to Hunter Reed further away in the hills of Morris County.
Papa usually had a speech of his own to make. Bill couldn't go because
he was always out somewhere being handsome and singing love songs
to the girls. Greg couldn't go because he was always off somewhere
working. So yearly it fell to the lot of "old faithful" Hunter Reed to accompany Mama, the featured speaker. Now, at last, at age fifteen, he
was released from those long, cold trolley-car journeys to places like
Madison, Morristown, or somewhere even more distant.

According to Hunter's almanac, it snowed every Emancipation

Day. Traveling from Montclair to Morris County was difficult on any day. Plus, Mama, among all of her other crusades, had one against being late. No C.P.T. (colored people's time) for her. The year before the car, it was way before sundown when they left the house to trudge down to Bloomfield Avenue through the snow. Back then, it seemed no matter where in New Jersey you wanted to go, you had to first take a trolley car to Newark. The year before the car, they arrived in Newark just in time to see the old Morris Line trolley car pulling away. They had to wait half an hour for the next one.

"To hell with emancipation," Hunter Reed had thought as he stood in the cold, rubbing his aching hands together, and cursing the trolley car for not coming sooner.

As Hunter Reed tells it, the old Morris Line trolley was special, equipped with a potbelly stove right in the center for long, cold distances. His practice was to get as near the stove as possible — three seats away and you had only visual evidence of heat. When he finally saw the lights of the approaching trolley, he practically pushed Mama aside in his haste to scramble aboard. After what seemed like a two-hour ride, they arrived at the little church somewhere in Morris County. They met the sexton carrying in wood to build a fire and Mama, of course, volunteered Hunter's services.

"Oh, how do you do, Mr. Barton? My son here will be glad to help you," she offered, beaming.

"Yes, sir," Hunter said, thinking, I'll do anything to get some heat.

"It's a very cold night out, Miz Allen," the sexton said. "I'll get the fire going and fix you some tea."

"Oh, bless you, you're an angel." Mama smiled.

Yeah, Hunter Reed thought, might could be, way up here.

After they'd had their tea and warmed up a little by the fire, people started coming in slowly. Though the program was scheduled for 7:00, nobody expected it to start until at least 8:00. In any Baptist church there are always about six musical selections and many prayers and announcements before the speaker is introduced. During the fifth solo,

Hunter Reed had dark thoughts about coming up here so early, and why in the heck he always had to be the one, but he kept a sanctimonious expression on his face, good son that he was.

Finally the minister introduced Mama:

"I know you all remember Mrs. Allen and the very inspirational talk she gave us last year." A few people in the front row nodded. Not in recognition, Hunter Reed says: they had just fallen asleep during the preliminaries. But best to wake up good now, Hunter Reed thought. Mama had been known to walk down the aisle and wake up a sleeper by saying, "Young man, I think *you* especially should hear this."

Hunter Reed said he could understand having to go way up to Morris County the first time, 'cause it was so far away maybe the emancipation news hadn't gotten there yet. But he just couldn't understand all these other trips. He distinctly heard Mama tell them last time, "We have been free a long time." Although, upon reflecting, he did admit she always added, "But until we can feel and act free and have all of the advantages of our fellow Americans, we cannot call this *full freedom*."

He particularly remembered that line because it always brought thunderous applause, which woke up all the nodders. He guessed Mama's purpose after that first trip was not only to see if we were feeling and acting free, but to see if this year's freedom was any fuller than last year's.

The year before the car, he remembers, Mama started her speech eloquently:

"It was on January 1, 1863, that Abraham Lincoln made his historical Emancipation Proclamation, freeing all of our forebears with these famous words: 'I, Abraham Lincoln . . . do proclaim that on the first day of January, A.D. 1863, all persons held as slaves . . . shall be then, thenceforward, and forever free.'" This brought the usual applause from her audience, but Hunter Reed was thinking to himself, "With all due respect to the gentleman from Illinois, I wish he coulda seen fit to make that speech in July."

Mama went on with her speech, and then dramatically ended with the wonderful quotation from James Weldon Johnson's "Fifty Years—1863–1913," his poem celebrating Lincoln's signing of the Emancipation Proclamation. She stood straight with her unshakable conviction, and spoke the lines ringingly:

> This land is ours by right of birth
> This land is ours by right of toil
> We helped to turn its virgin earth
> Our sweat is in its fruitful soil

As usual, she remained standing, and when the applause died down, she looked proudly at Hunter Reed and smiled. "I think you may all remember my son Hunter Reed. Come up here, son. Hunter Reed comes with me faithfully every year."

This part embarrassed him, but he went and stood beside Mama. The congregation applauded for him. He knew that the fat lady on the aisle of the first row would, as she usually did, run up to hug him. He bowed, and before he could raise his head, the fat lady had him.

"Amen, God's gonna bless you, chile, for looking out for your Mama." When he got back to his seat, the congregation stood to sing James Weldon Johnson's "Lift Every Voice and Sing," a song Negroes back then sang at the beginning of almost every important program. We knew every word growing up. The words still move me, especially those of the last verse, which ends with a pledge of loyalty to our country:

> God of our weary years,
> God of our silent tears,
> Thou who hast brought us thus far on our way
> Thou who has by Thy might
> Led us into the light,
> Keep us forever in the path, we pray.
> Lest our feet stray from the places,

our God, where we met thee,
Lest our hearts drunk from the wine of the world, we forget thee
Shadowed beneath Thy hand,
May we forever stand
True to our God,
True to our native land.

When the song ended and the minister had said the benediction and the audience had come up to Mama to thank her for her inspirational talk, finally, then, Hunter Reed could lead Mama back on the cold journey home.

BUT THAT WAS all now a thing of the past, that was last year, before the car. Hunter Reed stood beside Papa beaming with his own reasons as they looked out at the shiny black Essex.

"There she is—Miss Betsy," Papa said, smiling down upon his lady-in-waiting, "ready to take us anywhere we want to go. She's right fine, isn't she, Mary?"

"She's beautiful," Mama agreed.

"Yeah," said Bill, "but she's too fine to be called Miss Betsy." With a sweeping bow he said, "We'll call her Miss Felicia Fenimore."

We all stood at the window watching Miss Felicia gliding away with our parents inside. Mrs. Bengler was at her window, too. Mama had told her about the new car, so its arrival was no surprise. What was a surprise was that the sound of our "new" car pulling off was as loud as an earthquake. Relieved, she waved and moved away from the window.

My mother and father looked right regal, with Papa sitting up straighter than ever and Mama, in her red hat, looking her most beautiful as she smiled and waved good-bye to us. When they were out of sight, Hunter Reed made a beeline for the kitchen, poured himself a tall glass of milk, cut himself a big piece of chocolate cake, and sat down in the most comfortable chair, wallowing in his new freedom.

Then, suddenly, we heard the persistent clanging of trolley cars and tooting of car horns. Hunter Reed went to the front window to see what was going on, and what he saw was Miss Felicia in a very unbecoming position, straddling the trolley tracks down on Bloomfield Avenue. Hunter Reed put on his coat and hat and ran down to help. Not only had one of her tires blown out, but something underneath her had fallen down on the track. Papa, who knew nothing about the mechanics of a car, had gotten out and opened the hood, as any good mechanic would do. The clanging continued and became louder and more insistent. By now, trolley cars were trying to come up Bloomfield Avenue and trolley cars were trying to go down Bloomfield Avenue and the unhappy Felicia, stalled there between them, could not budge. A few sympathetic bystanders helped push her over to the side. Miss Felicia could not be revived. Complications set in, and for every quick repair that was made, something else would immediately break down. It was evident from the death rattles that Miss Felicia was failing fast. Mama, Hunter Reed, and Papa stood mournfully by as a tow truck came to carry Miss Felicia to what turned out to be her final resting place.

Once traffic started to move, Papa assured Hunter Reed that he would go on with Mama as planned, but on the trolley car. Hunter Reed hurried home to finish his chocolate cake and enjoy his freedom. Next year, he figured, he'd probably be riding that old Morris Line trolley again, huddling near that old potbelly stove, rubbing his poor cold hands together, and praying for "full freedom" to please hurry up and come on.

One of the great
measures of a people is its culture.

— Paul Robeson

Chapter 29

AN HOUR WITH STERLING BROWN

—

*O*ne of the most exciting hours in my life was one spent chatting with Sterling Brown, first about poetry and then about his memories of Mama's literary gatherings. I was teaching at Talladega College in the 1970s when the great Harlem Renaissance poet came to our Spring Arts Festival as one of the presenting guests. I was in a classroom working on something when he wandered in. He saw that I was busy and started to leave.

"Oh no!" I said. "Come sit down. This can wait."

He sat beside me, and after we'd chatted awhile he asked, "Where are you from?"

When I said I was born in Lynchburg, Virginia, but grew up in Montclair, New Jersey, he said, "Oh, then you must have known Mary Rice Hayes Allen."

"Know her," I laughed, "she was my mother."

"Your mother!" he exclaimed as he gave me a big hug. "What a wonderful woman she was. Whenever her poet friend Anne Spencer visited, your mother would have a gathering of the Harlem Renaissance writers with the great early leaders of the NAACP."

"I know," I said, "but as children we did not know the house was full of writers and fighters. Usually when guests were there, Papa just introduced us, then sent us upstairs."

"You probably don't remember, but on one or two occasions, when I was living in New York, your mother was kind enough to invite this fledgling poet. Do you remember me?"

"I know you through your wonderful poetry, but at the time I wasn't aware of the greatness of the people at Mama's gatherings. Children remember the simple things."

"That's true," he conceded.

"Do you know what I remember of Walter White, who came to dinner several times? As great a man as I now know he was, all I knew then was he ate a lot. He always made Mama promise to have her lemon meringue pie and Sally Lunn bread when he was coming."

"Your mama was a good cook. I remember that."

"Yes," I agreed. "One time when Walter White came, I had my eye on the last piece of lemon meringue pie, and when Mama offered it to him, he ate it."

Sterling Brown laughed. "That man put his life on the line for us many times in the NAACP's fight for freedom. Have you forgiven him?"

"Ten times over," I said. "Now, with James Weldon Johnson, all I remember is that he had the most beautiful eyes. They were kind of light in color and he was very friendly toward us children, unlike W. E. B. Du Bois, who wasn't. We knew from Mama's stories how important a man Du Bois was, but he was not friendly like Walter White and James Weldon Johnson."

We also talked about Aun' Tannie, and Sterling Brown told me he'd known her when he taught at Virginia Seminary. He thought her poetry was outstanding. It must have been. Anne Spencer was the first Negro poet in the *Norton Anthology.*

"Wonderful woman too," Sterling Brown said. "I know why she and your mother were such good friends."

"Many reasons, their free spirit and love of flowers among them."

"Oh, Anne's garden was her sanctuary. I wrote a poem about her garden," he said "part of which goes:

"Lady, my lady come from out the garden,
Clay-fingered, dirty-smocked, and in my time
I too shall learn the quietness of arden
knowledge so long a stranger to my rhyme."

Later, I read his whole poem about Aun' Tannie's garden. There are several other verses, and it ends lightly with:

One time, while clipping bushes, tending vines
(making your brave, sly mock at dastard days),
Laugh gently at these trivial, truthful lines—
and that will be sufficient for my praise.

"Anne Spencer was quietly committed to her garden," Sterling Brown commented, "and in the same way to her fight for equality. I can see your mother and Anne together. Common causes do bring us together."

"Speaking of common causes," I said, "another dear friend of my mother's was a lady you must have known very well, since she was from your hometown, Washington, D.C.—Mary Church Terrell."

"Indeed, she was a fighter for rights all of her life, and helped to straighten out my hometown. She organized a group of citizens to protest segregation of public accommodations in the Capitol. That was back in the 1950s. She was up in age then."

"I know," I said. "She was around the same age as my mother's first husband, Gregory Hayes. They were at Oberlin College together. I suppose it was through him that Mama met Mrs. Terrell, or it could have been through their work in the NAACP. Whichever it was, they were close friends up until Mama's death."

"That figures," he said.

"I remember Mama taking us to Washington to visit her. But like with the other great Negro men and women back then, I just knew her as Mama's friend."

In fact, Mary Church Terrell was much more than Mama's friend. She was pivotal in starting the NAACP. She was one of the group of Negro and white men and women who gathered in New York City on May 30, 1909, to see what they might do to correct the many wrongs against the Negro—the disfranchisement, the lynchings, the riots. She was one of the three hundred people gathered there, along with W. E. B. Du Bois and Ida B. Wells Barnett, at the conference out of which the NAACP was founded. Yes, Mary Church Terrell was more than Mama's friend. She was a comrade in the battle for equality and fought right up until her death at age ninety.

As Sterling Brown and I continued our talk and got onto the subject of the Harlem Renaissance poets, I mentioned that Mama loved Countee Cullen for the dignity and lyricism of his poetry. I told him that I had the copy of *Color*, Cullen's first book of poems, which he'd given Mama when he came to one of her parties. I treasure it. I told him, too, that although Mama loved Countee Cullen as a person, she always said that it was poets like Sterling Brown and Langston Hughes who truly captured the ways of our people.

"I agree with Mama," I said. "I think of you and Langston Hughes as two of our greatest folk-poets."

"Well, thank you." Sterling Brown smiled broadly.

"It's true: like Mama, I too like the lyricism of Countee Cullen, but for capturing the hearts, minds, culture of our people, the jazz, the blues, the down-home food, the language and the loud laughter that seems to ring from our souls, you and Langston Hughes are the masters."

"Langston Hughes's poems cut across every aspect of Negro life. He could write the deep, soul-stirring 'I've Known Rivers' and be just as stirring about the blues or freedom," Sterling Brown said.

I agreed, and when I mentioned that, for me, Hughes expressed in poetry what Duke did in music, that *both* of them were into the "souls of black folk," he said he had not thought of that but if I didn't mind he would use my idea.

"Not at all," I said.

"You seem to know a lot about poetry."

"It's one of my loves," I said. "Mama introduced me early to it, and whenever we had to perform for her guests I read or recited poetry. I couldn't sing, dance, nor play the piano like my brother and sisters, so I read poetry. There was one of yours I did often."

"Which one was that?"

"'Sister Lou,'" I said and recited the first verse:

"Honey,
when de man
calls out de las' train
you're gonna ride,
tell him howdy.

I couldn't remember any more, but Sterling Brown was pleased that I'd used that one. I told him how Mama had liked the fighting spirit of Claude McKay's poetry too. We talked about Claude McKay, and I told him I often recited his poems, and how I especially liked "If We Must Die."

"If we must die — oh, let us nobly die
So that our precious blood may not be shed
In vain,"

Sterling Brown recited, and continued with

"then even the monsters we defy
Shall be constrained to honor us though dead!"

"That poem reminds me of a Yoruba proverb," I said. "You must be willing to die in order to live."

"I must remember that," Sterling Brown said, "but tell me more about your love of poetry."

"Our growing-up days were full of poetry and stories."

"Speaking of stories," he laughed, "I remember at one of your mother's parties a lady who kept us laughing with her stories. She was a lady of quite some size."

"That must have been Miz Nettie, one of Mama's dearest friends. She worked in service and visited us almost every Thursday, bringing her stories. Mama's friends in service, whom we called our Thursday people, were always invited to her parties.

"By the way," I said, "were you at the gathering when my appendix broke up the party?" He didn't remember this, and I told him the story.

"Mama's guests were downstairs having a great time, laughing and talking. Some, I'm certain, were feeling the effects of Papa's medicinal whiskey." Sterling Brown laughed, and I went on with my story.

"I was upstairs writhing in pain with what Mama thought was just a stomachache from overeating, not too unusual for me. She did, however, come up and check on me once in a while. Late in the evening she came up and saw I was bathed in sweat, so she ran downstairs and got Dr. Alexander, our family physician. He came upstairs, Dr. Kenny and Dr. Peter Murray following. They pressed and talked and decided I had acute appendicitis. I was taken to Dr. Kenny's hospital in Newark and Dr. Murray operated on me, just in time. Papa always said, when telling this story, that Mama's party saved my life."

"You've had a rich life," Sterling Brown said after I finished my story.

"Yes, it has been good. Like everyone, I've had ups and downs— mostly ups. My biggest down involves my son, who after a stretch in the Air Force, returned with a psychiatric problem that has plagued him for a while." Sterling Brown was sympathetic.

"I wrote a poem about him," I told him.

"That's good," he said. "Sometimes out of pain comes our greatest work. It's so good sitting here talking with you about poetry. Your mother's love of poetry has certainly filtered down to you."

"No doubt about it. The presents she gave me and my father were often books of poems. I still have a book of poems she brought back to my father from Silver Bay, a conference center in upstate New York, in 1925. *Christ in the Poetry of Today* is the title. There are poems in there by Vachel Lindsay, Joyce Kilmer, Sara Teasdale, James Weldon Johnson, Carl Sandburg, and many others.

"I don't know that book, but it sounds like something you would want to keep."

"Yes, there is a poem in there, "Philip to Christ," that either Papa or Mama marked. I don't know which one, but the poem holds out the kind of hope that both of them held onto in a time when there was so much hate against us. I remember only the last lines.

"Man will make the angels hear
Through the sky so crystal clear
How love cast forth hate and fear.

"I thought it might have been marked by Mama since it really embodies her always positive view of the future."

"It also speaks the same language that Martin Luther King did, doesn't it?" Sterling Brown suggested.

We talked on for a while more about poetry and then about his love of teaching. And how did I like it? he wanted to know. I said I enjoyed teaching, but in the beginning I'd found it a little unsettling, especially since I'd come to Talladega in 1966, right in the middle of the student protests. Finally, he said he must go on and let me do my work.

As I sit here now writing about that hour with Sterling Brown, I think back to Mama's "Papa Sir" and wonder about the "ifs" in our lives. If he had not instilled in Mama a love of poetry and if she had not instilled the same love in me, would I have been able to experience so fully that hour with one of the Harlem Renaissance's greatest folk-poets? Something to think about.

My bookshelves are filled not only with the Harlem Renaissance poets, but with poets of the world: the old Classics, Greek poetry, Chinese poetry, Japanese poetry, English, Irish, Native American, Hispanic, Armenian, *Three Thousand Years of Black Poetry,* and contemporary white and black poetry. Perhaps poetry is the thread that connects me most truly back to Mama's father, the white man who rode down dirt roads reciting poetry to his young black daughter.

Train up a child in the way he should go:
and when he is old, he will not depart from it.

—Proverbs 22:6

Chapter 30

LESSONS

—

$\mathcal{M}$ama had several ways of getting "lessons of life" across to us, sometimes through discussion, sometimes through whippings, and sometimes through allowing us the rope to hang ourselves.

I remember her discussion method all too well. When I was in the sixth grade, my classmate James Tibb's brother died. They told us that in assembly. We sang "Dear Lord and Father of Mankind," and a few words were spoken by his teacher. The impact of the first death of a schoolmate was evident in the silent heaviness of that assembly morning. Whenever I hear that hymn I think of that experience.

"The body is in the home for viewing," the teacher said. I remembered when we were in Virginia and Mrs. Jackson died. Also, when I was five years old our sister Minnie was laid out in the parlor for viewing, but neither of those deaths seemed to have upset me as much as when we went to view James' brother after school. When I got home, Mama saw that I was upset. I told her about the assembly and going to the home. She sat quietly with me and talked about death; some I understood then, and some later.

"Death is a part of life," she said. This I did not quite understand. "It is a summary of your life. Live life joyously and with purpose. Leave something behind for people to think about, so they may cry a little, but laugh a lot. Remember how James' brother was such a happy, cheerful boy and was always so helpful. Think of that and his laughter." At the time, however, all I could think of was the cold, gray-looking body in that casket. But later on, as I grew older, what Mama had said about death came back and stayed with me.

Another lesson from Mama came via the whipping method. The worst lickin' I got in my whole life was when Mama overheard me telling Rosemary and Dolly that I had called my classmate Tony a "wop." I really hadn't. But how can you back down when you're bragging to your sisters about how you fought back when someone has hurt you?

Tony had brought a special pencil sharpener to school, a little cannon with a blade of some kind in it. In just a whirl or two your pencil was sharpened. This magnificent device was the center of attraction and Tony was very proud. He passed it around for us to try, and when it got to me — I had barely touched it — it fell apart. Tony was so upset he grabbed it and yelled, "You clumsy nig—" He never finished the word, but I knew. With tears in his eyes he just stood there looking down at the broken pencil sharpener. He never even heard me say, "I'm sorry." The eyes of the whole sixth-grade class passed a silent sentence on me. Now at home I was getting the worst whipping in my life for something I didn't say and something I didn't do: I could never have called Tony a "wop." I was so shy, I couldn't even call Tony Tony. And I loved Tony in a sixth-grade kind of way.

Mama's whipping and words left a sting that stayed with me for the rest of my life. "Never, never call anyone out of their name, never. Always respect others. Never use a term like that again in your life." I guess that lesson paid off, as now I don't, and I don't allow anyone close to me to use derogatory names about others. My white friends at Shepherd Center, where I teach creative writing, laugh at me. One of them said something about "poor white trash," and just like Mama, I heard myself saying, "Never, never use a term like that about a human being." And, "Never in your life, never, never, never." Carole, my white friend who had used the term, laughed and said, "Carrie, in my whole life, you're the only one who has ever admonished me for using that term." I guess Mama's whipping method worked.

My sister Dolly said she never forgot the whipping lesson Mama gave her when she graduated from high school. It was during the Depression and she was supposed to go to the YMCA for the properly chaperoned after-graduation party. Instead, she and her fast little crowd went into New York City (the place Papa was going to keep his girls away from). Not only that, but they went to a nightclub called Dickie Wells. Mama had bought Dolly a beautiful pair of blue shoes to go with the blue graduation dress. (Mama had given Dolly the opportunity to pick out her own graduation dress, but when she came home with a slinky, red, low-cut satin gown, Mama went back with her and helped her exchange it for the blue.)

On graduation night, when Dolly returned home at 4:00 A.M., long after the YMCA party was over, Mama went into her room.

"Dolly," she said calmly, "did you enjoy yourself?"

"Yes, Mama."

"Did you dance in those lovely blue shoes I stretched a point to buy for you? These are hard times."

"Yes, Mama."

"Well, then lie on the bed and turn over." Dolly got a lickin' with those "lovely blue shoes." She said she never wore them again.

Your age did not matter if it was a lickin' lesson. Once when Gregory was about twenty-one, he came home drunk and Mama swatted him with the broom. These days that would be called abuse, but those lickin's didn't hurt us except momentarily, and we knew Mama loved her children. We were her greatest achievement.

Mama's "give 'em a little rope, sometimes experience is the best teacher" method is one all of us remember well, and often laugh about.

Once during a church conference Mama entertained a very special guest speaker, a gentleman from England. Mama believed in the simple life, but for some reason we children thought this Englishman's visit called for puttin' on the dog as we had never put it on before. Out of respect for the Britishness of the gentleman we even took the *Encyclopaedia Britannica* volume from under the leg of the dining room table and replaced it with *Early American Literature*. We decided that we must have a butler to serve the meal. After all, there was a "butler's pantry" between the kitchen and the dining room. Securing the butler created a problem. We went into a huddle and came out having selected my brother Bill as butler. Mama didn't like the idea too much, but she let us go on with it after Dolly convinced her that everyone in England, including butlers, had a butler. Dolly always had a way of making the simplest request sound like a matter of extreme urgency, and as usual won her point.

Now that we had a butler, we needed a maid. Another huddle. We came up with Mizannie. It looked as if we would lose out on this one. Mama's first response was an emphatic "No."

Mizannie was an old lady who used to come and go. Sometimes she would "just happen by" (suitcase in hand) and stay on with us for two or three months. She loved to cook and work around the house, but mainly just loved to be around Mama. There was something comfortable about Mama and something that gave others a feeling of well-being. And, as you know by now, our house was a haven for characters, forgettable as well as unforgettable. When we were children, we thought there was no one on earth quite like Mizannie. I'm even more convinced of it now. Just the way she looked was pretty special. Her hair was dark and always full of grease, so much grease that it seemed to seep into her scalp and make her face oily. Her color was deep brown, and she had a round face and strange piercing gray eyes with a very faraway look in them. Though her skin was dark brown, the insides of her hands were pink, the pink accentuated by the contrast. As a child, I was fascinated by those hands. Her walk was slow and soft, and she could come up behind you without a sound. I've often thought she might have startled us that way to emphasize the mystery of her connection with the spirits.

It was pretty exciting to have Mizannie in our house because she knew all about spirits, evil and good. She said she'd been given the powers to use the good ones and to do away with the evil ones. She carried a little black bag with her always. In it were "all the powers of life."

Mizannie worked at her calling in a diligent and patient manner. Besides having "all the powers of life," she had a "second sight" and could tell us what was going to happen tomorrow and even many years hence. She also claimed that, with this second sight, she could tell what we were thinking. That anyone could actually have access to all the fantasies and dreams of childhood makes me shudder, but this was what Mizannie was supposed to have had, and it sometimes got us into trouble. We were always apologizing to Mizannie for our not-nice thoughts. A certain look would come into her eyes and you'd feel you had to say, "I'm sorry Mizannie," because you knew she had just tuned in. She would then shake her head and say, "Shame on you, child, purgitate those thoughts." We knew what she meant and hastened to clean up our dirty little minds.

From time to time, Mizannie would go away and stay gone for a long time. When she came back she'd say she'd been visiting the spirits, but some people said she had been in the county asylum. It was an idea we rejected, but at any rate Mama had many reasons to dread Mizannie's returns.

One time, when Eugene Kinkle Jones of the National Urban League came to Montclair to discuss the formation of an interracial committee to work on alleviating racial tensions, he ate dinner with us. After dinner, Mizannie, who knew he was about to attend this meeting, asked Eugene Kinkle Jones to hold out his hand. She rubbed a little of her greasy "power of life" in his palm and told him, "Everything will be all right now." Mama apologized when she realized what Mizannie had done. Eugene Kinkle Jones was not disturbed, however. "It just might work," he laughed.

There was plenty to make Mama cautious about having Mizannie back in the house. We all remembered the Christmas when Mizannie and the spirits had been particularly active. Every morning for about two weeks, there was evidence of their presence when we came downstairs. As Mizannie was the first to arise, she was always the first to discover their evil doings of the night before. Mizannie would check and then call us down to see the little holes in the linoleum, put there the night before by these spirits. As if this were not enough, the spirits had also gone into the dining room and by some strange means turned all of the silver black.

These were the kinds of things Mama remembered, and we had more pleading to do before she would say Mizannie could come back to play the maid. When Dolly said, "Didn't we learn in Sunday school you should forgive?" Mama gave in. "Okay," she said, "but mark my word, there will be trouble."

On the day of the dinner party, we were all in a dither—all of us, that is, except Mama, who had gone about preparing her dinner with her usual ease, oblivious to the problems we were having to deal with. Every now and then she would open the oven of the old coal stove and say, "Umm-umm, look at that, kids." Out would come lemon pies heaped with clouds of meringue, baked ham, roast chicken, and her masterpiece, Sally Lunn, a kind of sweet bread she baked in a funnel-cake pan and browned just right. She'd stand back, look at whatever it was for a second, and say:

"You know something, kids, your mother is a pretty good cook." Some people merely cook meals; Mama created them. I will say, though, that we all participated in some small way in these productions. She had some help. During the preparation of most every meal, we found ourselves skipping to and from the store, as Mama never seemed to remember she was out of salt and vinegar at the same time. So it was "Skip to the store and get me some salt" and twenty minutes later, "Skip to the store and get me some vinegar." Sometimes several of us would be skipping and would meet each other halfway to or from that store.

On this particular occasion, everything seemed finally to have fallen into place just as the guests began to arrive. Dinner got under way. Bill, with a towel over his arm, was performing admirably. Mizannie, who had stayed in the kitchen taking broken doses of Papa's medicinal whiskey, was a potential problem. But so far everything was going well in spite of that. At the table they were discussing the theme of the conference.

"We think our theme for the conference is very timely," Papa was saying: "the role of the church in a changing world." It was when Bill sent Mizannie in to pass the bread that things started going downhill. Mizannie had heard Papa describe the theme.

"Oh," she sang, "it is a rollin' world, rollin', rollin', rollin'." She repeated the line as she laughed and sang her way back out to the kitchen.

Miz Nettie came bustling out to the kitchen in her wake. "Disgusting," she said to Bill. "Look at her. What in the world are you all doing having her here?"

"She's our maid," Bill said, nodding toward Mizannie, who was now slumped down in a chair.

"Lord, help this crazy house," Miz Nettie snorted and returned to the dining room shaking her head.

When Mama called to Bill to bring more string beans, he forgot he was the butler, and called back:

"Mama, there ain't no more string beans."

"That's my middle boy," Mama said, as if she'd never known about our plan. We were, by then, beginning to feel deflated. Our maid was intoxicated and the butler was our brother.

After everyone had left, Mama was the only one of us who was happy about the way things turned out. She looked at Papa and remarked, "Perhaps that will teach them a lesson. Always be what you are. Pretense gets you nowhere."

Papa laughed, quoting one of his eternal proverbs: "Pride goeth before destruction, and an haughty spirit before a fall."

Confiding a secret . . .
is like carrying grain in a bag with a hole.

—Ethiopian proverb

Chapter 31

OLD SECRETS

⟶

*W*hat do you do to open a secret buried so deep and kept so long, the hinges are rusty?

When I was a child I thought my father was flawless. He was a perfect father who always arrived home with those bags filled with popcorn, bananas, peanut brittle, and coconut candy. He was a good provider, a trustee of the church, the superintendent of the Sunday school. He was a smart man who had worked his way through college and law school.

Papa was also a compassionate man. He took on many law cases when he knew that payment might come in the form of chickens or a pig, if anything. Papa also lived by the Proverbs. One he quoted a lot was, "He that hath pity upon the poor lendeth unto the Lord."

Like Mama, Papa disliked pretension. Although most professional Negroes who were moving up in the world rode around in Packards and Cadillacs, Papa did not find that necessary. Mama would laugh and say, "Will's only status symbol is the silver butter knife." If we'd forget to put the butter knife on the table when we set it, he'd say,

"Wheah is the butter knife?" It was obviously important to him. Once, when he'd asked the question for the umpteenth time, Dolly got out the big silver tray, put the butter knife on it, and, making a sound like trumpets, pranced in, bowed low, and intoned, "Your butter knife." Papa smiled, as he almost always did when Dolly teased him. But I don't think the butter knife was a status symbol for Papa. He'd worked in fancy hotels for so many years that, for him, the butter knife was simply a necessary part of a table setting.

Papa was a very protective father who tried to shield us from prejudice and, as Aun' Tannie said, "from the male animal."

"Your father," she said, "loved to read Bacon's essays, and once when you three girls had beaux visiting downstairs, he was upstairs reading Bacon's essay 'Of Youth and Age.'" Aun' Tannie could not remember all of what about that essay upset him but thought it had something to do with an unready horse. Later I decided to find the essay and read it. Then I knew:

> Young men, in the conduct and manage of actions, embrace more than they can hold; stir more than they can quiet; fly to the end, without consideration of the means and degrees . . . use extreme remedies at first; and, that which doubleth all errors, will not acknowledge or retract them; like an unready horse, that will neither stop nor turn.

Aun' Tannie said Mama told her he jumped up, went to the stairs, and bellowed down:

"Rosemary, Carrie, Dolly! It's time for the young men to go to their homes now." The exodus was immediate.

I don't think Bacon had sex in mind when he wrote that essay, but evidently Papa did when he read it. Protecting his three girls from the male animal made him quite literally tear his hair.

Once when we were teenagers, Mr. Williams, the very progressive executive secretary of the YMCA, had a workshop on sex education (way ahead of his time). We brought home the book used at the workshop, *So Youth May Know*. Papa saw it and seized it. Although we have long since passed the age of consent, I have yet to see that book again.

Papa would not let us go to many of our friends' favorite places. Shady Rest was one of those. It was a colored country club where they had tennis matches and dances. It sounded like a pretty nice place, although only once in my life did I get to see it, and that was because his mood just happened to lift at the right moment.

In the mornings we could tell Papa's mood of the day while he was shaving. If he was reciting "To be or not to be," it was not a good time to ask for anything. He had a sister named Maggie whom he adored, and if he was singing "I wandered today to the field, Maggie," it was a reasonable time to approach him. We had a fifty-fifty chance of getting what we wanted. But if he was singing "Didn't he ramble, ramble, ramble all around in and out of town," we took immediate advantage of the great mood.

It was on a rambling morning that we got Rosemary, the soft, sweet-voiced one, to ask Papa if we could go to Shady Rest to a dance after the tennis match.

"Why yes, sweetmeats," was his reply. We were startled but delighted. We all went, and it turned out to be my single visit to Shady Rest. I can't remember if it was worth it.

Papa was very moralistic. When Bill was rumored to be responsible for the pregnancy of a high school classmate, Papa absolutely would not consider the possibility. I was only ten or eleven years old then and didn't understand what was happening. Much later I realized what that mean old girl in my class meant to imply about my brother when she sidled up to me and smirked, "Your brother knocked up a girl."

I responded indignantly, "My brother doesn't fight girls."

"You so dumb," she said, leaving me standing there bewildered.

In any event, there was talk around town that Bill had fathered a little girl. Papa would not let the mother bring the baby up to see us. I learned later that Mama went to see her and took her things. There had to have been conflict between Mama and Papa over this. Finally, when the little girl was three years old, Mama brought the mother and the child to the house. I was thirteen then, and remember every detail of that day. Holding Mama's hand was the prettiest, chubbiest, smoothest, little light brown Elberta. We loved her from the beginning. When we asked her how old she was she answered, "Three in March and March done passed."

Mama adored her, and from that day on she was at our house as much as she was at home with her mother and other grandmother. She told me recently she distinguished her two grandmothers by thinking of Mama as "uptown Grandma" and her other grandma as "downtown Grandma."

Bill and Alice, Elberta's mother, eventually married. And there would never have been any need to do a DNA test. Elberta was Bill's baby, all right. She had his beautiful voice and was a born entertainer. Mama took her everywhere to perform. Her speciality was a rendition of Irving Berlin's "Russian Lullaby." Mama would stand there, beaming, as Elberta ended the song with:

Rock-a-bye my baby
Somewhere there may be a land
That's free for you and me
And a Russian lullaby.

Irving Berlin wrote it in 1927, ten years after the Russian Revolution. The Communists were in control and the song spoke to what some thought were harsh times there. Elberta was just four or five years old when Mama had her singing "Russian Lullaby" all over New Jersey. She continued to sing it for years. I have a copy of a program presented by the Montclair Unemployment Relief and Welfare Organization. There on the program for November 19, 1931, is:

Special Attraction:
Little Miss Elberta Wilhelmina Hayes
Miss Carrie Shepherd, at the piano

Mama smiled just as proudly when her granddaughter performed as she did whenever Bill performed. Elberta said she always felt the love and warmth of Grandma Allen.

But to her, "Mr. Allen was a cold fish."

I NEVER SAW my father in anything but a business suit and a starched white shirt. Every morning, on his way out the door, he kissed Mama three times. You can see why I couldn't comprehend what I discovered about him.

The summer I was seventeen and getting ready to go to college, I went down to Newark one day to do some shopping. When I finished, it was late afternoon, and since I was close to Papa's office, I thought I'd drop by and see if he was ready to go home. His second-floor office had an outer office. Because of the Depression, Mama was then his secretary, but she was home that day, not feeling well. So no one was in the outer office. The door to Papa's private office was closed, but the western sun struck the lightly frosted glass and silhouetted a woman in Papa's arms. I saw it, clear, sharp.

I turned and ran out of the office, hot tears in my eyes. I stumbled out of the building. I ran up the street to catch the trolley car I'd planned to ride home with Papa.

Dinner was late that evening, but for everyone at the table except me it was just like all other dinnertimes in our house. Stories were told, laughter burst out, events of the day were shared. I could not make myself join in the fun. I sat there, dumb, my eyes turned away from Papa at the head of the table and Mama on his left. She served the plates, Papa's first as always—always, the best of everything for Papa. Now and then, Mama and Papa bent their heads together to make some private comment and then laugh at a story some child of theirs had told.

But I was quiet. The sound of my mother's laughter was excruciating for me. I looked at her, but could not look at my father, not only because my faith in him was shattered but because I was afraid that if I did, something in my face would tell him I knew.

Anger and shame welled up in me. *My* father? I remembered a friend of mine telling me once in confidence about *her* father. But please, not mine. I looked across the table at Mizannie. I hoped her "second sight" wasn't working that night. I prayed that, at the very least, she could not read my mind. To protect Mama, I would guard this secret for the rest of my life. But from then on, whenever Papa came home late, the silhouette would flash into my mind. I never stopped loving Papa, but my love for him was not quite the same.

A few years ago, my sister Dolly and I were sitting around laughing and talking about home, as we often do. We reminisced over one funny story after another. Then we moved on to another favorite conversation: comparing Mama and Papa—the openness of Mama, her free spirit, and the staidness of Papa, his proverbs, his starched white shirts, his compulsive hand-washing. Dolly and I were looking at our parents now from our adult perspectives. When I got up and went into the kitchen to get two Cokes, Dolly called out to me, "Did you know Papa had a woman down in Newark for years?"

The rusty-hinged box would not open, and all I could do was answer back, "Really?" and stand there for a moment, before going back to join her.

I have sown beside all waters in my day
I planted deep, within my heart . . .

—Arna Bontemps,
"A Black Man Talks of Reaping"

Chapter 32

THROUGH MY MOTHER'S GARDEN

Miz Nettie was looking out the window watching Mama and Mrs. Bengler. They were both on their knees putting something on Mama's nasturtium plants to get rid of the little black bugs that seemed to love nasturtiums as much as Mama did.

Miz Nettie turned to Aun' Tannie, who was visiting. "I don' know how Mary did it. All the trouble that lady caused her, now look at 'em out there in the nasturtium bed—like nothing ever happened."

In her smooth, slow Southern drawl Aun' Tannie answered with lines from her poem "To a Nasturtium": "Day torch, flame flower, cool-hot beauty—"

"What'd you say?" Miz Nettie asked.

"That was for Mary. She understands. Flowers have healing powers."

Mizannie chimed in, "Some things you folks *don't* understand." For several years Mizannie had been sprinkling something that looked like salt between our house and Mrs. Bengler's. She told us, "If the spirits are brought into coherence of each other, they can bring people together."

"You and yo' damn spirits. Excuse me, children." Miz Nettie bristled. "Ain' no spirits did this."

"I said some things folks *don't* know about." Mizannie, with a superior sniff, continued her work at the sink.

PERHAPS AUN' TANNIE was right about the flowers. I remember that the first time Mrs. Bengler came inside our house, it was to see a flower. Mama had a night-blooming cereus, which bloomed just once a year and lasted only until the end of the next day. When it bloomed, Mama would ask some of her Baptist ladies to tea to see this beautiful flower, which they said looked like "Jesus in the cradle." So it was that Mama's Baptist ladies were on hand the day Mrs. Bengler broke her taboo.

But first let me digress and tell you about the Baptist ladies. If it hadn't been for the ladies of Union Baptist Church, some of Mama's crusades would have ended up only temporarily resolved. After Alroy's coup at the beauty salon, Mama, of course, said to herself, "One haircut is not enough." She asked a few of the Baptist ladies to go and get *their* hair cut at the department-store salon. Thereafter, certain ladies scattered throughout the congregation sported less hair and more pride each Sunday. When Mama was trying to get a policeman hired on the Montclair force, a group of Baptist ladies went with her one day to petition the commissioner. When Mama was fighting the segregation in a theater, Baptist ladies (praying silently to the Lord to forgive them) marched into the movie house with her. Those Baptist ladies, who worked in white people's kitchens all week, responded to the call to arms, while some of the "high society" ladies in the church expressed disapproval of Mama's behavior and kept themselves in the background.

Looking back, I realize that when I was a child, the Baptist ladies symbolized a kind of strength and security for me. These were strong, hardworking, solid, laughing women. I loved the ladies on the usher board, who walked firmly down the aisle, each with a white-gloved right hand held behind her back. I loved the high, screechy, out-of-tune soprano in an otherwise beautiful choir; I loved the ladies of the Willing Workers club who prepared those church dinners, every one of them secretly in love with the minister and hoping it would be her fried chicken that graced his plate. I loved when the congregation would join the high soprano voice that broke forth with "Gimme that ole-time religion" at the end of a really good sermon.

And I loved the women's day meetings, when all the members of all the women's clubs marched down the aisle to competitively present the church with money they'd raised. That army of women parading in rhythmic step with the beating music stirred me. Surely that proud, pulsing march step comes straight from our African heritage.

To say that the church was important to our social life is to greatly understate the case, forgetting the dinners; the BYPU (Baptist Young People's Union) meetings, where we girls encountered *boys*; the socials, and all the endless opportunity for theatrical expression. There was a lady in our church, Miz Martha Tucker, who fought as hard to pay off the church mortgage as Mama did for freedom. She was always producing plays, pageants, cantatas, and "musicales," and each one, she boasted, was always "the biggest thing I've ever done." She believed in putting her whole self into her productions—literally.

Miz Martha Tucker's "Pageant of Nations" could have laid justifiable claim to being the "biggest" of her productions, even though it ended up as one of the worst local "international" crises. Miz Tucker divided all the church women into nations, each of which was charged with raising money. At the end of the campaign she planned a grand pageant. A representative from each group was dressed as her nation—and after much ceremony, each nation was to dramatically present all the money it had raised to the Union Baptist Church, a wonderful fantasy. Miss America, played, of course, by a stately, dignified lady, was to make a grand entrance to climax the affair. But things got mixed up backstage, and Miss America came out too soon. Whereupon Miz Martha Tucker came running up to the front of the stage. "Go back, America, go back," she yelled. "You know France ain' been out there yet." This international incident almost had us on the brink as poor America had to retreat to the wings, never to quite recapture the glory that was her due.

We would promise to die if we couldn't be in Miz Martha Tucker's productions. One year Dolly almost did die. Miz Martha Tucker was tired of Dolly changing the scripts to suit herself and often leaving the next player with no cue. She did it one time too many and Miz Martha Tucker ran in from the wings yelling, "Get off this stage," whereupon Dolly trudged off, dragging her fallen wings behind her.

But Miz Martha Tucker actually loved Dolly and gave her another chance. Once Dolly, who had shown artistic ability at a very early age, asked if she could paint the posters for a "beautiful and grand" religious pageant. At first Miz Martha Tucker said no, she would get posters printed at her same old place. Then Dolly's big pleading eyes turned Miz Martha Tucker into jelly and she said yes.

"They better be good though; I can't risk any foolishness with this. This is absolutely the biggest thing I've ever done."

Dolly swore she would not let her down, and set about getting her poster paints and paper. Two weeks before the production, we went to rehearsal and found Miz Martha Tucker beside herself.

"Oh, that Dolly, that Dolly, she's going to drive me crazy. Talk, talk, talk — she never stops to listen. I bet in school she never stops talking long enough to learn how to spell. Here I'm putting on the biggest, and grandest, religious pageant in the history of the church, and she has fifty posters all over town advertising the SCARED pageant! Oh, me! Why do I bother. *Why do I bother!* If it wasn't for your mama. . . . Why do I bother," she said, pacing up and down with one of the posters in her hand. Then she approached Dolly as if she would like to have done away with her at that moment. But Dolly just looked up at her with those big brown eyes and said, "I'm sorry."

"Well," Miz Martha Tucker said, softening, "you did try — bless your heart . . . and I guess with all your mama tries to do for the whole race, I should be able to keep on trying with one of hers. But I tell you," she yelled in afterthought, "sometimes I do wonder whose job is the hardest."

Miz Martha Tucker not only helped pay off the church mortgage with her dramatic productions, she raised considerable money for the national office of the NAACP. In the Library of Congress files, I found a statement indicating that she had raised twice and in some instances three times as much money for that cause than any other single person. A copy of a letter to her from William Pickens, field secretary in 1925, reads:

> My dear Miss Tucker:
> We are happy to notify you that on page 77 of the December *Crisis* your picture appears as winner of first prize in the popularity contest.
>
> With best regards from,
William Pickens
Field Secretary

Miz Martha Tucker was a strong role model, as were many of our other Baptist ladies. They were our "other mothers." If they saw us doing anything wrong, they would punish us themselves, then tell our mothers, and we'd be punished again. Sadly, that "village" raising of children has all but disappeared today.

So THOSE WERE the Baptist ladies sitting now in Mama's parlor with Mrs. Bengler, the very same ladies who served as our intelligence agents when Mrs. Bengler tried to put us out of the neighborhood. Here they were now, gathered to see "Jesus in the cradle," and waiting to have tea and cakes.

Mama told me and Rosemary to come serve the tea. Carrying the tray with the tea, I stepped into the parlor and into an odd silence that hung heavily in this cheerful room, usually so full of talk and laughter. Keeping my eyes on the tray, I went self-consciously from lady to lady, smiling as each took a cup and thanked me politely. I was standing in front of Miz Nettie, watching as she took her cup off the tray, when I realized who was sitting beside her. Right there, in among all the Baptist ladies, was Mrs. Bengler. I could hardly believe my eyes.

When I finished serving Miz Nettie, I moved to Mrs. Bengler, acknowledged her greeting, and offered her tea. The cups left on my tray were rattling, and I don't know exactly how it happened, but as she picked up the cup, the tray hit against it, splattering tea on her and on the rug. Several of the Baptist ladies, uttering gasping sounds, rushed over with their napkins and started wiping the tea off Mrs. Bengler's dress, while she kept saying, "Oh, that's all right, that's all right," and I stood there as if I'd been struck by some curse and was fixed to that spot for the rest of my natural life.

"Take the tray out into the kitchen, Carrie, and get some more tea," Mama said, breaking the curse. I returned with a fresh tray and served Mrs. Bengler again, and then, uneventfully, the rest of the ladies.

The tea and cakes still did not quite break through the polite cautiousness. Maybe it was remembering how Mrs. Bengler had treated us in the beginning that made the Baptist ladies uncomfortable. Or maybe it just seemed strange, sitting there having tea with a white lady. I don't know which, but Mama soon had things in hand. As usual, she got us to perform. Rosemary played "Meditation" on the piano. "Meditation" was the only piece Rosemary knew, and the Baptist ladies had heard her play it a hundred times. But Mrs. Bengler clapped her hands long and loud and told Rosemary how wonderful it was. Then Dolly tap-danced for them and I recited a poem. Having gotten the lesser talents done to make way for the great performance, Mama announced, "Now my granddaughter, little Elberta Hayes, will sing for you." The Baptist ladies started clapping for her even before she began. Elberta took her place, bowed, and sang "Russian Lullaby." The ice broken, everyone laughed and talked, and Mrs. Bengler became just part of the group.

She was in and out of our home from that day on. Elberta remembers once when Dolly wanted to spend their lunch money on candy and so made Elberta come home from school with her for lunch. Dolly couldn't open the can of spaghetti. Elberta loved spaghetti, and spaghetti is what Dolly had used to bribe her. Dolly knew she had to get that can open somehow. After trying everything, she said to Elberta, "Let's get on our knees and pray." Just as they were saying "Amen," Mrs. Bengler knocked on the back door. She was looking for Mama, but, in answer to the prayer, she opened the can and left. Dolly thanked her, turned to Elberta, and asked, "What did I tell you?"

Twice when Mama was ill, Mrs. Bengler brought over a special soup she had made for her. Mama always returned the favor, taking soup and homemade custard over whenever Mrs. Bengler was ill. It had been a long road, but perhaps their friendship was all the more solid and meaningful for it.

AUN' TANNIE, MIZ Nettie, and Mizannie were now discussing that long, bumpy road and how in the family's early days in Montclair, Mama had stuck to her guns and continued to talk to Mrs. Bengler whenever she was in the garden, even though there was no response. "Yes," Aun' Tannie said, "Mary would ask her how her phlox or snapdragons were doing. No response. But that didn't stop Mary."

"Could you have done it?" Miz Nettie asked Aun' Tannie.

"Mary and I are much alike," was her answer.

"Not me," Miz Nettie said, "not me. That takes somethin' I ain't got. But I guess for Mary it was worth it, 'cause look at 'em now."

Aun' Tannie stood by the window for a while, then softly, as if speaking to herself, commented, "In the center of a garden one finds peace and love."

Gracious in manner
Impartial in judgment
Ready for service
Loyal to friends

—pledge of the YWCA's
former Girl Reserves

Chapter 33

THE COLORED GIRLS' FINISHING SCHOOL

*A*long with all her other church and community activities, Mama was a guiding force of Montclair's colored YWCA. She served on the board for a number of years and according to Mrs. Hortense Ridley Tate, our Girl Reserves secretary, was president of the board for two or three terms. We spent so much time at the Y as children, Mama called it our second home. Now some of us call it the Colored Girls' Finishing School.

The wealthy white girls in Montclair were sent off to finishing schools in Switzerland, England, France, New York, and New England. We had to go no further than the colored YWCA on Glenridge Avenue. There we learned how to walk, sit, talk, and eat properly. We learned manners, how to dress, how to set a proper table, how to make a proper bed with hospital corners, and all those seldom discussed, girl-into-womanhood things we needed to know. However, the YWCA had a much deeper meaning for us colored girls. It was a safe gathering place, a nurturing place. We were barred from so many other places in those days and the YWCA was the young colored girls' haven from prejudice.

We were also barred from joining many of the extracurricular activities at the high school. If you were colored, you could join the Negro spiritual choir. But I couldn't sing. If you were a colored boy, you could play on the football team. But I was a girl. Colored girls could play basketball. But I was not athletic. Colored girls could join the sewing club. But I hated to sew (and still do). So, like I said, my sisters and I and our friends practically lived at the YWCA.

In 1921, the year after we moved to Montclair, Hortense Ridley, a young lady just out of Washburn College in Kansas, came to work at the Y as the Girl Reserves secretary. Lively, cheerful, and determined to "build our characters," she was our beloved mentor. If we didn't grow up with well-built characters, no one can blame it on Miss Ridley or the YWCA. In the winter we spent long hours there learning how to be "gracious in manner" and "impartial in judgment." Then in summer, it was off to YWCA camp for the away-from-home molding.

That the YWCA touched every aspect of our lives was something we all realized. But I did have to laugh recently when I read a 1920s fund-raising appeal for the colored YWCA. As a girl I hadn't realized that the YWCA was also charged with compensating for, of all things, the lack of boys in our town:

> The need for the work done by the Colored Y.W.C.A. is forcibly emphasized by our Negro population. There are [in Montclair] 3,728 females and only 2,646 males, or a ratio of approximately three females to two males. This indicates the degree to which Montclair Negro girls and women have to turn to leisure time pursuits to compensate for normal relationships.

Do you suppose our character builders really believed the Y was an adequate substitute for males? I guess they did or they would have raised money for our train fare out of town.

Not only were boys scarce, but we weren't allowed at many public entertainments. Some amusement parks were closed to us, and we couldn't attend dances at the high school. Dances we went to were held at the YMCA and, after the board decided dancing was not a sin, at the YWCA. Another insult was that although there was never a white YWCA in Montclair, ours had to be called "a branch," just in case the whites decided to open a white (thus main) Young Women's Christian Association.

When we were young, the colored YWCA was located in a wonderful old house known as the Crane house. We knew every nook and cranny of that old house, which wrapped itself around us like a comforting blanket. The staff members — Mrs. Foster, Miss Ridley, and Miss Seward — were like our "other mothers," watching over us, correcting us, and caring about our development into proper young ladies.

We also learned about our black heroes at the Y. We danced, played games, and made gifts for the old folks' home. We watched silent movies, and Wilber Jeter played the piano to accompany the movies. We had mother-and-daughter banquets, lectures, and concerts. We presented morality plays written by Miss Ridley. Two of our talented pianists, Millie Thornhill and Carrie Shepherd, gave concerts. Millie played jazz and classical; Carrie played the "Warsaw Concerto" like I've never heard it before or since. We met visiting poets and writers of the Harlem Renaissance — Langston Hughes, James Weldon Johnson, and many others. At Christmas we caroled outside the board members' houses.

The board comprised mostly lovely, sincere, and very rich white ladies whose husbands were more interested in the bull and the bear than any little Girl Reserves. Every year on Christmas Eve we were taken to the homes of different board members to sing and stand shivering outside, looking through the windows at their smiling faces, rosy from the bright fires burning in the fireplaces behind them.

One year Miss Ridley had a wonderful idea, one that fairly reeked of wholesomeness. Instead of taking her young Girl Reserves out at night, she'd take us to sing to the board members at Christmas dawn—

"just like little birds." Can you think of anything worse than having your Christmas morning slumber broken by the piercing sound of twenty high, screechy little Girl Reserve voices, even if they were "gracious in manner"?

But the very thought of our Christmas dawn serenade sent Miss Ridley into a state of euphoria. For weeks we practiced all the beautiful carols, including "Silent Night," "Joy to the World," and the other old favorites, ending with "Go Tell It on the Mountain," the Negro Christmas spiritual.

When we arrived at the first home and started singing "Silent Night," a man came to the window and banged it down. Undeterred, we went right on with our repertoire until we got to "Go Tell It on the Mountain." Evidently he had stood as much as he could. The window flew up again, and he leaned out and yelled:

"I wish the hell you *would* go up on the mountain and let me get some sleep."

Our sweet Girl Reserves secretary's perkiness collapsed and she was brought down to earth like a wounded sparrow. We tiptoed away, only to learn later, Mrs. Ridley Tate told me recently, that we'd been singing at the wrong house.

Why did so much of this character building have to take place before sunrise, anyway? The morning carol singing, the sunrise hikes, and, worst of all, those bird hikes we had to go on at camp. Granted, you have to get up before sunrise to see a sunrise, but why did we have to get up before sunrise to see the birds? In those days, the proper demeanor of the group leaders was sweetness and light. At camp, the bird hikes were started off by the sweet one, Miss Ridley, kissing everybody in the cabin, then bursting into cheerful song: "Yawning in the Mawning When the Breakfast Bell Has Rung" (although it hadn't yet). We'd have to get up, walk half a mile to take care of nature's first morning need, wash up in very cold water, dress, and start out on a five-mile hike, stumbling all over each other in the dark.

Once we arrived at the bird-viewing site, we had to sit on the ground and wait for the ruby-crowned kinglet and the black-capped chickadee, who hadn't gotten up yet. As soon as we spotted one or the other, though, we would exclaim in delight:

"Oh, there's a red-bellied so-and-so." Then our leader would tell us all about this bird, about his habitat, the color of his eggs, and how ugly the females are (information we resented). Then we'd walk the five miles back to camp, wash up again, and have breakfast.

Despite the hardships of camp, I have been a bird lover ever since. For many, many years the first thing I've done every morning is look out my window to see which birds are out there eating from the feeders I have hanging in my trees. If there's one I don't know, I look it up in Roger Tory Peterson's *Field Guide to the Birds*. What a joy this is. A belated thank-you, Miss Ridley.

RECENTLY MRS. RIDLEY Tate described for me "the beautiful way your mother handled meetings. She had such skill and always came prepared." From what I have read about Professor Hayes, Mama must have learned some of this from him. And she certainly must have learned about being prepared from Papa, the successful lawyer. She usually discussed the problems she wanted to solve with him.

Mrs. Ridley Tate told me this wonderful story to illustrate Mama's skillful handling of difficult situations.

As I've said, in its early years, the YWCA did not allow dancing on its premises. Mama was determined to change this, believing there was no better place for our young girls to dance than at the well-chaperoned YWCA. For a long time, however, she met determined resistance from others on the board. Dancing was not a "Christian activity," they said. Some of them expressed their belief that dancing was a sin, which sent Mama to the Bible. Mama came to the next meeting prepared.

"I would like to take some time to again bring up the question of allowing our young people to dance here at the Y."

The dissenters immediately protested.

"Mrs. Allen, I thought we agreed before that dancing is not a Christian activity."

"All of us did not agree," Mama said, "and there are those of us who still believe that was an unwise decision. Our young people are going to find some place to dance, and that place may not be one we would want our young people to be."

"I know we can't control that," one lady from our Baptist church said, "but if we let them dance here we'll be playing into the hands of the devil."

"Oh," said Mama, "that's exactly what I wanted to discuss. Today I would like to turn to the Bible for some guidance about dancing." Mama had drawn her weapon. "I'll read first from Psalm 149:3.

"Let them praise his name
in the dance: let them sing praises unto him
with the timbrel and harp."

Without flinching, she continued, "And the Psalmist, in thanking the Lord for his goodness, spoke of dancing." She quoted Psalm 30:11:

"Thou hast turned for me my mourning into dancing.

"And in Ecclesiastes," she continued, "we find

"A time to weep, and a time to laugh;
a time to mourn, and a time to dance.

"And one last one, although the Bible is *full* of dancing. When the Is-raelites were saved by God from Pharaoh and the waters closed over Pharaoh, there was much celebration and praise. I'd like to read from Exodus 15:20:

"And Miriam the prophetess, the
sister of Aaron, took the timbrel

in her hand; and all the women
went out after her with
timbrels and with dances."

Mama finished up with, "So it seems to me if dancing was allowed in the Bible, we certainly should allow it here at the YWCA."

Mrs. Tate told me that, after very little discussion, the board voted to allow dancing at the Y. Thanks to Mama, we attended many well-chaperoned dances there throughout our teens. A coup for Mama and a treat for us.

As I've mentioned, the Y, in those days, also took reponsibility for teaching. We learned much about our heritage from the black poets, writers, musicians, and historians Miss Ridley brought to the Y. They told us stories about our heroes, read their poetry aloud to us, and sang us our own beautiful spirituals. No matter what the occasion, all programs started with *us* singing, "Lift Every Voice and Sing." I notice now in my church that all the older folks sing it without using the hymnbook. This song was as much a part of our lives as "America the Beautiful." We not only learned how to be proper young ladies at our Y—we also learned to be proud of our heritage. It was a place where we could "Become."

As Narcissus bent over a clear pool for a drink
and saw there his own reflection, on the moment
he fell in love with it.

—Edith Hamilton, *Mythology*

Chapter 34

"NORTH IS AN OLD NARCISSUS"

—

When we left Virginia for Montclair, Aun' Tannie had warned Papa about the North being an "old Narcissus." We children had no idea what she meant then, but life has taught us the meaning: North was busy pointing a finger at South for its misdeeds and loved the reflection it saw of itself in the water. But North was deluded. It was not that beautiful back in the 1920s and 1930s.

In *The American Nation*, John A. Garraty says, "The postwar [World War I] reaction brought bitter despair for many Blacks. Aside from the barbarities of the Klan, Negroes suffered from . . . the persistent refusal of organized labor to admit Black workers to its ranks [in the North] . . . and the increasing presence of Negroes in the great Northern cities also caused social conflict." Race riots and cross and house burnings in the northern cities were certainly evidence of Garraty's statement.

James Weldon Johnson called the summer of 1919 the "Red Summer," because there was so much bloodshed. There were twenty-six race riots that summer, some of them in Northern cities such as Washington, D.C. The one in Washington was triggered by raids on black residential areas by white soldiers. There were six deaths and more than one hundred were injured in Washington. In the Chicago race riot, there were thirty-eight deaths and five hundred were injured. Seventy-six blacks were lynched in America in 1919. It was not only a "Red Summer," but a red year. Lynchings continued in high numbers throughout the early 1920s. Du Bois kept a record, and it was reported that from 1919 through 1923 there were 268 blacks lynched in the United States. That year, W. E. B. Du Bois wrote in the *Crisis*:

> We are cowards and jackasses if . . . we do not marshall every
> ounce of our brain and brawn to fight . . . against the forces of
> hell in our land.

The NAACP had been working on the problems Negroes were facing ever since its inception. Another organization, the National Urban League, grew out of a need to solve problems Negroes were encountering moving from the South into northern cities. The National Urban League was formed through a merger of three organizations: the Committee on Urban Conditions, the National League for the Protection of Colored Women, and the Committee for Improving the Industrial Condition of Negroes in New York. The Urban League is a social agency that deals with many problems. It was organized in 1911 and had as its first executive secretary Eugene Kinkle Jones.

Although Mama supported the National Urban League, she was more active with the NAACP and took Du Bois at his word. In Montclair she used every ounce of her brain to fight "the forces of hell in our land." Neither Mama nor Papa found the North to be the "Promised Land," the name used to lure workers from the South to northern domestic service and labor jobs. However, both of them believed their move north had been worth it. Despite the evil they encountered, they recognized some good things about the north. The educational system in Montclair was declared one of the best in the country and it was not segregated. Thorndyke of Columbia University did a study of school systems at the time and found Montclair, New Jersey, and Pasadena, California, to have the two best educational systems in the country. The way Mama felt about education as the "road to full freedom," she knew she had come to the right place.

Another plus for the North was that Papa's law practice thrived, before the Depression at least. He was able to buy rental property in East Orange and we lived quite comfortably. And Papa found more fairness in the judicial system in Montclair, New Jersey, than he had in Danville, Virginia.

The other thing Mama and Papa loved about Montclair was its closeness to New York City. They loved going into the city to the theater and concerts. And although we didn't go ourselves, Mama would always describe the shows in detail the day after and even acted out some of what she'd seen. Black theater was "hot" during the twenties and early thirties and I remember Mama and Papa dressing up often to go into Harlem to the Lafayette and to the Lincoln Theatre. In 1921, they went twice to the Sixty-third Street Theatre to see the smash hit *Shuffle Along*. The words were written by Noble Sissle, the music by the great Eubie Blake. Flournoy Miller and Aubrey Lyle wrote the libretto and starred in it. *Shuffle Along* ran for 504 performances at the Sixty-third Street Theatre and was called the greatest show of its time. At different times it starred Josephine Baker, Florence Mills, Paul Robeson, and Adelaide Hall. Most important, *Shuffle Along* proved to white producers that black talent would be accepted on Broadway. It turned the tide and it was Mama's favorite show.

Mama and Papa also saw shows like *Blackbirds* and *Hot Chocolates*. I'll never forget Mama trying to sing "Ain't Misbehavin'" the next day, completely off-key. She loved Adelaide Hall and Florence Mills. Later, she had us all singing "I can't give you anything but love, Baby." I think she believed we sounded like Adelaide Hall. Dolly would dance to Baby Cox's "Diga, Diga Do."

One unforgettable Sunday Mama and Papa took us to New York

to visit Reverend William Moses. Reverend Moses's daughters, Julia and Ethel, were showgirls who danced in some of the same shows Mama and Papa had been to see. I was overcome when we were introduced to them. I thought they were the most beautiful girls I had ever seen: slim, with peaches-and-cream complexions and lovely dark brown hair that they could shake. (It was what I always wanted to do with mine, but mine doesn't budge.) Julia and Ethel showed us some dances, which both thrilled and upset us. They were dancing on *Sunday*. I couldn't understand why they would do such a thing. In our Baptist church we were taught that dancing on Sunday was a sin. Then there were those older ladies in our church who thought it was a sin to dance on any day of the week. And here were Julia and Ethel Moses showing us the dances they did in the show, shaking their hips wildly, dancing to fast music like "Diga, Diga Do." It was confusing, and we were wide-eyed. Julia and Ethel were "sinning" right there in front of their minister father. And he was smiling proudly. Later in life we sinned a lot at many Sunday afternoon fund-raising dances at the Savoy and other places. But as children, we didn't know what to make of all this.

Mama and Papa also liked going in to New York to concerts. I remember once they went to hear the great black tenor Roland Hayes, in concert. The next day when Mama was telling us about the concert she said he sang "And He Never Said a Mumbalin' Word." Greg looked puzzled and asked, "How did he sing then, Mama?" We all laughed as she explained to him that those were words in one of his songs.

There were those good things about the North, but there was also a lot that should have convinced North that it was not as beautiful as it saw itself. We knew when Mama put on that red hat, she was on her way to, as Du Bois said, use her brain to fight the "forces of hell in our own land." I learned the details of her fight through documents I found in the NAACP file at the Library of Congress.

Mama was constantly at the schools to confront unfairness. One day when a sixth-grade classmate and I were walking down the hall, I heard a familiar voice coming from the principal's office. "We're not going to have it; we're just not going to have it." I had heard those words many times before and would hear them many times thereafter. The principal's office door was ajar, so we could see the small group of mothers standing at his desk shaking their heads, giving emphasis to the spokeswoman's words.

"That's my mother," I commented, head down, as if admitting some terrible human failing.

"Which one?" Josephine asked.

"The one in the red hat," I said softly, feeling a lot like Peter wanting to deny Christ. Well, maybe not three times, but at least once. (What does a sixth-grader know about the fight for equality?) My mother was arguing with the principal. *No one* argued with the principal, the terrifying man the teacher sent you to for punishment. I will say that Mama was not raising her voice. She never did. But I knew by the way that red hat was pulled down on her head, by her posture, and by the dead-in-the-eye look at the principal, that she was straightening him out about something.

It turned out that particular controversy had to do with a class trip that the black children couldn't go on. The young teacher, who had recently moved from New England to Montclair, hadn't realized that the amusement park she'd chosen didn't admit colored people. When she found out, she wanted to cancel the trip, but some of the white mothers objected. The teacher, finding herself in a bad situation, went to the principal for a solution. He suggested that she go ahead with the trip and he'd see that something else would be arranged for the Negro children. So of course Mama got into it. She gathered *her* group of mothers, the head shakers with her, and she threatened to go to the superintendent of schools, the mayor, the governor, and even President Coolidge, if necessary. I smile now as I think of Mama's threat to go to Coolidge. It was a pretty empty threat, since Coolidge proved to be a man devoted to the laissez-faire approach to everything. But when issues were not resolved at the lower levels, Mama's motto was, "Somebody is always over somebody and God is over all." She was perfectly willing, if need be, to appeal to higher and higher sources. In regard to that class trip, however, she had to go no further than the principal. Another site, where *all* children were welcome, was selected.

I didn't, of course, realize what a wonderfully courageous lady our mother was until much, much later. I found out about another school fight Mama joined in a 1929 newspaper article in the Library of Congress's NAACP files:

> Mrs. Mary Rice Allen, Secretary of the Montclair Branch of the National Association for the Advancement of Colored People, appeared before the board with a petition from a committee of the Negro race in Montclair which stated that the Negro citizens of the town feel that they are being discriminated against in the exercises connected with graduation students in the High School.

The article went on to say that the committee had taken this problem up with the principal and with Mr. Pickell, the superintendent of schools, with no redress. The committee took issue with the way the school organized the students to march into the graduation ceremony. The white students marched in first, in alphabetical order, and the Negro students had to walk in behind the whites.

The newspaper article also quoted the school board as saying it would not permit discrimination against any race or creed in the public schools. Mr. Pickell begged off, claiming that it was too close to graduation to change things, but that it would be changed the next year. And indeed it was. *All* the students walked in in alphabetical order. Mama's oldest living girl, Rosemary, graduated that year, 1930. And since our name was Allen she was right up there in front, in alphabetical order, preceded by only Ruth Albey.

AMONG THE NAACP file papers was a letter from Robert Bagnall, field secretary of the NAACP, dated November 9, 1932, about a young woman named Cecilia Cox, who had applied to the Montclair Normal School and been steered away to Newark State Teachers College. Mr. Bagnall wrote:

> I did not know that this discrimination existed in the Montclair Normal School. I would suggest that the branch and state conference take up this matter and try to end the discrimination.

To find out more about Montclair Normal School in the early 1930s, I recently talked with Florence Hampton, an early graduate. She told me that during those years, Montclair Normal accepted only two black women each semester. Most likely, the quota had been filled before Cecilia Cox applied. And the policy was that once the quota was met, the admissions office was to suggest that other black students apply to Newark State. She also told me that black students could not do their practice teaching in any school in Montclair except Glenfield (formerly called Maple Avenue School), where the school population was largely Negro and Italian. Great changes have been made since those years. The current and the former presidents of the present Montclair State University are black. (There have been many other changes in Montclair since we grew up there. For example, the *Montclair Times* of September 11, 1997, reported that Montclair was voted the "Number 1 interracially friendly town in America.")

Probably the most important school fight was one that involved both Mama and Papa. In the early 1930s, it became obvious that the Montclair school board was gerrymandering school-district lines to keep Negro students out of Nishuane School, always predominantly white. The board had transferred some white students to Nishuane even though they lived closer to Glenfield School. Norma Holcombe McCain was one of the black students who, though she lived in the

Nishuane district, was being sent back to Glenfield. She told me what had first made people suspicious.

"We couldn't understand it," she remembers. "White kids who lived close to Glenfield would pass our house every day on their way to Nishuane!"

There were about ten black students whose parents protested this: the Kenneys, Stones, Wilkersons, Leslies, and Holcombes. All those families lived in the Nishuane district, but their children were being sent to Glenfield. A newspaper article found in the NAACP files reports:

Montclair, New Jersey, September 22—The newest attempt at Jim Crow schools, and the first to be made in Northern New Jersey, is being fought by citizens led by the NAACP branch. The school board is trying to transfer all white students from Glenfield School and send Colored students, in other districts, to Glenfield.

The protesting parents kept their children out of school while the fight was going on. That summer, Mr. Holcombe, the father of Norma Holcombe McCain, organized a school called the Holcombe/Kenney school. The teachers were students home from college. I was one of those teachers, along with Elsie Leach, Lavinia Holcombe, and Vinnie Thomas. My most delightful little student was Norma Holcombe. She wrote a composition I've kept all these years.

The House on Valley Rod

On Valley Rod there lived a family. Gregor was in the kitchen washing the dish. Rosuare was prety and played the piano. Bill was singing in the dining room. Doly was dancing with her brothe Hunter. Carrie was reading the bok and Gregor was in the kitchen washing the dish. Everybody was very happy.

"Probably everybody but poor Gregor," Mama laughed when she read it.

The school fight went on for several years. The NAACP appealed to the local and state school boards with no redress, so they appealed to the state commissioner of public instruction. A letter from Mama to Walter White, executive secretary of the NAACP, dated November 17, 1933, includes this news:

We are waiting to hear the decision of the Commissioner of Public Instruction, who has had the school question in hand since October 6th, when the Committee waited on him. I have written him, but received no reply. Dr. Love is urging the Governor to push the Commissioner. . . . I'm wondering if a strong letter from you to Commissioner Elliot, State House, Trenton, would strengthen the situation.

Walter White responded that he would be "very glad to write to Commissioner of Public Instruction Elliott" and did. But when time passed and there was no settlement of the situation through this avenue, the NAACP decided to take the case to the state supreme court. Papa worked on this along with another lawyer, Louis Fast. A February 19, 1935, letter from Mama to Walter White mentioned:

I have written to Mr. Houston about coming to us on Sunday . . . a very appropriate time . . . since we are about to go to the Supreme Court with our school case. . . . Mr. Louis Fast, an attorney at law of Newark, a Jew, has offered his services free of charge and gave his service in the appeal to the State Board. . . .

Mary R. Allen
President Montclair Branch
NAACP

The case was heard in the Supreme Court and there was "jubilation when the NAACP won," Norma McCain told me. When the students enrolled in Nishuane, however, they were treated badly there. Even superior students were given failing grades, and it was all too evident that they were not accepted. To protect their children, some black parents withdrew them and sent them off to private schools, to Bordentown in New Jersey and others out of state. One student entered a public school in Bloomfield and two returned to Glenfield. Several years later, after a concerted effort to end the injustice, colored children entered Nishuane school and things went more smoothly.

The NAACP files make it clear that Mama was active in the association from the time we moved to Montclair until her death in 1935. She was appointed secretary of the Montclair branch soon after arriving from Virginia. A letter from Robert Bagnall, field secretary of the NAACP, written in 1930, pleads with Mama to accept the presidency of the Montclair branch. Mama did accept and worked very hard with the branch during that year. It was reported that she was largely responsible for the sharp increase in members. Her "enthusiasm is catching," one report stated.

Sometimes the fights the NAACP took on were political ones, as was true when ex-Senator Baird was running for governor of New Jersey. The NAACP was against Baird because he had, while in the Senate, voted to confirm a judge considered by Negroes to be anti-Negro. A note from Mama to Walter White informs him of this and reports that Baird "refuses to answer telegrams and letters sent to him by the NAACP." The national office organized all the New Jersey branches to fight against the election of Baird as Governor.

During the early 1930s, when the NAACP was accused of courting the Communists, Walter White wrote Mama on August 5, 1931, to say:

I am enclosing a statement prepared by William Pickens for guidance of the Branches in the event that the Communists try to disturb the meetings. A great deal of this has happened in the last few months and it would be well for the Branch to be on guard.

Walter White had plans to come to Montclair to speak, and his letter goes on to say, "The Communists wait until almost the end of the meeting then demand to speak. As soon as I finish speaking, without music . . . launch into a request for funds. There have been 'obstructionist tactics' at this point in other meetings."

Walter White did not, in fact, get to this meeting, but sent William Pickens in his place. He wrote Mama to explain: "I am most sorry to have to write you that a serious crisis has arisen in Alabama with the Scottsboro case, which makes it necessary for me to leave New York." (Walter White, who had very fair skin, often went into the Deep South on serious cases because no one bothered him and he could go wherever he wished.) A postscript to this letter said, "For obvious reasons, please give no publicity to the fact that I am going to Alabama." (Walter White did put his life at risk for us many times, as did John Shillady, the white secretary of the NAACP, who had gone into the South earlier and had been severely beaten by a group of white men.)

Bagnall wrote to Mama on December 15, 1931, asking her to consider serving another year as president of the Montclair branch. She answered that she would have to consult Papa. Bagnall pleaded with her again, saying that he had been very glad to have been present at the annual meeting of the Montclair branch to hear of the splendid work done during the year and to see the deep appreciation she was accorded by the branch. "The Branch's future hangs on your decision," he said. Papa conceded and she did accept, but Mama had hesitated because the timing was bad. The call to continue as president came at the bottom of the Depression, when she was working long hours in Papa's office as his secretary. Rosemary and I were both in college and weren't aware of the extreme stress Mama was under. Nor did we know that Papa had lost his rental property or that finances were of great concern to Mama and Papa. Even so, Mama continued as president for the next *several* years. A number of issues arose that needed the branch's attention: housing segregation, discrimination at swimming pools, discrimination in the welfare department, and a continuing limit on the number of black students accepted by Montclair Normal. She was also working with the Montclair Unemployment Relief and Welfare Organization, set up by Negroes to help the needy during the Depression.

Now I realize, with hindsight I've gotten from reading letters in the NAACP files, that Mama's health was beginning to fail during that time. Our parents kept all this away from Rosemary and me while we were away—Rosemary at Fisk University in Nashville, Tennessee, and I at Talladega College, in Talladega, Alabama. A letter in the NAACP files (3/23/33) from William Pickens to Mama congratulates the branch for its contributions and adds:

> I know under what difficulties you worked, being sick-a-bed most of the time while we were conducting the campaign and being faced with the worst financial crisis in your or my lifetime. . . . When you are able to be up and about again why not try an entertainment.

Papa was also very busy and pressured. Even though he was struggling now to make ends meet because of the Depression, he was active as a lawyer for the Montclair branch of the NAACP, and was on its board as well. He was also serving on the YMCA board and on the executive committee of the Unemployment Relief and Welfare Organization. So both Mama and Papa were struggling to maintain enough energy for their community work.

Scattered throughout the NAACP files are letters containing personal communication between Mama and the national NAACP staff members. Mama was late in sending some information to the national office and says in her letter to Bagnall of December 16, 1930:

My dear Mr. Bagnall:

I am sorry not to have been able to send these [reports] earlier, but I have been busy and am just able to settle down. Now, do not get nervous. I do not have the complex [of a certain person]. It has not been contagious. . . . I hope Mrs. Bagnall is improving.

Bagnall answered:

My dear Mrs. Allen:

I did not for a moment think that you had a complex like that certain gentleman we know. I knew that at this time of year you were very busy and that you would send the list. . . .

Wishing you and your family a most happy New Year.

R. W. Bagnall
Director of Branches

Reading my mother's deepest convictions expressed in these letters, which I had been searching to find for many years, has been thrilling for me. In a letter written in January 1931 to William Pickens of the NAACP, who was coming to the Montclair branch as a speaker, she said:

I wish you would stress race consciousness or whatever it is we need that we haven't much of.

Yours truly,
Mary Rice Hayes Allen

Race consciousness to Mama meant having pride in your race. She wanted us — and everyone else — to have pride in ourselves and in our race. Her "Papa Sir" and her Uncle John let her know early in her life that she was "somebody," and she spent her life trying to do the same for her own children and everybody else's. Didn't Anne Slaughter say, "She always made each one of us feel we were important and that we could be anything we dreamed of. The sky was the limit."

Mama was also active in the Interracial Committee of Montclair. A letter from R. W. Bagnall to Mama commends her work there:

> Indirectly I heard of the splendid stand you took at the meeting of the Interracial Committee. It was a fine and brave presentation and I hope that the Colored members of the Committee will hold a meeting and outline a definite program, taking a united stand in order that the Committee may be able to do more than make nice and empty gestures.

The committee, under the leadership of Reverend Norman Fletcher of the Unitarian Church, did more than make "empty gestures." Reverend Fletcher was active in the segregated movie theater fight and in every aspect of discrimination in our town. Some of his sermons were on race relations. In 1935, Mama sent an account of one from the *Montclair Times* to Roy Wilkins of the NAACP:

> Unless Christians are personally and collectively active in breaking the color line, their doctrine of goodwill is a sham and their preachment of brotherhood a hypocritical mouthing," declared Rev. Norman D. Fletcher in his sermon Sunday on "Break That Line — the Color Line," at Unity Church in its observance of Inter-racial Sunday.
>
> Mr. Fletcher said that the Christian church had not only those to save who were suffering from the color line, but its own soul as well. To the extent that Christians deliberately break the color line in their own actions, said Mr. Fletcher, to that extent they really live the religion they profess.
>
> "The color line is drawn sharply in the field of economics.

The colored man, generally speaking," said Mr. Fletcher, "has been the last hired and the first fired. He has never known 'equal pay for equal work.'"

Reverend Fletcher pointed at the color line even when it was drawn by the federal government in some of the New Deal's projects, in federal loan banks, and in the government subsistence homestead projects. Since Negroes, like whites, paid federal taxes, Reverend Fletcher saw no excuse. He was a white man who was courageously outspoken at a time when fighting for Negro rights was an unpopular cause among whites. Prior to Reverend Fletcher's arrival in Montclair, Mama worked on the Interracial Committee with Reverend Edgar Swan Wiers, also of the Unitarian Church, and another white fighter for justice for Negroes in our town.

At the beginning of Mama's crusade she had a lot of energy to give. But by the 1930s the Depression was taking its toll on her. Those were harsh years for most everyone. Before I could go away to college I had to work in service, and I remember one of Mama's "bourgie" friends asking her, "How can you, a lawyer's wife, allow your daughter to work in service?" Mama's answer was, "I allow it now so she won't have to do it for the rest of her life. We are going to see that all of our girls get a good education, and right now this is our only way."

Actually, we had several ways of making summer money while we were in college. One of them was the Allen Sweet Potatoe Pie Company. Mizannie made the pies. Rosemary, the mathematician, kept the books and was the boss. Dolly and I did the cleanup work, and our friend Earl Davis delivered the pies. We always sold out our total production and, in fact, the firm still owes Dolly and me $1.75 each, which we never were able to collect from the boss.

Once I got to Alabama in September, there wasn't enough money for me to come home until June. Since most of my college friends were from the South, they all went home for Christmas, so those were sad Christmases for me. Even though I understood about hard times, I couldn't help being sad that my parents couldn't come to my graduation. My mother had gone to Rosemary's the year before. I understand now why they couldn't come to mine. Reading about Mama's failing health during that hard time has moved me deeply. My eyes fill with tears when I remember the words Mama wrote in a letter to Walter White in May 1934:

> Mr. White, I have stuck to the Branch at great sacrifice, even in the face of poor health and poorer pocketbook.

And there was that earlier reference to Mama's health in a letter from William Pickens to Mama. Rosemary and I never knew about any of these illnesses. Parents kept so much from their children back then, and our being away at college made it even harder for us to know what was really going on. Parents should discuss situations like this with their children, who understand better than adults think. Nowadays parents do. But they didn't back then.

Your crown has already been bought
and paid for. All you must do is put
it on your head.

—James Baldwin

Chapter 35

HOW ARE YOUR PHLOX DOING THIS YEAR?

It was early October in 1935. A light rain had softened the soil, and although she had a slight cold, Mama decided it was time to get her tulip and daffodil bulbs into the ground. That done, she climbed the steps, stopped for a moment in the shed next to the kitchen, and for the last time put her watering pail and trowel on the old shelves. The next day her cold was worse and she stayed in bed. Mizannie made a tea, lemon, and whiskey toddy, which we carried upstairs to her. On the third day it was clear she had more than a cold.

Dr. Alexander came as soon as we called him. He prescribed medication, and implied the seriousness of her condition by suggesting we get a nurse. I went to Newark with Gregory to pick up the nurse. When we returned, Mama was having chills and struggling to breathe. We called Papa, who rushed home. Dr. Alexander was summoned again. He and Papa stayed in the room with Mama for several hours; then Papa called us in.

All of us except Dolly, who was at Howard University, stood around Mama's bed. This was the first time I'd heard the sound of impending death. Mama's breathing was hard and had a rattling sound. Dr. Alexander tried to prepare us, but with her last breath, it was like a light had gone out of our lives. In March, she'd been so excited when we celebrated her sixtieth birthday. Mizannie made the birthday cake. Bill made a freezer of strawberry ice cream, and we put on one of our best ever performances for her. It was very hard to see her lying so still now, our Mama, always so vibrant, so full of life, so full of wit, so ready to tackle whatever needed tackling. Rosemary and I left the room together. No words came, but each of us knew how the other was feeling. We went to the bedroom we shared and broke down. Papa came to us, sat with us, tried to hold himself together, consoled us.

Later Mr. Woody, the undertaker, came and took Mama away. Once he'd brought her back, many people came to view her lying there in our parlor.

The day of the funeral, the church was overflowing with the people of our town and others who came from both near and far: the poor, the rich, the Thursday people, our neighbor Mrs. Bengler, the mayor, the chairman of the Democratic Party, Walter White of the NAACP, Eugene Kinkle Jones of the National Urban League, Reverend Norman Fletcher of the Unitarian Church, and even the superintendent of schools, with whom Mama had waged her bitterest fights. All of them came to pay respect to "the lady in the red hat." At the gravesite, a cruel reality struck us all. Mama, who had integrated the living of our town, was being lowered now into the segregated corner of the graveyard.

Back home again, surrounded by those closest to us and eating the food they had prepared, we felt some comfort. This day, with its quiet autumn sky and consuming sadness, still seemed somehow to vibrate with Mama's life. The house was full of warm stories of her. In all the rooms there were friends who'd come to console us, but the stories were in the kitchen, where they'd always been. Mama's kitchen was the place for friends and stories. Now we listened to many different stories, but the theme was the same: "the fighting spirit of the lady in the red hat."

"I don't know where Mary got her fighting spirit from," Miz Nettie commented, "but she sho' had it, thank goodness."

"It's clear to me," Aun' Tannie said. "I figured it out a long time ago. I think her father, the Confederate general, had a great deal to do with it. Strange, isn't it? But he adored her and gave her big doses of self-esteem. And then there was her Uncle John, the proud ex-slave who raised her. He added more and more of the same, so she *knew* she was as good as the next person. She was told so every day she was growing up."

"Yeah, I guess you're right," Miz Nettie commented. "And she wasn't just fighting for herself, but everybody."

"Yes, and the great thing about Mary, she could not be compromised. I remember her telling me a story about her fight with the school superintendent over the gerrymandering of school districts. She and the superintendent had practically been at each other's throats in a meeting and after the meeting he came over to Mary and said, 'Mrs. Allen, I'd like to shake your hand.'" Aun' Tannie laughed as she continued, "Mary said she stood up straight, looked him in the eye, and said, 'I'll shake your hand as one human being to another as long as it's clear to you that I still disagree with everything you said here tonight and plan to fight you with everything I've got.' And the principal answered, 'There could be no doubt about that, Mrs. Allen.' He smiled, and they shook hands as 'one human being to another.'"

"Lawd have mercy," laughed Miz Nettie. "I know she did it. I know she did. But you know sumpin' I'll never forget? 'Member when she got 'em to put the first colored cop on the police force and Gregory was made that cop. I came by so excited and said, 'Ain' that good, Lady, ain' that good. We got our first colored policeman in this town.' She said, 'Yes, it's good, Nettie, but I'm tired of hearing 'bout the first Negro. We won't have full freedom until we can stand up and say somebody was the *last* Negro to be kept out, that's when we can call it full freedom. And that day will come, Nettie, that day *will* come.' She was always talking 'bout 'full freedom,' you know." Miz Nettie shook her head, unable to go on.

Mizannie was moving around the kitchen serving cider and cake. When Eugene Kinkle Jones came in, he smiled and said, "Did I ever thank you for helping me out with the organization of the Interracial Committee?"

"Oh, yes." She smiled. "But it's all right to do it again. You may need more power."

He didn't hold his hands out this time, probably remembering too well what the weird greasy "power" felt like.

Aun' Tannie had another story about the school district gerrymandering. She told us Mama was attending a high school P.T.A. meeting and, as usual, raised the problem. She told the meeting that she believed the high school was an example of all races coming together, and perhaps the P.T.A. should send a letter of protest to the superintendent of schools about his segregation efforts. One angry white mother got up and in a shrill but very proper voice, said:

"No one has wanted to say this before, but the intelligentsia here knows that we are quite different, and I believe that not only should we have separate schools but where we don't, we should certainly have separate P.T.A. meetings."

Mama told Aun' Tannie the words of that woman provoked her into a speech about democracy and Kellogg's cornflakes. Aun' Tannie acted it out for us:

"'Madam Chairman,' your mama said, rising elegantly, and never raising her voice, 'the lady's use of the term "intelligentsia" already separates most of us, colored *and* white, from her elite group. However, I'm certain the *intelligent* among us would disagree with her. She spoke of differences. Yes, we are different. The English are different from the Irish, the Irish from the Dutch and the Italian and the English, the Irish and Dutch from the Negro. These are blessings. Some of those differences are what each group has to be proud of. But more than that we have likenesses.' She paused for a moment. "We all speak English. We all pledge allegiance to the same flag. We all eat Kellogg's cornflakes, and we all send our children to this school to learn the principles upon which our country was founded—democracy, freedom, and that all men are created equal. So it is not only our differences but our likenesses, as well, that say we *should* be together.'"

According to Aun' Tannie, the chairman said, "You stated that very well, Mrs. Allen. I agree with you. Now let's move on. I, too, think we should send a letter to the Superintendent." And evidently, they did just that.

"Yep, she was some lady," Miz Nettie said.

Walter White leaned forward into our circle and said, "I will never forget something your mother said to me once when I was here to dinner. After thanking her for one of those good meals she cooked, I said to her, 'But tell me something, Mary, how can you reconcile the fact that your Sally Lunn is about the best around with that fighting spirit of yours?'

"Your mother smiled and said, 'Well, Walter, Sally Lunn is not at its best until it rises to a level where you can be proud—and neither will we be. The only difference is the ingredient that will make each possible. In Sally Lunn it's a simple fermenting thing called yeast; in us, it's got to be a strong fighting spirit, amounts of which it seems we have to keep adding and adding and adding.' And with that as an analogy she smiled at me and said, 'And I daresay, Walter, you could make a pretty good Sally Lunn yourself.'"

The day after Mama died, Papa had received a telegram from Walter White:

We are shocked and grieved beyond words to learn of Mrs. Allen's death. The entire NAACP joins me in deepest sympathy to you and the family in the loss of a gallant comrade and a faithful, uncompromising fighter for justice.

Walter White
NAACP

Now we were glad to have his story about Mama and Sally Lunn to make us laugh. Papa took that moment to thank him again for the words in his telegram. Then he turned to Reverend Fletcher and said, "I want to thank you, too, for your beautiful letter in the newspaper."

I have kept my clipping of that letter for all these years:

MRS. WILLIAM P. ALLEN

To the Editor of the *Montclair Times*:

May I ask for space in your columns to pay personal tribute to the late Mrs. William P. Allen, whom I regard as one of the most heroic community and racial leaders I have ever known. People who choose popular causes, by deliberation or otherwise, and rise to a conspicuous position of leadership, usually receive the acclaim of their fellow citizens, while those who choose unpopular causes almost invariably receive considerably less. These leaders of unpopular causes are recognized by those for whose welfare they fight, and by a pathetically small number of others whose mind and conscience have led them into the cause. Lest this latter group be not articulate, I take it upon myself to pay tribute to Mrs. Allen for them and for myself.

Mrs. Allen was an heroic and persistent fighter for justice for the Negro Race in a community and a nation in which there is incalculable need for waging such a fight. The sword of her spirit was always drawn and it was not sheathed when the battle went hard, or when her fellow fighters retreated to safer spots. In any great cause there are two types of leaders, the fighters and the conciliators, those who fight the battle when a battle is needed, and those who gain ground for the cause by the less militant means of conference, mediation, conciliation. Although Mrs. Allen was not altogether lacking in the qualities of the latter type of leader, she was primarily of the former type.

She never considered the position of the Negro in Montclair or in America as hopeless, and never gave way to that debilitating defeatism which from time to time settles like a sultry haze over the minds and spirits of many of us. More than once have I sat in the meetings of the Interracial Committee with Mrs. Allen and noted how her extraordinarily keen ability to apply the ideal of inter-racial justice to concrete community situations, in which some seem singularly lacking, and how her undiminished courage shamed the rest of us into speech and action.

I look in vain throughout the Negro community of Montclair for anyone to take Mrs. Allen's place. I know, however, that leaders have a way of appearing when the social situation demands it, and I fervently hope that the one who does appear from Mrs. Allen's race will in great measure rise to her courage and devotion.

Norman D. Fletcher

Montclair, N.J., Oct. 15, 1935

While the stories were being told, Mrs. Bengler knocked on the back door. She had brought a cake she'd made for us. Rosemary accepted it and thanked her. Then Mrs. Bengler went over to speak to Papa, brushing tears from her cheeks. "My best friend," we heard her say to Papa. She said she had to leave, and Papa went with her to the door. When he sat down again, the stories continued. In a quiet moment he got up and walked over to the window to look out into Mama's garden (something he did every day of the two years he lived after her death). I went over and stood beside him. It was dark by then, but by the dim light from the car barn, we could see the chrysanthemums were still in bloom. And there in the middle of Mama's garden, in the dark, was Mrs. Bengler plucking the dead blossoms.

Miz Nettie had the last word that evening: "I almost went to pieces at the cemetery," she said, "her having to be buried in that segregated grave, the way she fought so living. Then the only thing that saved me, while I was standing there, I looked up toward the sky and said, 'Lord, you better have things straight up there, 'cause she's on her way.'" Everyone had a good laugh; then Miz Nettie continued, "If angels have gold crowns, I know Mary has one."

I thought to myself, You're right, Miz Nettie, Mama will have a gold crown, but I'm certain, somewhere tucked under one of her wings is her red hat—just in case.

Selected Bibliography

—

I. Books and Essays

Alloway, David Neslon, and Mary Travis Arny. *A Goodly Heritage: Montclair—a Commemorative History, 1664–1964.* Montclair, N.J.: Tercentenary Committee, Board of Commissions, 1964.

Bacon, Francis. "Of Youth and Age." *Essays, Advancement of Learning, New Atlantis.* Ed. Richard Foster Jones. New York: The Odyssey Press Inc., 1939.

Beilensen, John, and Heidi Jackson, eds. *Voices of Struggle, Voices of Hope: A Collection of Quotes of Great African-Americans.* White Plains, N.Y.: Peter Pauper Press, Inc., 1992.

Bennett, Lerone, Jr. *Before the Mayflower: A History of Black America.* 5th ed. New York: Penguin Books, 1984.

Blassingame, John W. *The Slave Community: Plantation Life in the Antebellum South.* New York: Oxford University Press, 1979.

Bradford, Phillips Verner, and Blume Harvey. *Ota Benga: The Pygmy in the Zoo.* New York: St. Martin's Press, 1992.

Brandt, Nat. *The Town That Started the Civil War.* Syracuse, N.Y.: Syracuse University Press, 1990.

Brown, Sterling. *The Collected Poems of Sterling Brown*. The National Poetry Series. Selected by Michael S. Harper. New York: Harper and Row, 1980.

Campbell, D. C., Jr., ed., with Kym S. Rice. *Before Freedom Came*. Charlottesville, Va.: University Press of Virginia, 1991.

Carr, Maria G. *My Recollections of Rocktown—Now Known as Harrisonburg. 1892*. Harrisonburg, Va.: Rockingham Historical Society, 1984.

Crow, Martha Foote. *Christ in the Poetry of Today: An Anthology from American Poets*. New York: The Women's Press, 1923.

Cullen, Countee. *Color*. New York: Harper and Brothers Publishers, 1925.

Davis, Charles T., and Henry Louis Gates, Jr., eds. *The Slave Narrative*. New York: Oxford University Press, 1985.

Du Bois, William E. B., James Weldon Johnson, and Booker T. Washington. *Three Negro Classics: Up From Slavery* [Washington], *The Souls of Black Folk* [Du Bois], *The Autobiography of An Ex-Colored Man* [Johnson]. New York: Avon Books, 1965.

Dunbar, Paul Laurence. *The Complete Poems of Paul Laurence Dunbar*. New York: Dodd, Mead and Company, 1913.

Ellison, Ralph. *Shadow and Act*. New York: Random House, 1964.

Fox-Genovese, Elizabeth. *Within the Plantation Household*. Chapel Hill: University of North Carolina Press, 1988.

Franklin, John Hope. *From Slavery to Freedom: A History of Negro Americans*. 6th ed. New York: Alfred A. Knopf, 1988.

Freeman, Douglas Southall. *Lee's Lieutenants: A Study in Command. Volume 1: From Manassas to Malvern Hill*. New York: Charles Scribner's Sons, 1942.

Furguson, Ernest B. *Chancellorsville 1863: The Soul of the Brave*. New York: Alfred A. Knopf, 1992.

Garraty, John A. *The American Nation: A History of the United States*. 3rd ed. New York: Harper and Row Publishers, 1975.

Greene, J. Lee. *Time's Unfading Garden: Anne Spencer's Life and Poetry*. Baton Rouge: Louisiana State University Press, 1977.

Gutman, Herbert G. *The Black Family in Slavery and Freedom (1750–1925)*. New York: Pantheon, 1976.

Gwin, Minrose C. *Black and White Women in the Old South: The Peculiar Sisterhood in American Literature*. Knoxville: University of Tennessee Press, 1985.

Haizlip, Shirlee Taylor. *The Sweeter the Juice*. New York: Simon and Schuster, 1994.

Hughes, Langston, and Arna Bontemps, editors. *The Poetry of the Negro (1746–1949)*. Garden City, N.Y.: Doubleday and Company, 1949.

Hurmence, Belinda. *My Folks Don't Want Me to Talk About Slavery*. Winston-Salem, N.C.: John F. Blair, Publisher, 1984.

Johnson, James Weldon. *God's Trombones*. New York: Penguin Books, 1976.

Johnston, James Hugo. *Race Relations in Virginia and Miscegenation in the South (1776–1860)*. Amherst: University of Massachusetts Press, 1970.

Kellogg, Charles Flint. *NAACP: A History of the National Association for the Advancement of Colored People. Volume I, 1909–1920*. Baltimore: Johns Hopkins University Press, 1967.

Holy Bible (King James Version). Chicago: John A. Dickson Publishing Co., 1973.

Leslau, Charlotte, and Wolf Leslau. *African Proverbs*. White Plains, N.Y.: Peter Pauper Press, Inc., 1985.

Lester, Julius. *To Be a Slave*. New York: Scholastic, Inc., 1968.

Lissauer, Robert. *Encyclopedia of Popular Music in America, 1888 to the Present*. New York: Paragon House, 1991.

Lyons, Mary E. *Letters from a Slave Girl: The Story of Harriett Jacobs*. New York: Charles Scribner's Sons, 1992.

Mattox, Cheryl Warren. *Shake It to the One That You Love the Best: Play Songs and Lullabies from Black Musical Traditions*. El Sobrante, Calif.: Warren-Mattox Productions, 1989.

McLaurin, Melton A. *Celia, a Slave*. Athens, Ga.: University of Georgia Press, 1991.

Ploski, Harry A., and Roscoe C,. Brown, Jr. *The Negro Almanac*. New York: Bellwether Publishing Company, Inc., 1967.

Probert, Christina. *Hats in Vogue Since 1910*. New York: Abbeville Press, 1981.

Reavies, Ralph. *Virginia Seminary: A Jouney of Black Independence*. Richmond, Va.: First Associates Publishing, 1989.

Richings, G. F. *Evidences of Progress Among Colored People.* Philadelphia: George S. Ferguson Co., 1902.

Root, Marla P., ed. *Racially Mixed People in America.* Newbury Park, Calif.: Sage Publications, 1992.

Scott, Bvt. Lieut. Col. Robert N., preparer. *The Peninsular Campaign.* Series 1, volume 11 of *The War of the Rebellion: A Compilation of the Official Records of the Union and Confederate Armies.* Washington, D.C.: Government Printing Press, 1884.

Stein, Grun. *Timetables of History.* New York: Simon and Schuster, 1979.

Sterling, Dorothy. *We Are Your Sisters.* New York: W. W. Norton, 1984.

Thoreau, Henry David. "Civil Disobedience." *Henry David Thoreau: Studies and Commentaries.* Ed. Walter Harding, George Brenner, and Paul A. Doyle. Rutherford, N.J.: Fairleigh Dickinson University Press, 1973.

Tucker, Susan. *Telling Memories Among Southern Women.* New York: Schocken Books, 1988.

Turnbull, Colin M. *The Forest People.* New York: Simon and Schuster, 1968.

Tyree, Marion Cabell. *Housekeeping in Old Virginia.* Louisville, Ky.: John P. Morton and Company, 1879.

Van Zant, Iylana. *Acts of Faith.* New York: Fireside (Simon and Schuster), 1995.

Washington, James Melvin. *Frustrated Fellowship: The Black Baptist Quest for Social Power.* Macon, Ga.: Mercer University Press, 1986.

Wayland, John W. *A History of Rockingham County, Virginia.* Harrisonburg, Va.: C. J. Carrier Company, 1980.

———. *Historic Harrisonburg.* Harrisonburg: C. J. Carrier Company, 1973.

Weiss, Nancy. *The National Urban League, 1910–1940.* New York: Oxford University Press, 1974.

West, Cornel. *Race Matters.* Boston: Beacon Press, 1993.

Woll, Allen. *Black Musical Theatre, from Coontown to Dreamgirls.* Baton Rouge: Louisiana State University Press, 1989.

Woodward, C. Vann. *Mary Chesnut's Civil War.* New Haven: Yale University Press, 1981.

II. ARCHIVES, MANUSCRIPTS, AND CENSUSES

James Madison University Library, Carrier Special Collections Library, Harrisonburg, Va.

Library of Congress, Washington, D.C. (NAACP Branch Files for Lynchburg, Va., and Montclair, N.J.)

Library of Virginia (Formerly Virginia State Library and Archives).

Montclair, N.J., Library, Montclair, N.J.

Oberlin College Archives (Alumni Records) Oberlin, Ohio.

Perkins Library, Duke University, Durham, N.C.

Rockingham Historical Society, Harrisonburg, Va.

Virginia Seminary Archives, Lynchburg, Va.

III. NEWSPAPERS AND PERIODICALS

The Afro-American, Baltimore, Md.

The Crisis. The official magazine of the NAACP.

The Montclair Times, Montclair, N.J.

The Newark Evening News, Newark, N.J.

Opportunity. The official magazine of the National Urban League.

The Pittsburgh Courier, Pittsburgh, Pa.

The Rockingham Register, Harrisonburg, Va.

IV. ARTICLES

"Black Higher Education Among American Baptists in Virginia from the Slave Pen to the University." Ralph Reavies, Sr., in *American Baptist Quarterly*, December 1992, vol. 11, no. 4.

"Ignored by History." Article on General John R. Jones by Dale Harter in *Montpelier*, the James Madison University newspaper for alumni, parents, and friends. Vol. 15, no. 2.

CREDITS

Lyric excerpts on page 223 of "Russian Lullaby" by Irving Berlin. Copyright © 1927 by Irving Berlin. Copyright renewed. International copyright secured. All rights reserved. Reprinted by permission.

Excerpts from "To a Certain Lady in Her Garden" and "Sister Lou" from *Southern Road* by Sterling Brown. Copyright © 1932 by Sterling Brown. Reprinted from the Literary Estate of Sterling Brown by special permission of his son, John Dennis.

Excerpts from "Near White" and "For a Mouthy Woman" from *Color* by Countee Cullen. Copyright © 1925 by Countee Cullen. Copyright © renewed 1952 by Ida M. Cullen. Copyright administered by Thompson and Thompson, New York. Reprinted by permission.

Excerpt from "Cross" and "Democracy" from *Collected Poems* by Langston Hughes. Copyright ©1994 by the Estate of Langston Hughes. Reprinted by permission of Alfred A. Knopf, Inc.

Excerpt from "If We Must Die" from *Harlem Shadows* by Claude McKay. Copyright © 1922 by Claude McKay. Reprinted by permission of Harcourt Brace & Co.

Lyric excerpts from "The House I Live In" by Earl Robinson and Lewis Allan. Copyright © 1942 by Earl Robinson and Lewis Allan/Administered by Warner Chappel Music, Inc. International copyright secured. All rights reserved. Reprinted by permission.

Excerpts from "I Have a Friend," "Lines to a Nasturtium," and "Life-long, Poor Browning" by Anne Spencer from *Time's Unfading Garden: Anne Spencer's Life and Poetry* by J. Lee Greene. Copyright © 1977 by J. Lee Greene. Reprinted by permission of J. Lee Greene.

Excerpts from "For My People" and "October Journey" from *For My People* by Margaret Walker. Copyright © 1942 by Margaret Walker. Reprinted by permission of Margaret Walker.